TEXAS TOWNS

FROM ABNER TO ZIPPERLANDVILLE

Second Edition

Don Blevins
Revised by Paris Permenter
and John Bigley

LONE STAR BOOKS

Guilford, Connecticut
Helena, Montana

LONE STAR BOOKS

An imprint of The Rowman & Littlefield Publishing Group, Inc.
4501 Forbes Blvd., Ste. 200
Lanham, MD 20706
www.rowman.com
A registered trademark of The Rowman & Littlefield Publishing Group, Inc.

Distributed by NATIONAL BOOK NETWORK

Maps: Melissa Baker © The Rowman & Littlefield Publishing Group, Inc.

British Library Cataloguing in Publication Information available

Library of Congress Cataloging-in-Publication Data available

ISBN 978-1-4930-3239-6 (paperback)
ISBN 978-1-4930-3240-2 (e-book)

∞™ The paper used in this publication meets the minimum requirements of American National Standard for Information Sciences—Permanence of Paper for Printed Library Materials, ANSI/NISO Z39.48-1992.

Printed in the United States of America

CONTENTS

REVISERS' PREFACE

What's in a name?

Well, when it comes to Texas towns, quite a lot. Whether they're named for an early settler, for a barroom brawl, or for a natural feature, towns across the Lone Star State wear their monikers with pride.

Over a decade ago, author Don Blevins sniffed out the origins of even the remotest Texas communities, digging through courthouse records and interviewing county personnel for clues into the story of these names.

Sadly Don Blevins passed away in 2014 after an Air Force and then a writing career. We are proud to update his work for a new generation of Texas travelers.

Some of these towns exist in memory only, the early community now memorialized with school and street names. Others thrive as hubs of commerce and growing communities.

We hope you'll enjoy this look at the fascinating origins of Texas town names—and that it inspires you to explore the towns of Texas.

DON BLEVINS'S PREFACE

In 2000, Cumberland House (Nashville) published my book *Peculiar, Uncertain, and Two Egg*, which covered some 3,000 American communities with unusual names and how those names came about. Texas, naturally, was included in the book, but there was only room for a small portion of the hundreds of villages and hamlets that dot the Texas state map. It is the intent of this book to bring more of these communities to the forefront.

As the Sources section at the back of this book indicates, a great number of people and entities were most helpful in gathering the data compiled herein on the many settlements. Without their assistance, the gathering of information would have been impossible. Most all of my inquiries were answered in a friendly and rapid manner. Some supplied information of value, others steered me to sources that might satisfy my questions, and some were unable to provide any data at all. I was surprised at the number of community names, the origins of which were unknown, even by current residents and old-timers.

Some of my inquiries were answered by letter, which I have indicated by showing the date. Others were simply answered with copies of histories or stories or recordings at hand, often forwarded without the benefit of a letter or note. I appreciate each and every response I received.

While some of the data I was provided was not in official format, I deem the sources reliable and believe the origins shown in this publication to be the most accurate at this time. Where there is doubt as to the validity of the name source, I have listed it as "believed to be" or with some similar statement. If anyone out there has a better version of the community name origin, I would appreciate hearing from that person. My aim has always been to provide the most accurate information available.

To all of those who provided me with information or led me on down the path to other sources, I extend my heartfelt appreciation. I hope I listed you properly in the sources. For those of you who answered my queries and sent me information, but do not find your data listed in the book, my apologies. When pressed for space, as all publications are, cutting is a necessary chore. I would like to have included even more communities, but that was not possible. All cuts were made subjectively and the decisions were mine, as much as I regret each and every snippet. My deepest apologies to all whose contributions I could not include here.

I would like to point out that I used the *Texas Almanac 2002–2003* as my source for locations and distances. I veered from *The New Handbook of Texas* because I wanted to keep landmarks within the county. The *Handbook* makes the reference points easier to follow by listing the larger cities as landmarks, whether they are in the same county as the community or not. I used my trusty ruler to judge the distances and locations within each county. Any mistakes are, therefore, mine.

The name in parentheses after each community name refers to the county in which it is located.

ABBREVIATIONS

CR	County Road
FM	Farm to Market Road
IH	Interstate Highway
int	Intersection
jct	Junction
LP	Loop
LR	Local Road
PR	Park Road
RM	Ranch to Market Road
TX	Texas Highway
US	U.S. Highway

Note: Directions are standard (i.e., N = North, SE = Southeast, C = Central, etc.)

ANIMAL KINGDOM

From Antelope to Wild Horse

ANTELOPE (Jack): near int LP 187, US 281, and FM 175, twenty miles NW of Jacksboro. Walter S. Jones platted and surveyed the town in 1875. The site acquired its name from a rather unusual, and comical, event. In 1881 a cowboy chased an antelope down the main street of the settlement and roped the animal in front of the general store.

BEE CAVE (Travis): at int TX 71 and FM 620 and 2244, twelve miles W of Austin. Also known as Beecaves and Bee Caves. Will Johnson organized the community around 1870. It was appropriately named for a large cave of wild bees discovered nearby.

BEE HOUSE (Coryell): on FM 183, eleven miles W of Gatesville. The community was established in 1850 and first called Boyd's Cove for James Boyd. Early settlers discovered cliffs and caves full of beehives in the vicinity. They erected a communal house and called it Bee House Hall. In 1884 residents wanted to name the site Bee Hive. Whether by mistake or by design, postal authorities recorded the name as Bee House.

BEEVILLE (Bee): at int US 181 and TX 59; county seat. The first settlers were the Burke, Carroll, and Hefferman families in 1830. It

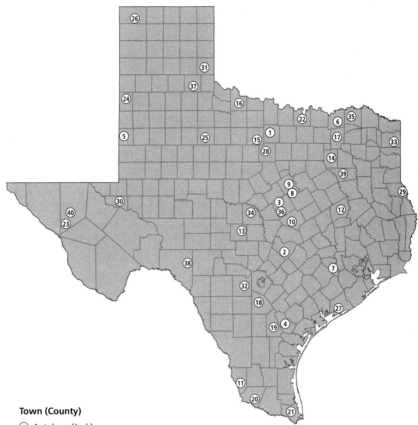

Town (County)

1. Antelope (Jack)
2. Bee Cave (Travis)
3. Bee House (Coryell)
4. Beeville (Bee)
5. Bronco (Yoakum)
6. Bug Tussle (Fannin)
7. Cat Spring (Austin)
8. Cayote (Bosque)
9. Coon Creek (Bosque)
10. Dog Ridge (Bell)
11. Falcon (Zapata)
12. Flo (Leon)
13. Fly Gap (Mason)
14. Frog (Kaufman)
15. Gooseneck (Young)
16. Grayback (Wilbarger)
17. Hogeye (Hunt)
18. Kyote (Atascosa)
19. Lagarto (Live Oak)
20. La Grulla (Starr)
21. La Paloma (Cameron)
22. Leo (Cooke)
23. Lobo (Culberson)
24. Muleshoe (Bailey)
25. Peacock (Stonewall)
26. Perico (Dallam)
27. Pheasant (Matagorda)
28. Possum Kingdom (Palo Pinto)
29. Possum Trot (Shelby)
30. Pyote (Ward)
31. Quail (Collingsworth)
32. Quihi (Medina)
33. Roach (Cass)
34. Skeeterville (San Saba)
35. Tigertown (Lamar)
36. Topsey (Coryell)
37. Turkey (Hall)
38. Vinegarone (Val Verde)
39. Wildcat (Henderson)
40. Wild Horse (Culberson)

was originally named Maryville for Mary Hefferman, the only surviving heir of James Hefferman, who was killed by Native Americans in 1835. When it was discovered that another Maryville already existed in Texas, residents chose Beeville as the name, honoring General Bernard E. Bee, who founded the Texas army and later served as secretary of war and secretary of the treasury for the Republic of Texas.

BRONCO (Yoakum): on US 380, twenty miles NW of Plains. H. "Gravy" Fields opened a store on the site in 1903. The community was christened for its location in range country where many cowboys engaged in the skill of "bustin'" broncos. On the other hand, a shoe salesman traveling through the area offered a cowboy five dollars to exhibit "bronc" riding. When the feat was completed, the salesman asked the storekeeper why the settlement didn't have a name. Upon being informed that postal officials had rejected all the suggested names, the salesman said, "How about 'Bronco'?"

BUG TUSSLE (Fannin): jct FM 1550 and TX 34, five miles N of Ladonia. Site established in the 1890s. Initially called Truss for John Truss, settler. The current handle comes from either the time an ice cream social was held and bugs came out in such force that they ruined the party or, after picnic festivities were over, there was little to do except sit around and watch the tumble bugs "tussle" (scuffle).

CAT SPRING (Austin): at int FM 2187 and 949, eleven miles SW of Bellville. Settled in 1834 by German immigrants. The spot received its name when the son of Leopold von Roeder killed a puma at the springs of the San Bernard River.

CAYOTE (Bosque): on FM 56, some twenty miles SE of Meridian. John Cox opened a mercantile business near here in 1866 or 1867. Cox sold out a couple of years later and the new owners moved the enterprise to this site to take advantage of the water supply. The name is a misspelling of "coyote," which referred to the wild canids that roamed nearby Bosque Prairie and for which the hamlet was supposedly christened.

COON CREEK (Bosque): on FM 56, two miles S of Lake Whitney. Jackson Smith and his wife Margaret, from Mississippi, bought several thousand acres in 1854 and the site became known as Smith Bend. The present handle probably came about from someone sighting raccoons near the stream.

DOG RIDGE (Bell): on US 190, three miles W of Belton. Settlers found dogs running wild in the region in 1836. That, coupled with the geography, accounts for the community name.

FALCON (Zapata): on US 83, twenty-six miles SE of Zapata. Due to flooding in August 1953, the site was moved from its original location at the junction of Medio Creek and the Rio Grande in southeast Zapata County. In the mid-1700s, José Clemente Gutiérez was granted 6,123 acres by the king of Spain. Gutiérez later sold the land to José Clemente Ramírez. The year 1780 witnessed the marriage of Ramírez and Margarita de la Garza Falcón. The couple moved to the original site of Falcon, which was then called Ramireño de Abajo. Following the opening of a post office in 1915, the village changed its name to Falcon in honor of the wife of the founder.

FLO (Leon): on FM 1151 and 831, twelve miles NE of Centerville. Site settled around 1855 and had a number of names throughout its history: Kidds Mill, Wheelock, Bethlehem, Oneta, New Hope, Oden, and Midway. The current name, tagged in 1891, was for the postmaster's dog.

FLY GAP (Mason): one-half mile W of RM 1900, twelve miles NE of Mason. A dozen or more families were in the area by mid-1883. Legend has it that the community name came from the time settlers pursued Native Americans from a raiding party and hid in a gap in the Kothmann Mountains in an attempt to ambush their prey. The horses were tied to trees in a nearby thicket. The outcome of the battle is unknown, but when the settlers went to retrieve their steeds, they found that horseflies had bitten them. The incident influenced the community's name.

FROG (Kaufman): on FM 316, S of US 80, seven miles E of Terrell. African Americans developed the settlement in the late 1800s. Lore tells us that the site was named for an early pioneer.

GOOSENECK (Young): one mile E of FM 1287, five miles S of Graham. First known as Honey Bend for the wild bees in the vicinity. The name was changed to its present designation for a prominent curve in the Brazos River.

GRAYBACK (Wilbarger): on FM 1763, fifteen miles SE of Vernon. Settlement began in the late 1880s and the town is sometimes referred to as Rock Crossing. A cowboy camp was once located here. The site became overrun with lice, referred to locally as "graybacks," and later, when a town name was considered, Grayback was chosen.

HOGEYE (Hunt): on FM 1566, ten miles N of Greenville. A Masonic lodge was established on the site in 1858, but there had been some semblance of settlement prior to that date. The Masonic emblem influenced the naming of the community because "to some of the unlettered natives, [the eye] looked like a hog's eye."

KYOTE (Atascosa): at int FM 2504 and TX 173, sixteen miles NW of Jourdanton. William D. Rogers, the first postmaster, chose the community name in 1927 because of the numerous coyotes in the vicinity. He varied the spelling because there was already a post office in Texas by that name. Ironically, that facility's name was also misspelled (as "Cayote").

LAGARTO (Live Oak): on FM 534 and 3162, eighteen miles SW of George West. While settlers were in the vicinity as early as 1836, the town was not developed until later. John W. Ramey, saddle manufacturer, platted the site in 1856. The settlement was first known as Roughtown for the wild times that went on there. The name was changed after saloons were banned. The current title comes from the Spanish for "lizard" and reflects the fact that numerous alligators were found along a nearby creek.

LA GRULLA (Starr): on US 83, three miles S of Alto Benito. Spanish settlers were on the scene as early as the 1780s, but a post office was not opened until 1912. The word is Spanish for "crane," denoting that the sandhill crane was once common to the ponds of this region. By the late 1980s, the ponds had been drained for farming.

LA PALOMA (Cameron): at jct US 281 and FM 732, five miles SW of San Benito. A post office was in operation here as early as 1912. Manuel Saldona, an early landowner, operated a general store on the site. He christened the community for the numerous doves (*paloma* in Spanish) found in a nearby grove of trees.

LEO (Cooke): on a LR, twenty miles SW of Gainesville. Settled before the Civil War. A Dr. Stamper from nearby Era named the site Leo ("lion"), because he believed the town to be a "rather rough place."

LOBO (Culberson): on US 90, twelve miles S of Van Horn. This had been a mail stop in the 1850s and 1860s. A post office was established in 1907, but a town was not organized until two years later. Bill Crist purchased the entire site in the mid-1970s, then put it up for sale, lock, stock, and barrel. The site was named for the wolves (*lobo* in Spanish) that roamed the region.

MULESHOE (Bailey): on US 84; county seat. Founded with the arrival of the railroad in 1913 and named for Muleshoe Ranch.

PEACOCK (Stonewall): on FM 2211, seventeen miles W of Aspermont. The railroad developed the site in 1909 and tagged it Alluvia.

In 1910 the name was changed to honor J. W. Peacock, the site's first postmaster.

PERICO (Dallam): on US 87, twenty-five miles NW of Dalhart. The site was developed in 1888 as a railroad shipping point. It was named Farwell for the Farwell Park line camp of the XIT Ranch. In 1905 George Findlay of the Capitol Syndicate asked the railroad to change the name. He requested it be called Perico, which in Spanish refers to a parakeet. What connection it has to the town is unknown.

PHEASANT (Matagorda): six miles N of Palacios. Also known as Pheasant Switch. The railroad built through here in 1903 and supposedly named it through error. Northern settlers mistook the local prairie chicken for a pheasant.

POSSUM KINGDOM (Palo Pinto): on FM 2951, two miles W of Morris Sheppard Dam. Tagged for the Possum Kingdom Bend in the Brazos River.

POSSUM TROT (Shelby): in SE Shelby County near Huxley. This predominantly African American community was probably developed in the latter part of the nineteenth century. It took its name from a regular opossum trail that ran through the site.

PYOTE (Ward): on FM 2355, TX 115, US 80, and IH 20, seven miles SW of Wickett. Settled sometime before 1881 and known as Pyote Tank. The present name seems to have come from the Chinese, who were working on the railroad, and their pronunciation of "coyote." However, there are those who believe the moniker came from the peyote cactus, which is common to the region.

QUAIL (Collingsworth): at int TX 203 and FM 47, fifteen miles W of Wellington. The families of brothers T. S. and W. I. Atkinson were the first settlers in the region, arriving in late 1890. The community was christened for the large number of quail in the region.

QUIHI (Medina): at int FM 2676 and a LR, eight miles NE of Hondo. While this name has long applied to the community, it has had various spellings, depending on the particular occupants of the land. Henri Castro laid out the site in 1845. He named it for the white-necked Mexican eagle, the "quichie," or "keechie." A nearby lake and stream carry the same name. Mexicans spelled the word "quichi," and the Germans, who came in last, altered the pronunciation and the spelling, changing the "ch" to "h," which is its present form.

ROACH (Cass): six miles NE of Linden in E Cass County. A post office was in operation here in 1898. The community name probably comes from Dr. J. Roach, a Cass County physician.

SKEETERVILLE (San Saba): on FM 502, six miles N of Richland Springs. The Church of Christ held services here around 1915. Roy "Dogie" Wilson is credited with naming the community in 1920. He thought the moniker appropriate because his horse was always covered with mosquitoes ("skeeters") after riding across the surrounding marshy ground.

TIGERTOWN (Lamar): sixteen miles NW of Paris. Called Co-thran's Store as early as 1873 for an early settler. A saloon owner hung a picture of a tiger over the bar, and cowboys soon acquired the habit of saying, "Let's go over and take a shot at the tiger." Another source of the town's name is that some drunks riding through town saw buildings covered with advertisements for a circus. Most of the posters depicted a tiger, and the drunks rode down main street shouting, "Tigertown! Tigertown!" A third rendition is that at a dance one night, local boys bested a group of boys from nearby Bonham. The out-of-towners slipped back later that night and painted a large tiger on a wall to symbolize the fierceness of the fight.

TOPSEY (Coryell): on FM 580, eight miles NW of Copperas Cove. The community came into being around 1900 and was named by a resident for his mule.

TURKEY (Hall): at int TX 86 and 70, twenty-seven miles SW of Estelline. The first settlers were in the area in the early 1890s and originally called the spot Turkey Roost. Its current tag comes from the creek, which was christened for wild turkeys in the vicinity.

VINEGARONE (Val Verde): on US 277, two-and-one-half miles NE of Lorna Alta. Developed as a ranching community in the 1920s, the settlement was named for the whip scorpion, common to the area. When excited, the insect emits a vinegar-like aroma that is called "vinegarone."

WILDCAT (Henderson): fourteen miles SW of Athens. Until the 1860s, this area was known as the Shepherd School District. During this period, a wildcat ran across the schoolyard while students were enjoying recess.

WILD HORSE (Culberson): on IH 10, eight miles E of Van Horn. In the 1800s, Native Americans attacked a wagon train and a young girl was tied to a wild horse and dragged to death. From this incident came the name of a nearby stream and, ultimately, of the hamlet.

COLORS

From Black to Yellowpine

BLACK (Parmer): on US 60, seven miles NE of Friona. Emerged as a railroad stop in 1898. In 1901 E. B. Black bought farmland from J. E. English, his brother-in-law.

BLACK ANKLE (San Augustine): on a LR off FM 3153, six miles E of San Augustine. The naming of this village apparently came from the time a local belle tore her black silk stockings at the ankle just before a dance. Improvising, the young lady covered the tear by applying stove soot to the area.

BLACK CREEK (Medina): on FM 2200, six miles NW of Devine. The town was settled prior to 1877 and named for a nearby stream. The creek probably obtained its moniker from the soil in the creek bed.

BLACK HILL (Atascosa): on FM 478, nine miles NW of Pleasanton. Also known as Lorna Prieta, Spanish for "black hill." The Black Hill School was in session in 1920. The site acquired its name from the black rocks that cover the landscape.

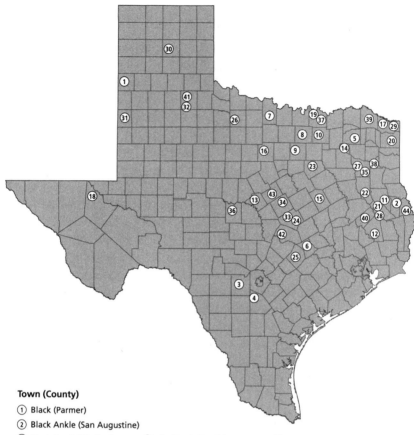

Town (County)

① Black (Parmer)
② Black Ankle (San Augustine)
③ Black Creek (Medina)
④ Black Hill (Atascosa)
⑤ Blackoak (Hopkins)
⑥ Blue (Lee)
⑦ Bluegrove (Clay)
⑧ Blue Mound (Denton)
⑨ Blue Mound (Tarrant)
⑩ Blue Ridge (Collin)
⑪ Blue Springs (Nacogdoches)
⑫ Bluewater (Polk)
⑬ Ebony (Mills)
⑭ Ginger (Rains)
⑮ Lavender (Limestone)
⑯ Palo Pinto (Palo Pinto)

⑰ Red Bank (Bowie)
⑱ Red Bluff (Reeves)
⑲ Red Branch (Grayson)
⑳ Red Hill (Cass)
㉑ Redland (Angelina)
㉒ Red Lawn (Cherokee)
㉓ Red Oak (Ellis)
㉔ Red Ranger (Bell)
㉕ Red Rock (Bastrop)
㉖ Red Springs (Baylor)
㉗ Red Springs (Smith)
㉘ Redtown (Angelina)
㉙ Redwater (Bowie)
㉚ White Deer (Carson)

㉛ Whiteface (Cochran)
㉜ Whiteflat (Motley)
㉝ White Hall (Bell)
㉞ White Hall (Coryell)
㉟ Whitehouse (Smith)
㊱ Whiteland (McCulloch)
㊲ White Mound (Grayson)
㊳ White Oak (Gregg)
㊴ White Rock (Red River)
㊵ White Rock (Trinity)
㊶ White Star (Motley)
㊷ Whitestone (Williamson)
㊸ Whiteway (Hamilton)
㊹ Yellowpine (Sabine)

BLACKOAK (Hopkins): at jct FM 69 and 269, eight miles W of Winnsboro. The region was settled about 1850 and took its moniker. from its location in a forest of black oak trees.

BLUE (Lee): on FM 696, eight miles W of Lexington. Brothers Joseph, William, and Isaac Jackson settled the site around 1846. It was originally called Blue Branch for a nearby stream. It was shortened to Blue in 1897 with the opening of the post office, supposedly christened for the "bluest water that anybody ever saw" in a nearby stream.

BLUEGROVE (Clay): on FM 172, eleven miles S of Henrietta. The first permanent settlers were in the vicinity in 1882. The community was named for its location in a grove of post oak trees that, from a distance, had a bluish haze.

BLUE MOUND (Denton): on IH 35, six miles NW of Denton. German settlers arrived here in the late nineteenth century. The site was originally known as Indian Mound, but was renamed for the blue prairie flowers.

BLUE MOUND (Tarrant): on FM 156, eight miles N of Fort Worth. John Kennedy, an immigrant entrepreneur, set up Globe Laboratories, Inc., here in 1920. The firm produced serum with which to immunize cattle against black leg, a toxemia especially fatal to young cattle. In time, a community grew up around the laboratory and Kennedy Airport and took the name Blue Mound for its proximity to a nearby hill of the same name.

BLUE RIDGE (Collin): at int TX 78 and FM 1562, ten miles N of Farmersville. The town is situated on land originally owned by Matthiss Mowry, which he received for his service in the Texas Revolution. The settlement was organized in 1876 and acquired its handle for its hilltop location and the blue-flowering grass in the region.

BLUE SPRINGS (Nacogdoches): on FM 226, twenty-five miles SE of Nacogdoches. A school was in operation here by at least 1904. The village was christened for an area spring.

BLUEWATER (Polk): on a LR S of FM 943, sixteen miles SE of Livingston. The area was settled as early as the 1890s, and the community supposedly was named for Blue Branch Creek.

EBONY (Mills): twenty-three miles W of Goldthwaite. The site was settled in the 1880s and first called Buffalo. Postal officials rejected Buffalo as a place name in 1891. Residents then chose Ebony for a local cowboy, Ebony Shaw.

GINGER (Rains): on FM 779, three miles SE of Emory. The hamlet was organized in the late 1870s as a railroad stop and supposedly takes its moniker from the color of a nearby deposit of clay.

LAVENDER (Limestone): on TX 164, seven miles W of Groesbeck. A post office opened here in 1900. The community is thought to have been named for an early pioneering family.

PALO PINTO (Palo Pinto): on US 180 and FM 4; county seat. Settlers arrived in the vicinity as early as 1855. A state legislative act of 27 August 1856 formed the county and specified that the county seat be called Golconda; the latter was laid out that same year. The name was changed to Palo Pinto, for the county, in 1858. This is Spanish for "painted stick" and probably refers to a marker used by early-day Native Americans.

RED BANK (Bowie): on FM 1398, four miles N of Victory City. The village was developed between 1830 and 1845 and tagged for the color of the soil in the surrounding area.

RED BLUFF (Reeves): on a LR off US 285, fifty miles NW of Pecos. Construction on Red Bluff Dam began in November 1934, and this little hamlet grew up nearby. It takes its moniker from the color of the bluffs on the Pecos River.

RED BRANCH (Grayson): on FM 901, twenty miles NW of Sherman. The hamlet was developed around 1860. Its naming was influenced by the red buds and red banks of an early creek.

RED HILL (Cass): at jct TX 8 and FM 995, eight miles N of Linden. There was a post office on the site by 1878. William Lambert, an early settler, christened the village for the red clay banks of Frazier Creek.

REDLAND (Angelina): at int US 59 and FM 2021, five miles N of Lufkin. The community was settled sometime before the Civil War and christened for the color of the soil on a ridge that forms the center of the village.

RED LAWN (Cherokee): on US 69, eight miles S of Rusk. The region was settled sometime before the Civil War, but the community was not developed until 1891, when the railroad came through and Red Lawn was set up as a station. This is an old name, coming from the time when residents did not have grassy lawns in the front of their houses, only red clay.

RED OAK (Ellis): on IH 35, twenty miles S of Dallas. This site on Red Oak Creek was first settled around 1844 by James E. Patton. The little hamlet was first called Possum Trot for the abundance of possums in the area. Considering the name a bit undignified, residents renamed their home Red Oak in 1849, taking the name of the stream for the community.

RED RANGER (Bell): at int FM 437 and 940, eleven miles SE of Temple. Developed by Czech immigrants around 1900. One claim is that when it was time to select a name for the settlement, a cigar salesman happened to be sitting in on the discussion and suggested the name Red Ranger. His offer was from the fact that most of the old homes at the site were painted with red barn paint. The salesman was partially ignored because the residents were looking for a name to rhyme with Frank for Frank Reznicek, a local citizen. The salesman was adamant, however, and offered Reznicek a deal: "If you name your community Red Ranger, I will name my cigar the Rymund Cigar, after your son, Rymund, and put his picture on the lid of the box." This was too good an offer to pass up, and so the community became Red Ranger.

RED ROCK (Bastrop): on FM 812, two miles N of Bateman. Thought to have been called Hannah Land at one time, the current designation comes from the red rock chimney attached to the first house built here in the early 1850s and owned by James Brewer.

RED SPRINGS (Baylor): on US 82, ten miles W of Seymour. A trading post had been set up on the site in the 1890s. The settlement was named for the spring flowers growing on a clay bank of the Salt Fork of the Brazos River.

RED SPRINGS (Smith): at int FM 16, 14, and 2710, six miles NW of Winona. The site was originally a railroad stop in the late 1840s and was developed as a community in 1855. The place took its name from springs located just northwest of the local crossroads.

REDTOWN (Angelina): on FM 1819, fourteen miles W of Lufkin. The settlement was founded about 1900 and probably named for the red color of the lumber company houses. Many of the families had been moved to the area from nearby logging camps to work for the company. They were housed in railroad boxcars, which were painted what was known as "boxcar red."

REDWATER (Bowie): at int FM 2148 and 3098, twelve miles SW of Texarkana. First called Ingersoll, named by religious nonbelievers for Bob Ingersoll, the agnostic and anti-Bible cleric. E. T. Page moved here from London, England, in 1889, when the settlement was undergoing a great religious revival. The time was ripe for a name change, so Page suggested Redwater for the nearby sulfurous springs that spouted red-tinted water.

WHITE DEER (Carson): on US 60, fifteen miles NE of Panhandle. The first occupant of the land was the Francklyn Land and Cattle Company, which began operation in 1882. The railroad built a station in 1888 and called the place Paton for John Paton, settler. The name then took a political turn when it was called Whig. The present designation came in 1889 for a creek, which was so labeled because a white deer was once spotted nearby.

WHITEFACE (Cochran): at int TX 125 and 114, fifteen miles SE of Morton. Organized in 1924 by Ira P. DeLoach. The following year, residents moved the community some four miles southwest to be near the railroad. Colonel C. C. Slaughter brought the first Hereford (whiteface) cattle to this section and grazed them in a special pasture, which became known as Whiteface Pastures. The town took its name from the pasture.

WHITEFLAT (Motley): on TX 70, ten miles NW of Matador. Either Bill Tilson or Mrs. H. H. Campbell named the settlement in 1899 for its location in flat country covered with white needlegrass.

WHITE HALL (Bell): on FM 2409, nine miles NW of Temple. The region was settled prior to 1856; a Masonic lodge was organized here around that time. Early settlers in northwestern Bell County had a verbal landmark they used to set up meetings: "Meet you at the white hall," which probably meant the lodge. The phrase, "the white hall" was used so often that when a little village grew up around the two-story frame building, the site became known as White Hall.

WHITE HALL (Coryell): on FM 215, nine miles N of Gatesville. A school was established on the site in 1890, and the community took its name from the White and Hall families, early settlers in the region.

WHITEHOUSE (Smith): on FM 346 and TX 110, six miles SE of Tyler. In 1836 travelers from several deep-southern states traversed this region. Later, the families moved back in a wagon train and settled down. It is believed the spot took its name from a whitewashed building situated near the railroad tracks. Locomotives following the rails through here stopped to take on water near the "white house." It wasn't long before the village became known by that term.

WHITELAND (McCulloch): ten miles W of Brady. This was a railroad stop when the line was built through in 1911. The White family donated land for the town site.

WHITE MOUND (Grayson): on FM 902, eight miles SE of Sherman. Also known as Whitemound. Henry Lackey and his family settled here in 1849, moving from Missouri. The settlement derived its name from two conical white mounds situated nearby.

WHITE OAK (Gregg): at jct US 80 and FM 3272, fifteen miles W of downtown Longview. The site grew up around a school established in 1887. The christening of White Oak began earlier in the 1880s, when T. J. Tuttle and J. E. (Uncle Bee) Shelton built a small frame school for children in the vicinity. That structure burned down in 1885, and the two men set about, with the aid of volunteers, building another school. Pleas Harris and Kaleb Bumpus donated land near a spring between two white oak saplings. When the new school was completed Bumpus, who was foreman during the work, suggested that the school be named White Oak for the two trees outside the door. The community also took the name.

WHITE ROCK (Red River): at jct FM 1158 and 1699, eight miles NE of Clarksville. Settlers were in the region as early as 1823. It was during this period that John Stiles crossed the Red River and settled at a spot identified by a large white rock.

WHITE ROCK (Trinity): on TX 19, fifteen miles N of Groveton. Billy and Elizabeth Skains, from Georgia, settled here about 1845. It is possible the community label relates to White Rock Creek. The stream acquired its moniker from the chalky gravel of its bed, which turns whitish when removed from the water and exposed to air.

WHITE STAR (Motley): on FM 2009, six miles SE of Flomont. In the 1880s, the region was called Hide Bug Junction. During buffalo days, a small beetle, or bug, favored the thick hide and hair of buffalo as home. The bugs were grayish-black with a white star on their backs. Buffalo hunters, naturally associated with the bugs, often camped here and the site acquired the label White Star.

WHITESTONE (Williamson): at int TX 183 and FM 1431. Acquired its name early in the twentieth century for pale limestone quarries in the vicinity.

WHITEWAY (Hamilton): on TX 36, twelve miles SE of Hamilton. A school was in session here as early as 1936. The community honors Steve White, a local resident. His sons operated several enterprises at the site.

YELLOWPINE (Sabine): at jct FM 2426 and TX 87, five miles S of Hemphill. A one-teacher school was on the site in 1896. The community takes its tag from the fine quality of yellow-pine lumber that was milled here in early days.

THE BUSINESS AT HAND

From Adsul to Yard

ADSUL (Newton): off FM 82, ten miles S of Newton. The post office was established in 1905, and the community was named for the *Ad*ams-*Sul*livan Lumber Company sawmill.

CELOTEX (Fisher): on FM 668, seven miles SW of Hamlin. The community was known as Plasterco in 1907 for a gypsum plant. The Celotex Corporation bought the plant in March 1945 and changed the name of the surrounding settlement.

CLAIRETTE (Erath): on TX 6, fifteen miles SE of Stephenville. Established in the early 1880s with the arrival of the railroad. The moniker relates to a popular brand of soap.

COLTEXO (Gray): on FM 1474, three miles NE of Lefors. The community was organized in the late 1920s and christened for the *Col-Tex* Refinery Company.

COMBINE (Kaufman-Dallas): at int FM 3039 and 1389, twenty miles SE of Dallas. Developed in the late 1880s or early 1890s. The town received its label when a blacksmith shop, grocery store, and post office "combined" their operations into one building.

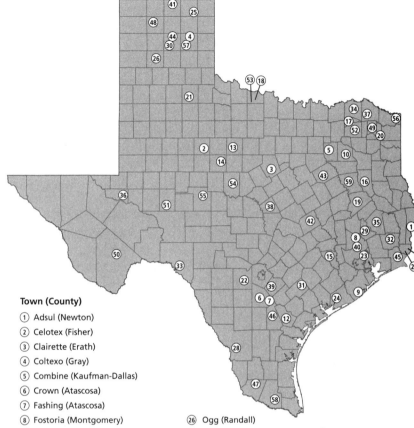

Town (County)

1. Adsul (Newton)
2. Celotex (Fisher)
3. Clairette (Erath)
4. Coltexo (Gray)
5. Combine (Kaufman-Dallas)
6. Crown (Atascosa)
7. Fashing (Atascosa)
8. Fostoria (Montgomery)
9. Freeport (Brazoria)
10. Grand Saline (Van Zandt)
11. Gratis (Orange)
12. Humline (Bee)
13. Ibex (Shackelford)
14. Impact (Taylor)
15. Industry (Austin)
16. Ironton (Cherokee)
17. Jot Em Down (Delta)
18. Kamay (Wichita)
19. Latexo (Houston)
20. Lone Star (Morris)
21. Matador (Motley)
22. Mico (Medina)
23. Moonshine Hill (Harris)
24. Northern Headquarters (Matagorda)
25. Notla (Ochiltree)
26. Ogg (Randall)
27. Oilla (Orange)
28. Oilton (Webb)
29. Palmetto (San Jacinto)
30. Pantex (Carson)
31. Pearl City (DeWitt)
32. Plank (Hardin)
33. Pumpville (Val Verde)
34. Razor (Lamar)
35. Rock Island (Polk)
36. Royalty (Ward)
37. Rugby (Red River)
38. Rumley (Lampasas)
39. Saspamco (Wilson)
40. Security (Montgomery)
41. Sher-Han (Hansford)
42. Silver City (Milam)
43. Silver City (Navarro)
44. Skelleytown (Carson)
45. Sun (Jefferson)
46. Sunniland (Live Oak)
47. Sun Oil Camp (Starr)
48. Sunray (Moore)
49. Talco (Titus)
50. Tesnus (Brewster)
51. Texon (Reagan)
52. Thermo (Hopkins)
53. Thrift (Wichita)
54. Trickham (Coleman)
55. Veribest (Tom Green)
56. Wamba (Bowie)
57. Wesco (Gray)
58. Weslaco (Hidalgo)
59. Yard (Anderson)

CROWN (Atascosa): on FM 1334, ten miles W of Jourdanton. This locale was settled by freed slaves shortly after the Civil War and was known as Lagunillas, Spanish for "small lagoons or lakes." It was renamed in 1900, with the new title supposedly coming from the Crown trademark of a sewing machine.

FASHING (Atascosa): at jct FM 2924 and 99, twenty-nine miles SE of Jourdanton. This area had been settled by the 1850s, but a settlement wasn't in place until around 1916. It was originally called Hickock for the Hitchcock Ranch, which had been sold off as farming plots. Later, the community took the handle Hindenburg, probably for an early settler. Citizens gathered at the general store to consider a new name for the community. The storekeeper noticed a stock of Fashion Tobacco on a shelf and suggested that name. Apparently the handwriting was difficult to read because officials in Washington recorded the name as Fashing. Some believe the name relates to *Fasching*, Germany's carnival season.

FOSTORIA (Montgomery): on TX 105, seventeen miles E of Conroe. The town was known as Clinesburg in the early 1900s for the owner of a mill. The Foster Lumber Company bought the mill in 1901 and renamed the site Fostoria for the firm.

FREEPORT (Brazoria): on FM 1495, sixteen miles S of Angleton. A post office has been in continuous operation here since 1898. The town was not officially organized, however, until November 1912, when the Freeport Sulphur Company dedicated the site.

GRAND SALINE (Van Zandt): on US 80, fifteen miles NE of Canton. Known as the "Salt Capital of Texas." Originally called Jordan's Saline, apparently from an early entrepreneur or settler. The name was changed to Grand Saline in 1873 with the arrival of the railroad, recognizing the extensive area salt mines. An Indiana firm, Grand Saline Salt Company, started mining the site in 1875. This company would become better known as the Morton Salt Company.

GRATIS (Orange): on TX 62, six miles NW of Orange. There was some settlement at the site by 1905. In 1909 the Gratis Townsite Land and Development Company of Dallas was organized to encourage settlement. Although the company's plans did not materialize, the hamlet's name still lives.

HUMLINE (Bee): in SW Bee County. It was christened for the *Hum*ble Pipe *Line* Company in 1927 or 1928.

IBEX (Shackelford): on FM 601, twenty miles E of Albany. Founded in 1921. The name relates to the Ibex Oil Company of Colorado, not to the wild goat.

IMPACT (Taylor): off US 277, eight miles NE of Abilene. This village carries the name of an advertising firm, Impact, Inc. The owner, Dallas Perkins, gave the name to the small trailer park area, which was incorporated in 1960, for the main purpose of voting for legal liquor sales at the northern edge of then-dry Abilene.

INDUSTRY (Austin): on TX 159, fifteen miles W of Bellville. This is the site of the first permanent German settlement in Texas. Johann Freidrich Ernst and his family settled here in 1861 on a grant ceded by the Mexican government in April 183l. Ernst platted the town site in 1838 and then planted fruit trees and began to grow crops. From his tobacco planting he rolled cigars and sold them in San Felipe, Houston, and Galveston, as well as other places in between. The cigar industry is supposedly how the town received its moniker.

IRONTON (Cherokee): six miles SW of Jacksonville. C. H. Martin, an immigration agent from Jacksonville, began promoting the site in 1904. He also named the place, taking the tag from nearby ruins of the Chapel Hill Iron Manufacturing Plant.

JOT EM DOWN (Delta): at int FM 904 and 1532, ten miles W of Cooper. Settlers were in the area by 1885. The site has been called

Mohegan, Muddig Prairie, and Bagley. Dion McDonald built a store here in 1936. At the time, and for many years thereafter, a favorite radio show was *Lum and Abner,* whose characters' antics took place in their hometown of Jot 'Em Down, Arkansas. Residents started referring to McDonald's store as "Jot Em Down." The store owner considered the title undignified and refused to accept the name. Later, a Jot Em Down Gin Corporation was organized, and when state highway officials marked the area, they wrote the name Jot Em Down, and it became the community's official designation.

KAMAY (Wichita): on TX 258, twelve miles SW of Wichita Falls. Joseph A. Kemp, W. Munger, and Reese S. Allen developed the site in 1912. The goal of their land company was drastically changed when oil was discovered. The firm was reorganized into the K-M-A Oil Company, taking its name from the first letters of the three founders' last names. In 1928 the town was known as Kemp City, taking that label from one of the company founders. Citizens learned that there was already a Kemp in Texas. By the late 1930s, the town had started using the initials of the company [K-M-A] as its name. Postal officials accepted Kamay as the official designation.

LATEXO (Houston): on US 287 and TX 19, five miles N of Crockett. Earlier known as Stark's Switch. In the 1900s, the *Louisiana Texas* Orchard Company platted the town.

LONE STAR (Morris): on US 259, six miles S of Daingerfield. Although the town was first settled during the 1860s, it didn't begin to develop until the 1930s, when Lone Star Steel established a mill here.

MATADOR (Motley): on US 62/70, TX 70, and FM 94; county seat. The current designation came from either the Matador Land and Cattle Company, established in 1879, or from the Matador Ranch, which could have also been the cattle company name. Interestingly, Motley County was organized in 1891. There was no town on this site at the time. To qualify for status as an incorporated town, twenty businesses had to be in place at the time of organization. To meet this requirement, twenty "businesses" were set up by ranch hands from the Matador Ranch for a period of one day. A county seat charter was granted, and the "business owners" closed their doors and returned to their routine as cowhands at the ranch.

MICO (Medina): on a LR off FM 1283, twenty-two miles NE of Hondo. A post office was in operation here by 1911. Christened by the Medina Irrigation Company. The name was changed to Medina Lake in 1916, but renamed Mico in 1923.

MOONSHINE HILL (Harris): two miles E of Humble. Charles F. Barrett from Houston secured a lease on Moonshine Hill near what is now FM 1960 and struck "liquid gold" in May of the following year. The site was probably named for the Moonshine Air Jammer Company pumping station.

NORTHERN HEADQUARTERS (Matagorda): seven miles N of Markham. The community was developed in the early 1900s and founded by and named after the Northern Irrigation Company, which had a headquarters here from 1902 to 1907.

NOTLA (Ochiltree): on FM 281 in the SE corner of Ochiltree County. The village was born in 1906 when Bud Westerfield and Frank L. Hamilton bought acreage in the region. First called Half Way for its location on the freight line between Canadian and Ochiltree. Frank L. Hamilton levied the current designation in 1920, which is Alton spelled backward. Alton was Hamilton's partner in the Alton Grocery Company.

OGG (Randall): on US 87, in SC Randall County. Originally called Ralph for the settler who donated land for a school in 1893. The Ogg Grain Company elevator and loading facilities were prominent here in the early 1980s.

OILLA (Orange): in extreme WC Orange County. Ernest Williams and Robert Walles developed the town in 1913. It is believed that they christened the community, naming it for oil production in the area near Kishi Colony.

OILTON (Webb): on TX 359, thirty-two miles E of Laredo. Jose M. Garcia opened a store here in 1900. It was called Torrecillas, or "little towers," for two limestone rock formations in the vicinity. The discovery of oil brought about not only a sudden spurt in population, but also the new name of Oilton.

PALMETTO (San Jacinto): on FM 946, in N San Jacinto County. Also called Palmetto Park. The community was developed in 1902, and its name pays homage to the Palmetto Lumber Company.

PANTEX (Carson): between US 60 and TX 293, some ten miles SW of Panhandle. This was established as a federal munitions center, the Pantex Ordnance Plant, which loaded bombs with TNT for the United States Army between 1942 and 1945. The site takes its name from its location in the Panhandle section of the state.

PEARL CITY (DeWitt): at int TX 111 and FM 951, four miles E of Hochheim. This little village supposedly takes its name from the quantity of Pearl beer that was sold in Walter Hagen's store. The store was built on the site in 1935.

PLANK (Hardin): near int FM 1003 and US 287/69, some five miles NW of Kountze. This site was originally called Noble's Switch, presumably for the Noble and Shulton Mill, established prior to 1882. The new name relates to the many lumber operations in the vicinity.

PUMPVILLE (Val Verde): on FM 1865, twenty miles W of Langtry. Established as a pumping or water station for the railroad in 1882. The railroad drilled wells at Samuels, the site's original name, to supply water for use by the trains. The station was renamed Pumpville accordingly.

RAZOR (Lamar): on FM 197, sixteen miles NW of Paris. The site was settled prior to 1900. When a name for the town was being considered, someone noticed a popular brand of tobacco by the name of Razor that was sold in a store owned by A. K. Haynes.

ROCK ISLAND (Polk): on FM 942, in Polk County. Established sometime before 1900. Carl Bergman, Jim Lewis, and Tom Manry opened a sawmill that later became the Rock Island Tie and Lumber Company.

ROYALTY (Ward): at int FM 1219 and TX 18, two miles N of Grandfalls. First known as Allentown for an early landowner. Oil was discovered in the vicinity in 1927, and the town name was changed for the "royalties" received by landowners.

RUGBY (Red River): at int US 271 and FM 410, four miles NW of Bogata. Settled sometime before the Civil War. The name relates to a brand of bicycle owned by T. J. Lemens.

RUMLEY (Lampasas): NE of jct FM 580 and 2527, twelve miles SE of Adamsville. This was ranching territory in the late 1870s. The moniker is believed to have come from the brand name of a large threshing machine owned by Smart and Clay, two settlers.

SASPAMCO (Wilson): on a LR, off US 181, fourteen miles NW of Floresville. The *S*an *A*ntonio *S*ewer *P*ipe *a*nd *M*anufacturing *Co*mpany developed the town about 1901.

SECURITY (Montgomery): thirteen miles E of Conroe. While pioneers were in the region by the mid-nineteenth century, a community was not developed until the coming of the railroad in 1889.

The village title reflects the name of the promoter, the Security Land Company.

SHER-HAN (Hansford): in Hansford County, near the Oklahoma border. This is a World War II settlement organized by the Phillips Petroleum Panhandle Eastern Pipeline and the Michigan Wisconsin Pipe Line companies. Its name was derived from the Phillips *Hans*-ford natural gas liquid extraction plant and its *Sher*man plant.

SILVER CITY (Milam): on FM 485, four miles NE of Cameron. At one time, the community's only telephone was situated on the porch of the store operated by Tom Hamilton. A person making a call paid by placing fifteen cents (silver) in a box over the telephone.

SILVER CITY (Navarro): at jct TX 31 and FM 55, two miles N of Purdon. Developed before the Civil War. As lore has it, the site was referred to as Silver City when a German merchant refused to accept Confederate money during the war and demanded payment in silver coinage only.

SKELLEYTOWN (Carson): on TX 152, ten miles N of White Deer. The Skelly Oil Company brought in the nearby oil fields during the 1920s.

SUN (Jefferson): on TX 347, five miles SE of Beaumont. The Sun Oil Company bought the town site in 1901 following the discovery of the huge oil pocket at Spindletop.

SUNNILAND (Live Oak): W of US 281, eleven miles N of Three Rivers. First known as Fant City for Dillard R. Fant. Its present designation comes from the Sunniland Railroad Depot.

SUN OIL CAMP (Starr): four miles SW of San Isidro. The community derived its name from the Sun Oil field in which it was situated.

SUNRAY (Moore): at jct FM 119 and 281, fourteen miles N of Dumas. Developed in 1929 by E. S. Collins, the town was soon called Altman. The Sunray Oil Company took over the industrial plant in 1931.

TALCO (Titus): at jct US 271 and FM 719, sixteen miles NW of Mount Pleasant. A post office was opened here in 1856. The town took its name from the initials on the wrapper of a candy bar marketed by the Texas, Arkansas, and Louisiana Candy Company.

TESNUS (Brewster): twenty-three miles SE of Marathon. Established when the railroad came through in 1882 and originally known as Tabor. When residents applied for a post office in 1912, they wanted to name it Sunset, in honor of the sunset logo used by the Southern Pacific railroad line. There was already a facility by that name in Montague County. Residents then devised the current designation by simply spelling Sunset backward.

TEXON (Reagan): at jct FM 1555 and 1675, fifteen miles W of Big Lake. The Texon Oil and Land Company drilled the famous Santa Rita well here in 1923.

THERMO (Hopkins): on FM 1870, five miles E of Sulphur Springs. Founded around 1900 and called Crush, after a large rock crusher near the town site. The name was changed to Thermo in 1910, relating to the Thermo Fire Brick Company.

THRIFT (Wichita): off TX 240, six miles NW of Burkburnett. Refers to the Thrift Waggonner Bank, which opened here during the oil boom days of 1919.

TRICKHAM (Coleman): RM 1176, twelve miles SE of Santa Anna. This is the oldest settlement in the county and had a post office by 1879. The hamlet acquired its handle from the time Emory Peters, or maybe store owner Bill Franks, played tricks on cowboys, such as putting pepper in snuff, etc. The name for the store was originally Trick 'Em, but was changed when residents petitioned for a post office.

VERIBEST (Tom Green): on FM 380, eleven miles E of San Angelo. Originally called Mullins for Isaac "Ike" Mullins, landowner, who arrived in the county prior to 1875. The Mullins settlement was up and running in the early 1900s, but the name had to be changed due to duplication. The current name relates to a packing company's trademark, Very Best.

WAMBA (Bowie): at jct FM 559 and 1397, five miles NW of Texarkana. The community was christened sometime between 1855 and 1860, when Wamba was a popular brand of coffee.

WESCO (Gray): at jct FM 1321 and 1474, two miles E of Lefors. Settlement date unknown. This is the original site of a carbon black plant owned by Western Carbon Company.

WESLACO (Hidalgo): on US 83, fifteen miles W of Harlingen. This is part of the Llano Grande grant made to Juan José Ynojosa de Ballí in 1790. The current settlement was christened around 1919 for the W. E. Stewart Land Company.

YARD (Anderson): on FM 321, twenty miles NW of Palestine. This was originally part of Tennessee Colony and had a post office as early as 1903. Bruce Gray, store owner, was making a list of community names to send to postal authorities. Someone entered the store and asked for a yard of cloth. Gray wrote Yard on the list, and the Post Office Department accepted it.

KNOWN BY THEIR FIRST NAMES

From Abner to Zella

ABNER (Kaufman): on FM 2727, seven miles NE of Kaufman. Settled in the late 1840s and first known as Johnson's Point for the founder, Abner Johnson, a riverboat pilot. The community name was later changed to reflect the founder's first name.

ACE (Polk): on FM 2610, fifteen miles S of Livingston. In 1830 Samuel G. Hirams established a community about a mile south of the present site of Ace that was called Smith's Field, after early settler Robert Smith. The town moved nearer to the present site in 1840 to be closer to the Trinity River and was renamed for Ace Emanuel, the first postmaster.

ADA (Lampasas): six miles E of Lometa. Settled in 1875, the town name honors the daughter of William Malony, postmaster.

ADDIELOU (Red River): eleven miles NE of Detroit. The town was founded about 1910, and its name dates from 1914. A. B. "Bone" Wood built a store that also housed the post office. Sam Patterson, the postmaster, sent three names to postal authorities: Rex, Vea, and Addielou. The postmaster general chose the last. It has been stated that Patterson claimed Miss Addielou Walker was his sweetheart.

Town (County)

1. Abner (Kaufman)
2. Ace (Polk)
3. Ada (Lampasas)
4. Addielou (Red River)
5. Adell (Parker)
6. Adrian (Oldham)
7. Agnes (Parker)
8. Albert (Gillespie)
9. Alfred (Jim Wells)
10. Alice (Jim Wells)
11. Alief (Harris)

60. Dora (Nolan)
61. Dot (Falls)
62. Edhube (Fannin)
63. Edna (Jackson)
64. Edroy (San Patricio)
65. Elbert (Throckmorton)

12. Alma (Ellis)
13. Alsa (Van Zandt)
14. Alvin (Brazoria)
15. Ambrose (Grayson)
16. Amy (Delta)
17. Anarene (Archer)
18. Andice (Williamson)
19. Angelina (Angelina)
20. Anna (Collin)
21. Anna Rose (Live Oak)
22. Annetta (Parker)
23. Arlie (Childress)
24. Asa (McLennan)
25. Aubrey (Denton)
26. Audra (Taylor)
27. Augusta (Houston)
28. Azle (Parker-Tarrant)
29. Ben Franklin (Delta)
30. Benjamin (Knox)
31. Bessmay (Jasper)
32. Bettie (Upshur)
33. Birome (Hill)
34. Bonita (Montague)
35. Brad (Palo Pinto)
36. Bula (Bailey)
37. Buna (Jasper)
38. Calvin (Bastrop)
39. Camilla (San Jacinto)

40. Camp Ruby (Polk)
41. Catarina (Dimmit)
42. Cele (Travis)
43. Celeste (Hunt)
44. Charlie (Clay)
45. Charlotte (Atascosa)
46. Chester (Tyler)
47. Christine (Atascosa)
48. Clara (Wichita)
49. Claude (Armstrong)
50. Cleo (Kimble)
51. Clodine (Fort Bend)
52. Courtney (Grimes)
53. Dads Corner (Archer)
54. Daisetta (Liberty)
55. Delia (Limestone)
56. Delwin (Cottle)
57. Desdemona (Eastland)
58. Dicey (Parker)
59. Donna (Hidalgo)

66. Electra (Wichita)
67. Ellen (Hale)
68. Elmo (Kaufman)
69. Elroy (Travis)
70. Elsa (Hidalgo)
71. Elton (Dickens)
72. Emory (Rains)
73. Era (Cooke)
74. Estelline (Hall)
75. Ethel (Grayson)
76. Eunice (Leon)
77. Fairlie (Hunt)
78. Fairy (Hamilton)
79. Fate (Rockwall)
80. Fedor (Lee)
81. Floy (Fayette)
82. Foncine (Collin)
83. Fred (Tyler)
84. Gail (Borden)
85. Gary (Panola)
86. George (Madison)
87. Gladstell (Liberty)

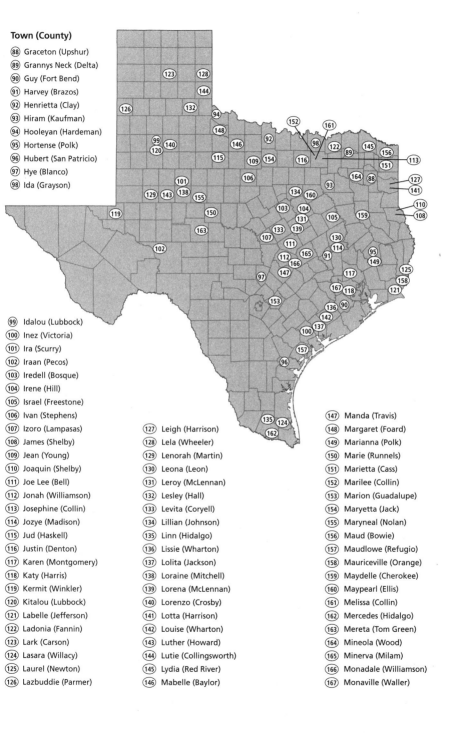

Town (County)

- 88 Graceton (Upshur)
- 89 Grannys Neck (Delta)
- 90 Guy (Fort Bend)
- 91 Harvey (Brazos)
- 92 Henrietta (Clay)
- 93 Hiram (Kaufman)
- 94 Hooleyan (Hardeman)
- 95 Hortense (Polk)
- 96 Hubert (San Patricio)
- 97 Hye (Blanco)
- 98 Ida (Grayson)

- 99 Idalou (Lubbock)
- 100 Inez (Victoria)
- 101 Ira (Scurry)
- 102 Iraan (Pecos)
- 103 Iredell (Bosque)
- 104 Irene (Hill)
- 105 Israel (Freestone)
- 106 Ivan (Stephens)
- 107 Izoro (Lampasas)
- 108 James (Shelby)
- 109 Jean (Young)
- 110 Joaquin (Shelby)
- 111 Joe Lee (Bell)
- 112 Jonah (Williamson)
- 113 Josephine (Collin)
- 114 Jozye (Madison)
- 115 Jud (Haskell)
- 116 Justin (Denton)
- 117 Karen (Montgomery)
- 118 Katy (Harris)
- 119 Kermit (Winkler)
- 120 Kitalou (Lubbock)
- 121 Labelle (Jefferson)
- 122 Ladonia (Fannin)
- 123 Lark (Carson)
- 124 Lasara (Willacy)
- 125 Laurel (Newton)
- 126 Lazbuddie (Parmer)

- 127 Leigh (Harrison)
- 128 Lela (Wheeler)
- 129 Lenorah (Martin)
- 130 Leona (Leon)
- 131 Leroy (McLennan)
- 132 Lesley (Hall)
- 133 Levita (Coryell)
- 134 Lillian (Johnson)
- 135 Linn (Hidalgo)
- 136 Lissie (Wharton)
- 137 Lolita (Jackson)
- 138 Loraine (Mitchell)
- 139 Lorena (McLennan)
- 140 Lorenzo (Crosby)
- 141 Lotta (Harrison)
- 142 Louise (Wharton)
- 143 Luther (Howard)
- 144 Lutie (Collingsworth)
- 145 Lydia (Red River)
- 146 Mabelle (Baylor)

- 147 Manda (Travis)
- 148 Margaret (Foard)
- 149 Marianna (Polk)
- 150 Marie (Runnels)
- 151 Marietta (Cass)
- 152 Marilee (Collin)
- 153 Marion (Guadalupe)
- 154 Maryetta (Jack)
- 155 Maryneal (Nolan)
- 156 Maud (Bowie)
- 157 Maudlowe (Refugio)
- 158 Mauriceville (Orange)
- 159 Maydelle (Cherokee)
- 160 Maypearl (Ellis)
- 161 Melissa (Collin)
- 162 Mercedes (Hidalgo)
- 163 Mereta (Tom Green)
- 164 Mineola (Wood)
- 165 Minerva (Milam)
- 166 Monadale (Williamson)
- 167 Monaville (Waller)

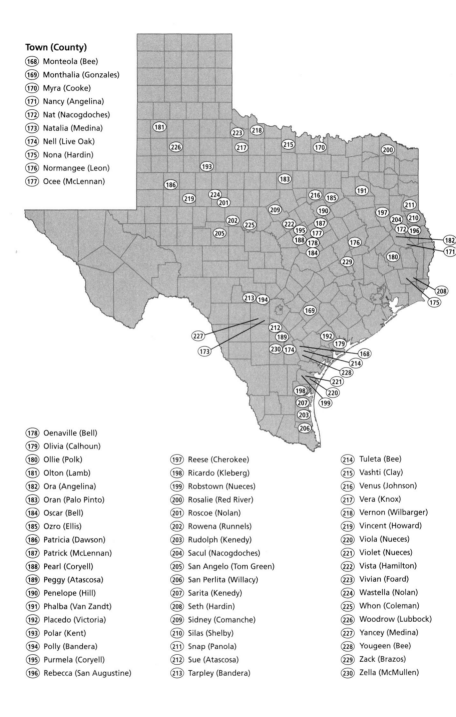

Town (County)
- 168 Monteola (Bee)
- 169 Monthalia (Gonzales)
- 170 Myra (Cooke)
- 171 Nancy (Angelina)
- 172 Nat (Nacogdoches)
- 173 Natalia (Medina)
- 174 Nell (Live Oak)
- 175 Nona (Hardin)
- 176 Normangee (Leon)
- 177 Ocee (McLennan)

- 178 Oenaville (Bell)
- 179 Olivia (Calhoun)
- 180 Ollie (Polk)
- 181 Olton (Lamb)
- 182 Ora (Angelina)
- 183 Oran (Palo Pinto)
- 184 Oscar (Bell)
- 185 Ozro (Ellis)
- 186 Patricia (Dawson)
- 187 Patrick (McLennan)
- 188 Pearl (Coryell)
- 189 Peggy (Atascosa)
- 190 Penelope (Hill)
- 191 Phalba (Van Zandt)
- 192 Placedo (Victoria)
- 193 Polar (Kent)
- 194 Polly (Bandera)
- 195 Purmela (Coryell)
- 196 Rebecca (San Augustine)

- 197 Reese (Cherokee)
- 198 Ricardo (Kleberg)
- 199 Robstown (Nueces)
- 200 Rosalie (Red River)
- 201 Roscoe (Nolan)
- 202 Rowena (Runnels)
- 203 Rudolph (Kenedy)
- 204 Sacul (Nacogdoches)
- 205 San Angelo (Tom Green)
- 206 San Perlita (Willacy)
- 207 Sarita (Kenedy)
- 208 Seth (Hardin)
- 209 Sidney (Comanche)
- 210 Silas (Shelby)
- 211 Snap (Panola)
- 212 Sue (Atascosa)
- 213 Tarpley (Bandera)

- 214 Tuleta (Bee)
- 215 Vashti (Clay)
- 216 Venus (Johnson)
- 217 Vera (Knox)
- 218 Vernon (Wilbarger)
- 219 Vincent (Howard)
- 220 Viola (Nueces)
- 221 Violet (Nueces)
- 222 Vista (Hamilton)
- 223 Vivian (Foard)
- 224 Wastella (Nolan)
- 225 Whon (Coleman)
- 226 Woodrow (Lubbock)
- 227 Yancey (Medina)
- 228 Yougeen (Bee)
- 229 Zack (Brazos)
- 230 Zella (McMullen)

ADELL (Parker): near FM 1885, twelve miles NW of Weatherford. The settlement was organized in the late 1880s. Alexander Sanger, owner of Sanger Mercantile Company in Dallas, suggested this name because he wanted the town christened "in honor of the prettiest girl in Dallas, his daughter, Adell."

ADRIAN (Oldham): on IH 40 and TX 214, sixteen miles W of Vega. Organized in 1900 as a railroad stop. The community was laid out in 1909 and remembers Adrian Cullen, an early farmer.

AGNES (Parker): on TX 199, eighteen miles N of Weatherford. Settlement began in the 1870s when B. B. Barnard opened a mercantile store. The community carries the name of Agnes Mull, daughter of a pioneer physician in north Texas.

ALBERT (Gillespie): on FM 1623, sixteen miles SE of Fredericksburg. The town dates back to 1877 and was first called Martinsburg for an early pioneer. The moniker was changed in 1892 to honor Albert Luckenbach, postmaster.

ALFRED (Jim Wells): on TX 359, twelve miles NE of Alice. Founded in 1888 when it was in Nueces County and known as Driscoll, probably for an early settler. The name had to be changed in 1904 because the discovery was made of another Driscoll in Texas. N. T. Wright was the postmaster of the original Driscoll and agreed to change the name of his locale to Alfred, in honor of his father, Alfred, who had been the first postmaster in the community.

ALICE (Jim Wells): at int of US 281 and TX 44 and 359; county seat. Was a railroad depot known as Bandana in 1883. In 1888 a post office was established and residents wanted to name it Kleberg, to honor Robert Justus Kleberg, of King Ranch fame. Since there was already a Kleberg in the state, they simply christened it Alice, thinking of Alice Gertrudis King Kleberg, R. J.'s wife and the daughter of Richard King. This was the site of Lyndon B. Johnson's infamous "box 13" during the primary election of 1948.

ALIEF (Harris): on Bray's Bayou in W Harris County. The town was platted in 1895 and first called Dairy and Dairy Station. The present tag is in remembrance of Alief Ozella Magee, the first postmistress.

ALMA (Ellis): on US 75, four miles S of Ennis. Developed in the early 1840s and christened Alma about 1881, possibly for the daughter of a local banker.

ALSA (Van Zandt): twenty-two miles N of Canton. As one report has it, Bill Starnes established the community shortly after the Civil War and opened a store on the site. He named the place for his childhood sweetheart.

ALVIN (Brazoria): on TX 6, twenty-two miles NE of Angleton. The settlement was on its way in the 1860s. It received a post office in 1881 and named it Morgan for an early settler. This name duplicated another Morgan, Texas, so residents renamed it Alvin. Alvin Morgan was hired by the Santa Fe Railroad in 1872 to supervise the loading and shipping of cattle at the local stock pens. Morgan built the first home there in 1879 and was instrumental in enticing other settlers to move into the region.

AMBROSE (Grayson): on FM 1897, six miles SE of Denison. Ambrose Bible came to Texas from eastern Tennessee and settled in the vicinity in 1883.

AMY (Delta): on East Fork of Big Creek, three miles N of Cooper. This region was settled in the early 1800s, but the town was not officially designated until 1894. It was called Hobbs Thicket for the four brothers that settled here in 1875. Residents submitted the name Hobbs in 1894 for the newly established post office. The name was rejected, probably because of duplication. It is believed that the present name honors a woman, while there are those who aver that the residents just wanted an "easy name."

ANARENE (Archer): in SC Archer County. The region was settled after the Civil War, but the town was not developed until 1908 when Charlie Graham laid it out. The village name pays tribute to *Anna Laurene* Graham, daughter of pioneer settler J. M. Keen and wife of Charlie Graham.

ANDICE (Williamson): at int FM 2338 and 970, five miles SW of Florence. Joseph Stapp settled the site in 1857. It has been known as Berry's Creek and Stapp. The name submitted to postal authorities was Audice for Audice Newton, son of an early settler. The word was misspelled somewhere along the line, and Andice was recorded as the town name.

ANGELINA (Angelina): eight miles N of Lufkin. Settled prior to the Civil War. A post office was opened here in 1855 under the name Angelina. It was changed to Durst in 1893, then back to Angelina in 1898. The present label comes either from Angelina Dickinson, daughter of the lone Anglo survivor of the Battle of the Alamo, or it could have simply taken the county's name.

ANNA (Collin): on TX 5 and FM 455, eleven miles NE of McKinney. John L. Greer arrived here in 1867, opened a store, and built the first permanent home. He is credited with founding the little village. There are several possible choices for the origin of the town's name: (1) the daughter of John L. Greer, (2) Anna Quinlan, daughter of George A. Quinlan, former superintendent of the Houston and Texas Central Railroad, (3) Anna Quinlan, wife of George Quinlan and the daughter of J. C. Greer, or (4) Anna Huntington, daughter of C. P. Huntington, who built the Dallas-Denison Railroad line. Take your pick.

ANNA ROSE (Live Oak): on FM 624, eighteen miles S of George West. A post office opened here in 1915. Harry Hyman, postmaster and real estate agent, came up with this name in 1912, taking it from the names of Anna Robinson, schoolteacher, and Hyman's stepdaughter, Rose.

ANNETTA (Parker): on FM 1187, six miles SE of Weatherford. Developed in the 1870s and named after Annetta, the daughter of a Mr. Fraser, who established a freight station on the site.

ARLIE (Childress): on FM 1034 in NE Childress County. The town was established in 1888 and christened for Arlie Griffith Weddington, early resident.

ASA (McLennan): at jct FM 2643 and 434. First called Norwood for early settlers. The railroad changed the name to Asa for Asa Woodward Warner, a businessman and farmer with vast holdings and enterprises.

AUBREY (Denton): at jct US 377 and FM 428, twelve miles NE of Denton. Originally known as Onega. This name was not popular with the townsfolk, so a drawing was held in 1881 to choose a new one. Three proposed names were placed in a hat, the selection was made, and Aubrey was the winner. Some claim it was the name of a girlfriend of one of the participants in the drawing. Another version was offered, but local historians do not look on it kindly. There is a yarn that a wagon master was driving a team of mules down the main street when he became quite peeved because the mules were braying rather loudly. The driver shouted, "Aw, bray, you blankety blanks." While this is not considered a valid origin, it seems that the town was once called AwBray, which evolved into Aubrey.

AUDRA (Taylor): on FM 1086, one-and-one-half miles W of TX 83. Named around 1900 for the daughter of Frank Shepherd, partner in a local mercantile store.

AUGUSTA (Houston): on FM 227, sixteen miles NE of Crockett. The first home is thought to have been built here around 1821. The community name is believed to honor Augusta Smith, daughter of a pioneer settler.

AZLE (Parker-Tarrant): on TX 199, sixteen miles NW of downtown Fort Worth. The first recorded settlers were in the region in 1846. This site was originally known as 0-Bar, most likely from a cattle brand, or possibly for the individual who acquired the post office. Anyway, the name was later changed to Azle for Dr. James Azle Steward, who donated land for the town site.

BEN FRANKLIN (Delta): on FM 38 and 128, four miles NE of Pecan Gap. The Simmons, Birdwell, and Hogue families arrived here in 1835, being among the earliest settlers in the region. Up until 1870, when Delta County was formed, this community was part of Lamar County. The site was named for the son of Benjamin Simmons.

BENJAMIN (Knox): at int US 82 and TX 6; county seat. Founded in 1885. It was christened for the son of Hilary H. Bedford, president and controlling stockholder in the Wichita and Brazos Stock Company, which donated land for the town site.

BESSMAY (Jasper): on US 96, one mile N of Buna. John Henry Kirby built a sawmill here in the early 1900s and honored his daughter by naming the community after her.

BETTIE (Upshur): at jct US 271 and FM 2088, six miles N of Gilmer. Established in the early 1880s as a railroad stop and named for Mary Elizabeth "Aunt Bettie" Anderson, early settler.

BIROME (Hill): on FM 308, fifteen miles S of Hillsboro. Developed in 1910 as a railroad shipping point. R. L. Cartwright, an early settler, wanted to honor his two grandsons, so he named the town for both of them: *Bi*ckham and *Je*rome.

BONITA (Montague): on FM 1815, nine miles NE of Montague. Established in 1886 and named for Bonita Hansen, daughter of a railroad engineer. Since this name derives from *bonito*, the Spanish for "pretty," a surveyor enthralled by the surrounding beauty could have tagged it.

BRAD (Palo Pinto): on US 180 and TX 16, twenty miles W of Mineral Wells. Settled prior to 1940. The name memorializes the town's founder, *Brad*ford Fitzgerald.

BULA (Bailey): on FM 54, thirty-two miles SE of Muleshoe. In 1924, W. B. and Tom Newsome subdivided their Bailey County ranch, designating a town site known as Newsome. When a post office was considered, they discovered that there was another postal facility with the name Newsome. Bula was chosen and came from either the daughter of the Rev. Roma A. Oakes or from Bula Thorn, wife of William Thorn, the first postmaster.

BUNA (Jasper): at jct FM 253 and 1004, US 96, and TX 62, thirty miles S of Jasper. Founded in 1892 and first called Carrolla for the Carrol family of Beaumont. The name was changed to Buna in 1893 to honor the cousin of Joe Carroll Sr., Buna Corley.

CALVIN (Bastrop): between TX 95 and Big Sandy Creek, five miles NW of Bastrop. Developed in 1910 as a company town for mostly Mexican coal miners. It was christened for Calvin Silliman, son of W. C. Silliman, founder of the Calvin Coal Company.

CAMILLA (San Jacinto): at int FM 222, 3128, and 3278, six miles E of Coldspring. Settled shortly after the Civil War and named for Camilla Hardin Davis, early pioneer.

CAMP RUBY (Polk): on FM 1276, sixteen miles E of Livingston. First known as Old Hope and also as Ruby, a settlement was here before the onset of the Civil War. Sources state that A. B. Clayton named the site in 1926 for an acquaintance, Ruby Moore.

CATARINA (Dimmit): on US 83, ten miles SE of Asherton. Asher Richardson, rancher, developed the site after electing to construct a railway line to hook up with his other development, Asherton. This moniker has been attached to the region since the late 1700s. There is a legend that it was the name of a Mexican woman killed by Native Americans near here.

CELE (Travis): two miles W of FM 973, seven miles N of Manor. Established in the 1890s, the town is said to have been tagged for Lucille Custer, daughter of a local store owner.

CELESTE (Hunt): on US 69, ten miles NW of Greenville. The town was laid out in 1886 by the railroad and carries the moniker of the wife of a Santa Fe Railroad official. This was once the home of Audie Murphy, reputedly World War II's most decorated soldier and later a movie star.

CHARLIE (Clay): on FM 810, twenty miles NW of Henrietta. Henry T. Dunn built a store on the spot in 1878 when it was called Big Wichita Valley. Dunn later sold out to Charlie Taylor.

CHARLOTTE (Atascosa): at jct TX 97 and FM 140, 1548, and 1333, twelve miles SW of Jourdanton. This village was carved from the Old Tobey Ranch, and in 1910, a town site was platted. One of the area's biggest landowners, Charles Simmons named the town for one of his daughters, as he also did for his other daughters, Imogene and Christine.

CHESTER (Tyler): near jct US 287 and FM 1745, thirteen miles NW of Woodville. This town site was part of a five-league grant ceded to Gavino Aranjo. It was established as a railroad stop in 1883, and the town that developed around it remembers Chester A. Arthur, who was at the time a senator from New York and who would later become the twenty-first president of the United States.

CHRISTINE (Atascosa): on FM 140, ten miles S of Jourdanton. See Charlotte.

CLARA (Wichita): on FM 1813 and TX 240, twelve miles NW of Wichita Falls. Herman Specht began development of a town site in 1886 and named the settlement for his wife.

CLAUDE (Armstrong): on US 287; county seat. First known as Armstrong City. The community name was changed to Claude for Claude Ayers, a railroad engineer who, in 1887, brought the first train through the region. Although the town is named for him, Ayers never set foot in the city once it was organized and christened to honor him.

CLEO (Kimble): on FM 2291, ten miles NW of Junction. A settlement was first attempted on this site in 1880. A post office was finally set up and called Viejo, Spanish for "old" or "ancient." Sam L. Pearson, the new postmaster, renamed the site in 1920 for his niece, Cleo Weston.

CLODINE (Fort Bend): at jct FM 1093 and 1464, twelve miles NE of Richmond. Established around 1888 as a railroad stop and most likely named by a railroad official for Clodine King of Houston.

COURTNEY (Grimes): on FM 2, eight miles S of Navasota. Although the region was first settled in the early 1820s, the town was not organized until 1860 with the arrival of the railroad. By tradition, this site was acquired by Jared E. Groce, one of Stephen F. Austin's early colonists, "for the price of a riding pony and a bolt of cloth." It received its moniker at the time of its development for Courtney Ann Fulton, Groce's daughter-in-law.

DADS CORNER (Archer): twelve miles NW of Archer City. Developed during the oil boom days of the early 1920s. The name relates to oilman C. M. "Dad" Joiner.

DAISETTA (Liberty): at jct FM 770 and 834, twelve miles NE of Liberty. Although occupied as early as 1850, the town was not founded until 1918 following the discovery of oil in the Hull oil field. Newt Farris, store owner, christened the site by combining the names of *Daisy* Barrett and *Etta* White.

DELIA (Limestone): on FM 341, ten miles W of Coolidge. Platted in the late 1870s, the town carries the name of Delia Copeland, daughter of an early pioneer.

DELWIN (Cottle): at jct FM 462 and 2278, fifteen miles SW of Paducah. Torn and Ora Drummond founded the community in the early 1900s and named the site for their son.

DESDEMONA (Eastland): at jct FM 8 and 2214 and TX 16, eighteen miles SE of Eastland. This is one of the oldest continually inhabited regions in Eastland County. Colonizers were here around 1857 and built a fort on land owned by C. C. Blair. William and Ben Funderburg bought the fort in 1875, and by 1877 a community was in the making. For many years the locale was known as Hogtown for its location on Hog Creek. The site was named Desdemona in 1877, in honor of the daughter of the local justice of the peace.

DICEY (Parker): on a LR off FM 730, eight miles NE of Weatherford. The first settlers were in place by the late 1850s. The town was originally called Power for Parson Power, early pioneer. Sometime later the name was changed to Dicey for the wife of another pioneer, W. G. Puryear.

DONNA (Hidalgo): off US 83 and State Spur 374, fourteen miles NE of McAllen. This site is situated in territory ceded by the Mexican State of Tamaulipas to Lino Cabazos in May 1834. The first Anglo settler in the region was John F. Webber, who arrived in 1839 with his wife Sylvia, a former slave. They moved to this area to escape persecution for their interracial marriage. The town, founded in 1904, remembers Donna Fletcher, a divorcee who settled here and established the Alameda Ranch.

DORA (Nolan): four miles E of Nolan. The village was established in 1877 and is said to be the oldest in Nolan County. Its moniker relates to the daughter of Edmond S. Collings, the first postmaster.

DOT (Falls): on FM 1950, four miles SW of Chilton. Originally known as Liberty. Application for a post office was made by William B. Murphy in 1894, and he suggested that it be named for his daughter, whose nickname was Dot.

EDHUBE (Fannin): near FM 1629, seven miles S of Bonham. *Ed*ward *Hu*gh *Be*nton arrived in the region in 1867, and this settlement was first known as Bentonville. The hamlet was probably developed in the mid-1880s. Apparently when the post office opened in 1894, the name had to be changed due to duplication.

EDNA (Jackson): on US 59; county seat. The town was established in 1882 and became the county seat the following year. It was first known as Macaroni Station, because it was a mercantile outlet for Italian-speaking laborers on the Texas and New Orleans Railroad, which came through the region in the 1880s. An Italian count, Joseph Telfener, was the builder and promoter of the railroad. Being of Italian extraction himself, he did not care for the name Macaroni. He started calling the site Ednaville for his daughter. The name was officially changed some four years later.

EDROY (San Patricio): on IH 37, fourteen miles SW of Sinton. *Ed* Cubage and *Roy* Miller bought the land on which the town is situated in 1913, following the arrival of the railroad. In 1921, the Heuermann brothers (E. J. and William) bought land from Cubage and Miller and developed the town site.

ELBERT (Throckmorton): on TX 79 and FM 1711, fifteen miles NE of Throckmorton. The area was settled in the late nineteenth century, but the town wasn't established until 1901. It remembers Elbert Keeler, early settler.

ELECTRA (Wichita): on US 287 and TX 25, fifteen miles NW of Wichita Falls. Daniel Waggoner began ranching in the area in 1852, and the site was known as Waggoner. In 1889 the settlement was renamed Beaver, most likely for nearby Beaver Creek. In 1902 the town took on the name of Electra for the daughter of Daniel's son, William T.

ELLEN (Hale): on FM 784, fifteen miles SE of Plainview. A post office was opened here in May 1904 and named for the wife of Edward M. White, founder of the town of Petersburg, Texas.

ELMO (Kaufman): on US 80, thirteen miles NE of Kaufman. The community came into being with the arrival of the railroad in the 1870s. Its moniker pays homage to Elmo Scott, a railroad surveyor and engineer.

ELROY (Travis): on FM 812, twelve miles S of Austin. Also known as Driskill, Dutch Waterhole, and Hume. It was developed in 1892 and carries the name of the son of a local store owner. There is a colorful legend surrounding the site that General Antonio Lopez de Santa Anna gave this land to one of his officers for duty well served. The officer, in turn, supposedly traded the entire region for a horse and saddle so he could return to Mexico.

ELSA (Hidalgo): at int of TX 107 and FM 88, seventeen miles NE of McAllen. This is part of the vast land grant ceded to Juan José Ynojosa de Ballí; the area served as ranchland before 1800. Anglos were not in the region until the early 1900s. The town, which emerged in 1927, is named for Elsa George, wife of a landowner.

ELTON (Dickens): on TX 70, five miles N of Dickens. L. W. Stark came to the area in 1895 as one of the earliest settlers. The site honors Elton Purcell, local schoolteacher.

EMORY (Rains): at jct US 69 and TX 19; county seat. Originally known as Springville for the abundance of springs in the vicinity. A colorful story accompanies Captain Tom Cain, who built a house here in 1881. As the legend goes, he brought with him a cutting from the ivy growing on General LaFayette's grave in Paris, France. He supposedly planted the ivy in the front yard of his house, and it is still growing there, in front of the original house. There were other settlers in the region before Cain, some as early as 1845. The site was laid out in the late 1840s. The name of the town was changed from Springville to Emory in 1870, recognizing Emory Rains, state representative for Wood and Upshur counties in the state legislature. Rains was instrumental in getting his namesake county organized.

ERA (Cooke): on TX 51, twelve miles from Gainesville. Although settlers were in the region as early as the 1850s, the town did not develop until 1878, when Judge Jim Lindsay donated six acres for a school. The community label remembers Era Hargrove, daughter of an early settler.

ESTELLINE (Hall): at int US 287 and TX 87, fourteen miles SE of Memphis. Brothers Elam and Math Wright established a colony here in 1892 and christened it for Estelle de Shields, daughter of an early settler. This used to be part of the Diamond Tail Ranch.

ETHEL (Grayson): on FM 902, fourteen miles SW of Sherman. Settlers were here as early as the 1850s. In 1878 William H. Burgin and his family moved to the area from North Carolina. He built the first store and became the first postmaster. When a name was required for the facility, Burgin submitted Beulah, Ethel, and Ola, names of his nieces. Beulah and Ola were eliminated due to duplication. There is another opinion, though, that the town was named for Ethel Hardy, daughter of early settlers.

EUNICE (Leon): on TX 7, fourteen miles E of Centerville. John Morrison founded the community in the mid-1800s, and it was called

Morrison's Chapel. The present moniker remembers the daughter of Charles J. Hogan, the first postmaster.

FAIRLIE (Hunt): on TX 11, twelve miles NE of Greenville. The site had a post office as early as 1892 and was named for Fairlee Webster, believed to have been an early resident. There apparently was a misspelling when the name was recorded.

FAIRY (Hamilton): at jct FM 219 and 1602, eight miles SE of Olin. The site was first called Martin's Gap for James Martin, early resident. The current label was bestowed in 1884 when the post office was created and remembers Fairy Fort, daughter of Confederate army captain Battle Fort.

FATE (Rockwall): on TX 66, four miles NE of Rockwall. A post office was established here in 1880. The town was christened either for Lafayette "Fate" Brown, onetime county sheriff, or Lafayette "Fate" Peyton, governor. With a forewarning of the coming of the railroad in 1886, many residents and businesses moved about half a mile east and settled on land owned by Dr. Wylie T. Barnes. To avoid confusion, residents took the old community name of Fate with them.

FEDOR (Lee): on a LR, off FM 1624, twelve miles NW of Lincoln. Also known as Moab, West Yegua, and Long Prairie. The town site was platted in the late 1850s by Wend pioneers from Serbia. It was christened for Fedor Soder, local merchant.

FLOY (Fayette): on FM 154, two-and-one-half miles SW of Muldoon. A railroad depot was in place in 1900 and carries the name of the daughter of E. A. Arnim, early settler.

FONCINE (Collin): near FM 720, five miles W of McKinney. The town was developed in the 1890s and remembers Foncine Fisher, daughter of R. C. Fisher, the community's most prosperous merchant.

FRED (Tyler): on FM 92, twelve miles S of Spurger. A post office was operating here in 1881. From local lore, the site was once called Yeller Corn, because local farmers grew "yeller" corn. At the time, this was the main ingredient in moonshine. The present, more acceptable name supposedly relates to Fred Weathersby, who used a mule team to haul logs out of the piney woods. Another theory, but one with little backing, is that the site was coined for a well-known alcoholic.

GAIL (Borden): on US 180; county seat. Named for Gail Borden, Jr., for whom the county also was christened.

GARY (Panola): on FM 10, ten miles S of Carthage. Settlers began moving into the region in 1844 or 1845. The town evolved in 1898 with arrival of the railroad and was christened for Gary Sanford, grandson of S. Smith Garrison, cofounder of the town site. Walter Prescott Webb, renowned author and historian, and Western movie actor and musician "Tex" Ritter were born in Gary.

GEORGE (Madison): at jct FM 39 and 1452, twelve miles NW of Madisonville. The community was developed about 1907 at the site of a small store owned by George Donaho.

GLADSTELL (Liberty): in NW Liberty County, between Cleveland and the East Fork of the San Jacinto River. A post office opened here in 1913. The site carries the names of *Glad*ys and E*stell* Grogan, daughters of George and Will Grogan.

GRACETON (Upshur): near jct FM 726 and TX 154, eight miles E of Gilmer. The community was developed in the early 1880s and christened for Grace Simpson, daughter of Judge Walter Simpson, who donated land for a church.

GRANNYS NECK (Delta): one mile W of TX 154, six miles SE of Cooper. Brigidier De Spain and his family, migrating from Tennessee, settled the region in 1846. The site was previously called Old

Grannys Neck and Harpers Crossing. The current designation comes from Mary "Granny" Sinclair, who raised goats on a "neck" of land that jutted into the South Sulphur River.

GUY (Fort Bend): at int TX 36 and FM 1994, eighteen miles S of Richmond. Philip F. Ward was the first settler in the region, arriving in 1890. The town name reveres a little disabled girl, Una Guy Rowland, daughter of Orr Rowland, the first postmaster.

HARVEY (Brazos): on FM 30, two miles SE of Bryan. First known as Bethel for Bethel Church. It was renamed in 1879 in honor of Colonel Harvey Miller, an early settler known as "Father of Brazos County," for his efforts in developing the region.

HENRIETTA (Clay): on US 287 and 82, TX 148, and FM 1197; county seat. There is a long history to this name, which was designated at the establishment of the county in December 1857. Some believe the moniker is the formation of two names, *Henry* and *Etta* Parish. Others relate the name to that of Henry Clay, for whom the county was christened. Another source contends that Mrs. Henry Clay, who was Lucretia Hart until her marriage to the statesman in 1799, changed her name to Henrietta Clay. This is conjecture because it seems that there was a daughter named Henrietta, but no record that Lucretia took the name. Finally, there are those who aver that the first name of Henry Clay was simply feminized.

HIRAM (Kaufman): on FM 2965, S of IH 20, in E Kaufman County. Also known as Locust Grove. The site was given the name Hiram in 1893 when the post office opened with James Hiram Hughes as postmaster.

HOOLEYAN (Hardeman): on FM 680, in extreme NW Hardeman County. Sometimes referred to as Hooley Ann. The village was laid out in the late 1890s and is said to carry the names of members of two early families.

HORTENSE (Polk): on FM 942, S of Moscow. Aaron Feagin and his family were the first white settlers in the vicinity, arriving in 1857. The site was sometimes referred to as the Bear Creek Settlement. John Handley was instrumental in acquiring a post office in 1891, and he named the site for his youngest daughter.

HUBERT (San Patricio): two miles W of Edroy in W San Patricio County. The hamlet was developed around 1914 as a railroad switch. It was christened for Hubert Odem, son of Sheriff David Odem.

HYE (Blanco): on US 290, ten miles W of Johnson City. The first Europeans arrived in the region in 1860 and began ranching on Rocky Creek, located some three miles east of the present town of Hye. The site was known as Rocky at the time. A general store was established on the Pedernales River in 1880 by Hiram G. "Hye" Brown.

IDA (Grayson): on FM 697, seven miles SE of Sherman. The community developed in the late 1870s. The village name was for either the daughter of Pete Matthews, the first postmaster, or for Ida Atchison, who operated the first store out of her home.

IDALOU (Lubbock): on US 62 and 82, twelve miles NE of Lubbock. The village was established around 1911, adjacent to a railroad depot. The origin of its name is anyone's guess. It could have come from early settlers *Ida* and *Lou* Bacon. Maybe it was derived from *Ida* and *Lou* Bassett, daughters of Julian M. Bassett, vice president of the local Crosby-Bassett Livestock Company.

INEZ (Victoria): on US 59, fifteen miles NE of Victoria. The town was settled by 1851 and called Arenosa for a nearby creek. The name was changed in 1882 to honor the daughter of Count Joseph Telfener, president and builder of the New York, Texas, and Mexican Railroad.

IRA (Scurry): at int TX 350 and FM 1606, fourteen miles SW of Snyder. Ira Green built a store on the site sometime before 1893.

IRAAN (Pecos): at int US 190 and TX 349, sixteen miles NW of Sheffield. The town was platted after oil was discovered on Ira G. Yates's ranch in 1926. The site carries the names of *Ira* and *Ann* Yates. The name was chosen in a contest that offered a town lot as the prize.

IREDELL (Bosque): on TX 6, sixteen miles NW of Meridian. Ward Keeler and Ranse Walker settled near the site in the 1850s and named the development for Keeler's son Ire.

IRENE (Hill): on FM 308 and 1946, twelve miles SE of Hillsboro. Settlers were moving into the region as early as 1848. First called Zollicoffers Mill for Alabama migrant Edwin Zollicoffer. J. T. Everette and Ramsey Armstrong moved into the region in the early 1870s. They were former Methodist ministers in Alabama. In about 1878, the name was changed to honor the daughter of one of the Armstrong brothers.

ISRAEL (Freestone): on FM 833, three miles NE of Kirvin. The Caney Baptist Church was serving the region before 1858. The hamlet has been called both Burleson and Caney. Its current name derives from Israel Traweek, probably an early pioneer or the first postmaster.

IVAN (Stephens): at jct TX 67 and FM 1148, sixteen miles NE of Breckenridge. The post office opened in 1898. J. O. Brockman christened the community for his son.

IZORO (Lampasas): on FM 1690, some twenty-five miles NE of Lampasas. Established in the early 1880s and called Higgins Gap for John Higgins, early settler. The name was later changed to honor Izoro Gillam, daughter of a prominent settler.

JAMES (Shelby): on TX 7, six miles NE of Center. The town site was probably laid out about 1890 and christened for James Rushing, postmaster.

JEAN (Young): at int TX 114 and FM 1769, ten miles SE of Olney. S. B. Lamar and his son James began ranching here in 1874. James coined the site for his sweetheart.

JOAQUIN (Shelby): on US 84, fourteen miles NE of Center. Benjamin Franklin Morris donated one hundred acres to the railroad in 1885, which marked the beginning of the settlement. The community that eventually came into being was christened for Morris's grandson, Joaquin Morris.

JOE LEE (Bell): four miles SW of Rogers in S Bell County. The first settlers arrived in the 1830s. Jefferson Reed donated land for a community, then named it Mud Springs, apparently for a large spring where livestock watered, keeping the ground thereabouts muddy. Millie Reed McLean, Reed's daughter, renamed the community in 1912, combining the names of two prominent businessmen in the area, *Joe* Reed, storekeeper, and *Lee* Underwood, blacksmith.

JONAH (Williamson): on TX 29, seven miles E of Georgetown. James P. Warnock and Joseph T. Mileham built a mill here in 1857. The site has been known variously as Water Valley and Eureka Mills. When residents applied for a post office in the early 1880s, postal officials rejected both names. Someone suggested that they baptize the place Jonah, meaning bad luck as far as obtaining a name was concerned. In 1884 Jonah became the official designation of the settlement.

JOSEPHINE (Collin): on FM 1777, eight miles SE of Farmersville. The town was settled in 1888 with arrival of the railroad. J. C. Hubbard donated land for the town site, and it was named for his daughter.

JOZYE (Madison): on TX 90 at FM 1452, three miles S of Madisonville. First settled around 1887 and named in honor of Joe Shannon, the first settler.

JUD (Haskell): on FM 617, eight miles SW of Rochester. The town was here before 1915. Jud Robertson and his family migrated from Knox County in 1901.

JUSTIN (Denton): at int FM 407 and 156, twelve miles SW of Denton. The region was colonized by a group of French settlers. In 1848 they established the short-lived Icarian Colony, which was abandoned the following year. No other settlers were in the area until the early 1880s. The current town was laid out in 1883 and christened in 1887 for Justin Sherman, chief engineer of the Santa Fe Railroad.

KAREN (Montgomery): on FM 149, fifteen miles SW of Conroe. A post office opened here in 1909. The general consensus is that the site was tagged for the daughter of John H. Bauer, postmaster.

KATY (Harris): on IH 10 and US 90, twenty-five miles W of downtown Houston. The site was occupied sometime before 1890 as a train depot and was once known as Cane Island. The present name comes from either that of a saloonkeeper's wife or the shortened name of the Missouri, Kansas, and Texas Railroad.

KERMIT (Winkler): on TX 18, 302, 703, and 115; county seat. Organized in 1910 and incorporated in 1938. It was named to honor the son of President Theodore Roosevelt, who had visited an area ranch.

KITALOU (Lubbock): N of int US 62/82 and TX 114, eight miles NW of Lubbock. First called Causey Hill for an early pioneer. The present name relates to the daughter of F. E. Clarity, a vice president of the Burlington Northern Railroad.

LABELLE (Jefferson): ten miles S of Beaumont. The area was populated prior to the 1830s. J. E. Broussard christened the town for his fiancée, Mary Bell Bordages.

LADONIA (Fannin): on TX 34 and 50 and FM 2456 and 64, sixteen miles SE of Bonham. James MacFarland and Daniel Davis colonized the region about 1840, and it became known as McCownville for Frank McCown, the site's first merchant. It seems that a wagon train from Tennessee traveling through around 1857 had as a passenger a lady by the name of La Donna Millsay. The lady so enthralled residents with her singing voice that they named their hamlet La Donna, which over time evolved into Ladonia.

LARK (Carson): on IH 40, ten miles E of Conway. The town was developed when the railroad came through in 1903 and honors Lark Stangler, rancher.

LASARA (Willacy): on TX 186 and FM 1015, eight miles W of Raymondville. The community was laid out in 1924. Whether spelled Lasara, La Sara, or La Saro, the village was named for *La*ura Harding and *Sara*h Gill, spouses of residents William Harding and Lamar Gill.

LAUREL (Newton): on TX 87 in SE Newton County. A logging camp was in place here in 1889. The site is named both for Laurel Gilmer, daughter of the company director of the logging camp, and for the laurel thickets so prominent in the vicinity.

LAZBUDDIE (Parmer): at jct FM 145 and 1172, twenty-five miles E of Farwell. In 1902 Thomas Kelly purchased some 55,000 acres of ranchland. He established his Star Ranch and later sold off some of the land. A school was in session in 1907. The hamlet is named for D. Luther "Laz" Green and Andrew "Buddie" Sherby, who in 1924 opened a store on the site.

LEIGH (Harrison): at int FM 134 and 1999, fourteen miles NE of Marshall. Also known as Antioch. This was supposedly once the site of a large Native American village. Anglos arrived in the early 1840s. The site acquired its present title in 1901, named for the wife of John W. Furrh, large landowner.

LELA (Wheeler): on IH 40, eight miles W of Shamrock. Established in 1902 as a railroad depot and called Story. Bedford F. Bowers, postmaster, changed the name in 1903 to honor his wife's sister, Lela Smith.

LENORAH (Martin): on TX 176, fourteen miles N of Stanton. This was ranchland in 1894. A post office was granted in 1925, and the town that grew up here took the name Lenorah for Lenorah Epley, county clerk.

LEONA (Leon): at int FM 977, TX 75, and IH 45, six miles S of Centerville. Settled before the mid-1800s. The Texas legislature directed that the people of the county choose a site for the county seat and name it Leona, apparently for the county.

LEROY (McLennan): at int FM 308 and 2311, fourteen miles NE of downtown Waco. Laid out in the late 1890s in a joint effort by the Great Northern Railroad and the Smith Land Company. The town remembers Leroy Smith, president of the joint endeavor.

LESLEY (Hall): on TX 256, eighteen miles W of Memphis. The locale was occupied before 1902 and carries the name of the son of James P. Montgomery, landowner.

LEVITA (Coryell): at jct FM 930 and 2412, ten miles NW of Gatesville. A post office opened here in 1886. Mont Simpson, entrepreneur, donated acreage for the town site, thus marking the beginning of the hamlet. For a while it was known as Simpsonville. Residents soon discovered that there was another Simpsonville in Texas. The new moniker came from Levita Jay, mother of Charles Jay, the first postmaster. There are some, however, who believe that the name came from the daughters of M. Simpson, *Lee* and *Vita.*

LILLIAN (Johnson): on FM 2738, fifteen miles NE of Cleburne. G. J. Renfro bought land from J. W. Cunningham in 1902 and established a town site. Each man had a wife named Lillian.

LINN (Hidalgo): off US 281, thirty miles NE of McAllen. Developed in 1927 as a railroad station and coined for Linn A. Dougherty, son of a land developer.

LISSIE (Wharton): on US 90A, fourteen miles W of East Bernard. Settlers moved into the area in 1878, establishing a center near West Bernard Creek. When a post office opened that same year, the site took the name New Philadelphia. New Philadelphia burned to the ground and, according to at least one source, the fire was set intentionally "to keep out the cattle thieves and squatters." The community that replaced New Philadelphia in the mid-1880s was named to honor Melissa Levridge, schoolteacher.

LOLITA (Jackson): on FM 616, five miles E of Vanderbilt. Isaac N. Mitchell was living here by 1840. The town site was platted in 1909 and named for Lolita Reese, great granddaughter of Texas Revolution veteran Charles Keller Reese, a prisoner at Perote, who managed to escape.

LORAINE (Mitchell): on US 20/80 and FM 644, ten miles E of Colorado City. The town site was developed in the 1880s as a rail shipping spur. There is some controversy over the origin of the community moniker. One version is that Loraine was designated for the wife of a railroad official. Another is that the name came from the daughter of a landowner, possibly Loraine Crandall. Others contend that the name refers to the French region of Lorraine. And, finally, some think the railroad threw off the wrong place marker, that the name Loraine was actually destined for another station on the line.

LORENA (McLennan): on IH 35 and US 81, thirteen miles SW of Waco. The area was being settled by the 1850s. A town site was laid out in 1881 with the arrival of the railroad and was named in honor of Lorena Westbrook, daughter of a prominent family.

LORENZO (Crosby): on US 82, twenty miles E of Lubbock. First settled before 1910. Originally known as San Lorenzo for Lorenzo Dow, an employee of the C. B. Livestock Company. Dow purchased the title to the settlement in April 1910, then sold it to the livestock company three months later.

LOTTA (Harrison): on FM 9, fifteen miles E of Marshall. Developed in the early 1900s, the town carries the name of J. E. McLemore's wife.

LOUISE (Wharton): on US 59, twelve miles SW of El Campo. Settled around 1846, the town was part of Jackson County until Wharton County was formed later that same year. The site was christened in 1882 for the wife of John Mackay and sister-in-law of Count Joseph Telfener, railroad promoter.

LUTHER (Howard): on FM 846, eighteen miles NE of Big Spring. A post office opened here in 1909, and the town carries the name of the first postmaster, Luther F. Lawrence.

LUTIE (Collingsworth): at jct US 83 and FM 1439, eleven miles N of Wellington. The town site was part of the Rocking Chair Ranch until 1890. In 1909 the place was christened for the wife of R. H. Templeton, county attorney.

LYDIA (Red River): at jct FM 44 and 911, eight miles S of Avery. Developed around 1870, the town honors Lydia Pritchett, daughter of David B. Pritchett, postmaster.

MABELLE (Baylor): at int FM 1790 and US 183/283 and 277/82, eight miles NE of Seymour. The hamlet was born in 1906 with the arrival of the railroad. The moniker remembers the daughter of an influential resident, J. T. Thompson.

MANDA (Travis): four miles N of US 290, two miles E of FM 973, in NE Travis County. The first settlers arrived here in 1885. In 1893 Otto Bengston, store owner, named the community for his sister *Amanda.*

MARGARET (Foard): at jct FM 98 and 3103, seven miles NW of Crowell. This was the first county seat of Hardeman County, when the site was in that county. It lost its status when it became part of Foard County, which was organized in 1891. Originally known as Pease, the town was renamed in 1884 for Margaret Wesley, supposedly the first white child born in Hardeman County.

MARIANNA (Polk): on the E bank of the Trinity River in SW Polk County. Settlers were here before the outbreak of the Civil War. At the time, it was named Drew's Landing for Monroe Drew, an early businessman. The name was changed in 1871 by Charles Fitze to honor Mary and Annie Goodrich, daughters of William Goodrich.

MARIE (Runnels): on CR just S of FM 384 in W Runnels County. Although pioneers were in place about 1900, the town wasn't christened until 1906. It was named for the wife of Walter "Buck" Gentry, landowner.

MARIETTA (Cass): at jct FM 1399 and 250, fifteen miles NW of Linden. The post office opened in 1880, and the site was first known as Oak Ridge. It was later changed to honor the wife of Newt Wommack, early pioneer.

MARILEE (Collin): five miles N of Celina in NW Collin County. The community had been developed by the 1930s. It carries the name of the first train that came through the village.

MARION (Guadalupe): on FM 78, eleven miles W of Seguin. The Galveston, Harrisburg, and San Antonio Railroad was chartered for this region in 1870. Colonel Thomas W. Pierce, a major stockholder in the railway, bought land in the vicinity. At the time, a small grocery store and hotel were located at the site. Pierce platted a town and christened it for his daughter.

MARYETTA (Jack): on TX 59, six miles NE of Jacksboro. Named for the daughter of Lee and Belle Graves.

MARYNEAL (Nolan): on FM 608 and 1170, twenty miles SW of Sweetwater. The hamlet came to life in 1907 as a railroad depot. There are several versions as to the origin of the place name. Some contend it came from the combined names of Neal S. Doran, a trustee of the Orient Land Company, and his wife, Mary. Others claim it was christened for the first girl born in the community. Then there are those who think it was named for Mary Neal, a stockbroker for the railroad.

MAUD (Bowie): near US 67, ten miles S of Boston. One of the earliest settlements in the region, but Spanish land claims, general lawlessness, and outlaws from the Neutral Ground deterred development until the railroad reached the vicinity in 1870. The town was named for Maud Knapp, daughter of Samuel D. Knapp, the first postmaster and donor of land for the town site.

MAUDLOWE (Refugio): on TX 35, in NE Refugio County. The community was developed about 1912 and carries the name of Maud Lowe, who, with her husband Martin O'Connor, owned the acreage where a railroad station was built.

MAURICEVILLE (Orange): at jct TX 12 and 62, twelve miles NW of Orange. Also known as Maurice. The town was established in the early 1900s along the railroad tracks. The label refers to Maurice Miller, son of the first president of the Orange and Northwestern Railroad.

MAYDELLE (Cherokee): at jct US 84 and FM 2138, nine miles W of Rusk. Also known as Camp Wright, which was established to cut wood for use in the prison iron factory at Rusk. The region was settled in the 1840s, but the town site was not laid out until 1910. The town honors the daughter of Governor Thomas Mitchell Campbell (1907–1911), who was instrumental in getting the State Railroad extended from Camp Wright to Palestine.

MAYPEARL (Ellis): on FM 66, ten miles SW of Waxahachie. First called Eyrie, an allusion to the area being considered a sanctuary for birds and animals. It had a post office in 1894. The name was changed in 1903 to honor the daughters of two officials of the International-Great Northern Railroad.

MELISSA (Collin): on TX 75, seven miles NE of McKinney. Settlers were here in the 1840s, but the town wasn't developed until 1872 with the coming of the railroad. The town carries the name of the daughter of either George A. Quinlan or C. P. Huntington, both railroad officials.

MERCEDES (Hidalgo): on US 83, twenty-five miles E of McAllen. Ranchers were here as early as the 1770s on land that was part of a Spanish grant ceded to Juan José Ynojosa de Ballí. In 1904 Lon C. Hill Jr. had obtained some 45,000 acres in the region, including land on which Mercedes is now located. In that year, Hill formed the Capisall Town and Improvement Company. He named the site Lonsboro, then sold out to the American Rio Grande Land and Irrigation Company, who dubbed the site Diaz. Finally, after more changes, the locale officially became Mercedes. The town was christened for the wife of Porfirio Díaz, president of Mexico at the time, as a sort of self-serving gesture. It was hoped that through flattery, Díaz would be influenced to exert his power to prevent Mexican banditry in the area. If the gesture worked at all, its effect was short-lived, because border trouble continued well into the twentieth century.

MERETA (Tom Green): near FM 1692, eighteen miles E of San Angelo. Also known as Fisherville and Lipan. The community was labeled in 1902 for twin sisters, *Me*ta and *Reta* Burns.

MINEOLA (Wood): at jct US 69 and 80, thirteen miles S of Quitman. Known as Sodom prior to 1873, the label apparently influenced by the rugged terrain and isolated location, which some early settlers connected to the biblical Sodom. The present moniker is believed to have come from Major Ira H. Evans, an International-Great Northern Railroad official, who platted the town. He supposedly named the town for his daughter *Ola* and a friend Minnie Patten. There is a possibility it carries the designation of the hometown of I. E. Ward, the railroad construction engineer from Mineola, New York. Then, there is the offering that Major Rusk, surveyor for the railroad, combined his daughter's name, Minna Wesley Patten, but the postal department misspelled the name.

MINERVA (Milam): on US 77, six miles S of Cameron. Honors Minerva Adeline Sanders, who donated land for a railroad station in 1891.

MONADALE (Williamson): on FM 1660, in SE Williamson County. Once called Springtown or Stringtown. A gin was in operation in the community in 1899. The town was renamed for Mona House, daughter of Edward Mandell House, a friend and advisor to President Woodrow Wilson. Emhouse, Navarro County, was christened for him.

MONAVILLE (Waller): on FM 359, twelve miles S of Hempstead. In 1886 Daniel C. Singletary opened the first grocery store/post office on the site. He named the community for his daughter Mona.

MONTEOLA (Bee): on FM 2985, twenty-four miles N of Beeville. George Cook and his daughter Eliza settled here sometime before 1880. The place was called Butler's Neighborhood, or Butler, for ranchers L. G. and A. B. Butler. A traveling salesman was advised that where Mase Lynch's store sat had no name. The salesman volunteered his name, Monty, and that of his wife, Ola, to come up with Monteola. The salesman's offer was accepted.

MONTHALIA (Gonzales): on TX 466, fourteen miles W of Gonzales. Settlers were in the region as early as 1848, but the town site wasn't developed until 1868. One of the earliest settlers, Phelps White, is reputed to have named the town Mount Thalia to honor the memory of his deceased sweetheart, Thalia. The name eventually evolved into its present-day spelling.

MYRA (Cooke): on FM 1198, twelve miles W of Gainesville. The town was established in 1887 with arrival of the railway and christened for the daughter of a railroad superintendent.

NANCY (Angelina): three miles S of Zavalla in SE Angelina County. The Angelina County Lumber Company set up the community about 1923. It was originally called Dunkin, but was renamed to honor both the wife of Charles A. Kecty, lumberman, and the daughter of Dave Thompson, a former secretary-treasurer of the lumber company.

NAT (Nacogdoches): on FM 343, fourteen miles NW of Nacogdoches. Henry Brewer was the first settler here, arriving around 1814. It was called Crossroads for Crossroads Cumberland Presbyterian Church, but was renamed in 1895 in memory of Nathan (Nat) Jarrell, storekeeper and the first postmaster.

NATALIA (Medina): off IH 35, sixteen miles SE of Hondo. The Medina Irrigation Company established and named the site in 1912. It was christened for Natalie Pearson, daughter of Fred Pearson, promoter of the irrigation project. The recording of the namesake was misspelled.

NELL (Live Oak): on FM 882, seventeen miles NE of Three Rivers. The community was most likely developed between 1910 and 1930, when it was subdivided into farms. It carries the moniker of the daughter of the Butler family, large landowners in the region.

NONA (Hardin): two miles S of Kountze. The site was opened in 1881 by lumber enterprises, brought on by the arrival of the railroad. It was originally called Carroll Station, probably for a local businessman or settler. This name was very similar to another Texas post office, so it is said to have been renamed for the girlfriend of one of the mill owners.

NORMANGEE (Leon): at int FM 39 and 3, seventeen miles SW of Centerville. This was set as a railroad station in 1905. The place name is a derivation of *Norman G.* Kittrell, well-known local judge and legislator.

OCEE (McLennan): on FM 185, six miles E of Crawford. The community was developed shortly after the Civil War and could have been christened for O. C. Ewing, son of Flem Ewing, postmaster.

OENAVILLE (Bell): at int FM 438 and 3369, six miles NE of Temple. C. D. Johnson opened the first business on the site in the late 1860s. The community was named in 1872 and most likely remembers Miss Oena Griffin.

OLIVIA (Calhoun): near jct TX 172 and 159, fourteen miles E of Port Lavaca. This was developed as a Swedish Lutheran colony in 1892. C. J. E. Haterious led the movement here, and the community carries the name of his wife.

OLLIE (Polk): on FM 942, twenty-two miles NE of Livingston. The first known settlement hereabouts dates to the end of the Civil War, and the site was called Rice, probably for the Nelson Henry Rice family. The present designation supposedly is the name of a female member of that family.

OLTON (Lamb): on US 70 and FM 168, twenty miles NE of Littlefield. Harry Baugh, T. F. Brown, and Luther Williams settled the region about 1900. A. B. Powell, postmaster, titled the village in 1903 either for his son or for an early-day preacher.

ORA (Angelina): twenty miles E of Lufkin in E Angelina County. Known as Breaker when the post office opened in 1884. The site was renamed in 1894, levied with the name of the daughter of George Medford, postmaster.

ORAN (Palo Pinto): on FM 52, five miles NE of Graford. A post office was opened here in 1886 in what was, at the time, cattle country. Longtime residents accept that the town was named to honor Oran M. Roberts, governor of Texas, 1879–1883.

OSCAR (Bell): on FM 3117, six miles E of Temple. Also called Jones Gin, probably for an early entrepreneur. Czech settlers developed the town site in the late nineteenth century, and the name is apparently that of an early-day farmer, Oscar Jones.

OZRO (Ellis): one mile west of FM 157, twelve miles W of Waxahachie. Received a post office in 1898. The site was christened for either Ozro High, son of an early rancher, or Ozro Cheatham, son of T. O. Cheatham.

PATRICIA (Dawson): at jct TX 349 and FM 703, twelve miles SE of Lamesa. The settlement was developed in 1923 as headquarters for the Binge-Forbes Land Company and known as Natalie. The moniker was later changed to Patricia, maybe for the granddaughter of a company official.

PATRICK (McLennan): eleven miles NW of downtown Waco. This area was settled in the 1850s and the small settlement was known as Garretts Mill. The place was renamed in 1882, possibly for Patrick Gallagher, postmaster.

PEARL (Coryell): on FM 183, twenty-two miles W of Gatesville. First known as Wayback. This rather unique name came about through error. A petition was sent to Washington for a post office with the name Swayback for a nearby mountain of the same name. Some postal official misread the entry and recorded the moniker as Wayback. Freighters didn't care for this label and refused to use it, referring to the site as Pearl. Finally, in 1890, the official handle was changed to Pearl for Pearl Davenport, son of the local storekeeper.

PEGGY (Atascosa): at int FM 99 and a LR, twenty-seven miles SE of Jourdanton. The hamlet was started in the early 1930s and was known for several years as Hollywood. It was renamed in the late 1930s for the niece of John Mowinkle, landowner and an original settler.

PENELOPE (Hill): on FM 308, fifteen miles S of Hillsboro. The Seley family established the Zee Vee Ranch in the early 1890s about a half-mile from the location of the present town. The Smith Land Improvement Company developed the community and christened it for the daughter of the president of the International-Great Northern Railroad, Penelope Trice.

PHALBA (Van Zandt): on TX 198 and FM 316, eleven miles SW of Canton. Also known as Snider Springs for John Snider, landowner, who settled here in 1853. The settlement was renamed in 1897 to honor the daughter of Joseph W. Jordan, local gin owner.

PLACEDO (Victoria): on US 87, fourteen miles SW of Victoria. There has been a settlement on this spot since the Republic of Texas era. Both Placedo Creek and the town relate to Placido Benavides, a member of Martín de León's colony in 1828.

POLAR (Kent): on FM 1142, some thirty miles SW of Clairemont. A post office was established here in 1906 and the site remembers Polar Singletary, daughter of county commissioner S. H. Singletary.

POLLY (Bandera): two miles N of TX 16, six miles NE of Bandera. Once called the J. P. Rodriguez settlement. The official name, levied in the 1850s, remembers José Policarpo (Polly) Rodriguez, rancher.

PURMELA (Coryell): near int FM 932 and 1241, thirteen miles NW of Gatesville. A post office was granted for the site in 1879 with

Martin Dremien, store owner, town founder, and postmaster. He supposedly submitted the name Furmela for his sweetheart, as the name for the site, but the postal service made a mistake in recording the moniker.

REBECCA (San Augustine): on TX 103, ten miles SE of San Augustine. This hamlet was at first a railroad station for the Gulf, Colorado, and San Francisco Railway, established in the early 1900s. In 1906, the community that developed around the facility acquired its name from that of Rebecca Phelps, daughter of J. A. Phelps, store owner and postmaster.

REESE (Cherokee): on US 175, twenty miles NW of Rusk. Settled around the time of the Civil War, but the community did not develop until the 1890s with the opening of a lumber camp. A post office was put in place the same year and called Andy for A. J. "Andy" Chessher. The locale's label was changed to Reese in 1901, after Reese Lloyd, conductor on the Texas and New Orleans Railroad.

RICARDO (Kleberg): on US 77, six miles S of Kingsville. This began as a railroad siding. Robert Kleberg Sr., who managed the vast King Ranch, asked in 1908 that the railroad build a depot where the siding was located. The station was named Richard in 1906, but the name was later changed to the Spanish Ricardo.

ROBSTOWN (Nueces): at int US 77 and TX 44, eighteen miles W of Corpus Christi. Real estate developer George Payl of Washington, D.C., developed this community around 1906 and named it for *Robert Driscoll.*

ROSALIE (Red River): on FM 909, S of Clarksville. The town was settled prior to 1880 and called Wayland. Originally, the site was situated about one and one-half miles northwest of its present location, which acquired the name Maple Springs soon after the population began to grow. The name was changed to Rosalie in 1880, apparently for Rosanna Nugent, wife of John Nugent. It seems that a mistake in spelling occurred once again.

ROSCOE (Nolan): on US 20/80 and 84 and FM 608, eight miles W of Sweetwater. Organized in 1890 and called Vista, supposedly for an official of the Texas and Pacific Railway. In 1892 residents applied for a post office, but discovered that there was already a Vista in the state. They then changed the moniker to Roscoe to honor a relative of one of the railroad officials.

ROWENA (Runnels): on US 67, and FM 2872 and 2133, eight miles SW of Ballinger. P. J. Barron laid out the town in 1898, and it has since been referred to as Barronville, then Bolf, and finally Rowena. There is a feeling that Rowena came from the Bohemian word *rovina,* meaning "level or plains," and serves as an apt description of the region. There are others, though, that think Jonathan Miles was permitted to name a railroad station between San Angelo and Ballinger. Miles's son, John S., persuaded his father to christen the town for the girl he was courting at the University of Missouri.

RUDOLPH (Kenedy): on US 77, thirty-eight miles S of Sarita. Christened about 1900 to honor Rudolph Kleberg, U.S. congressman.

SACUL (Nacogdoches): at jct FM 204 and 1648, twenty-eight miles NW of Nacogdoches. The community was developed sometime after 1900 with the arrival of the railroad. Residents submitted the name Lucas for their town, wanting to honor the original owners of the land on which the town site was situated. Postal officials turned the petition down because of duplication. Still determined, citizens resubmitted their application with the name Sacul, which is Lucas spelled backward.

SAN ANGELO (Tom Green): on US 87, 67, and 277, TX 208 and 126, FM 584, 765, 1223, 388, and 853; county seat. The community began in the late 1860s and was located across the Concho River from

Fort Concho. The fort was established in 1867, and shortly thereafter, Bartholomew J. DeWitt, founder of San Angelo, bought 320 acres from Granville Sherwood for a dollar an acre. The town laid out at the time was called Santa Angela. One story as to the naming of the settlement is that it honored DeWitt's sister-in-law, a nun in San Antonio. Another opinion is that he christened it for his wife, Carolina Angela, who died in 1866. Regardless, the name was changed to San Angela by 1883. The post office rejected the name because of "the ungrammatical construction." Officials directed that the moniker should be Santa Angela or San Angelo. The latter was chosen.

SAN PERLITA (Willacy): on FM 2209 and 3142, nine miles NE of Raymondville. This town site is situated on part of what was once the San Juan de Carricitos land grant. The land was acquired in 1881 through court action brought by Richard King and Mifflin Kenedy. Pyrle Johnson developed the town in 1926 and christened it for his wife, Perlita.

SARITA (Kenedy): off US 77; county seat. The settlement was once part of the John G. Kenedy Ranch. The community name honors his daughter.

SETH (Hardin): in SE Hardin County. Developed as a railroad siding in the late 1920s and coined for Seth Carter, logging contractor.

SIDNEY (Comanche): on FM 1689, eight miles NW of Comanche. William Yarborough and J. A. Wright settled this region around 1870, putting down stakes on Jimmie's Creek. The site was first called Jimmie's Creek for the stream, then later Round Mountain for a geographical feature. John Stapp became postmaster in 1886 and christened the community for his son.

SILAS (Shelby): on FM 415, six miles S of Timpson. Founded around 1880. In the beginning, the locale was called Battle Ridge, due to, of all things, an argument among residents over a name for the site. The issue was settled somewhat later when it was named for Silas Baines, the first merchant on the scene.

SNAP (Panola): off TX 315, six miles SW of Carthage. The community was settled following the Civil War and the name reveres Dr. "Snap" Cariker.

SUE (Atascosa): eight miles W of Poteet. Also known as Tank Hollow. The site was developed around 1890 and pays homage to Sue Collins, postmistress.

TARPLEY (Bandera): at jct FM 462 and 470, twelve miles SW of Bandera. A post office called Hondo Canon opened in the vicinity in 1878 and was situated on Williams Creek. The facility was moved several miles south in 1899 and renamed Tarpley for Tarpley Pickett, son of the postmaster.

TULETA (Bee): on TX 181, twelve miles N of Beeville. This was a Mennonite settlement founded in 1906. Owners of the Chittum-Miller Ranch sold Peter Unzicker, a Mennonite minister, some fifty-four acres, which was laid out as a town site and named for the daughter of J. M. Chittum.

VASHTI (Clay): at int FM 174 and 1288, eighteen miles SE of Henrietta. Dave Taylor developed the site between 1880 and 1891 and christened it for Vashti Strahan, the first postmaster.

VENUS (Johnson): on TX 67, twenty miles E of Cleburne. The area was settled in the late 1850s and, for reasons unknown, was once called Gossip. J. C. Smyth, landowner, established the village in the late 1880s and named it for the daughter of a local physician.

VERA (Knox): on US 82, sixteen miles E of Benjamin. The town is situated on a flat strip of land with grass of a whitish color. Due to this environment, the community was originally known as White Flat. The settlement had to be renamed in 1890 due to duplication and took its handle from either the daughter of Holt Kellogg, an early pioneer, or the daughter of J. J. Truscott.

VERNON (Wilbarger): on US 70, 183, 283, and 287; county seat. The Tonkawa tribe called the region Eagle Springs as early as 1858, taking the name from the abundance of nesting eagles. A huge number of Anglo settlers moved into the area following the Civil War, and a village was established in 1880 on land donated by Robert Franklin Jones. Residents wanted to name the site Eagle Flat, but this name was rejected by Washington, seeing as there were already too many "eagle" names in Texas. Vernon was the second choice and was recorded by officials in 1880. The name may be that of a traveling whiskey salesman, Vernon Brown, or it may refer to the home of George Washington, Mount Vernon.

VINCENT (Howard): on FM 846, twenty-two miles NE of Big Spring. A town site was laid out in 1908. However, Vincent Vinson had settled here in 1892, and the community carries his name.

VIOLA (Nueces): in N Nueces County at the far west extension of the Corpus Christi Ship Channel. This area is now referred to as the Viola Turning Basin. The town was established in 1912 and christened in honor of Viola McGregor Emmert of Corpus Christi.

VIOLET (Nueces): on TX 44, twelve miles W of Corpus Christi. The community was developed in the early 1900s and was originally called Land or Land Siding. In 1913, the town took the name of the wife of John Fister, the first storekeeper on the site.

VISTA (Hamilton): in SW Hamilton County. W. T. Mason set up a mercantile outlet and a gin on the spot in 1882. The place carries the name of his wife.

VIVIAN (Foard): on FM 2566, thirteen miles NW of Crowell. For a short time, the place was called Pealorville, most likely for Joseph H.

Pealore, whose family in 1890 selected the present designation from a list submitted by the postal service.

WASTELLA (Nolan): on US 84 and FM 1982, ten miles NW of Roscoe. The town was laid out in 1908 on land donated to the railroad by Will Neeley. The community moniker relates to Neeley's eldest daughter.

WHON (Coleman): at jct FM 2633 and a LR, four miles E of Rockwood. Sam H. McCain began organizing the village in 1903. The handle is an anglicized version of "Juan," and relates to a Mexican cowboy who once lived on the McCain Ranch.

WOODROW (Lubbock): on TX 87, ten miles S of Lubbock. The first school was holding class here in 1917. When a name for the town was discussed, there was debate whether to name it Woodrow or Wilson for then-President Woodrow Wilson. Backers of the former won out.

YANCEY (Medina): on FM 462, fourteen miles S of Hondo. A post office opened here in 1897. The settlement has been known as both Tehuacana and as Moss. Its present designation relates to two individuals, Yancey Kilgore and Yancey Strait, sons of local landowners.

YOUGEEN (Bee): on US 181, six miles S of Beeville. This region was originally part of the McMullen-McGloin colony. Eugenia McGloin donated five acres in 1911 for a railroad station. The station, and later the settlement, carry monikers derived from her name.

ZACK (Brazos): twelve miles NE of Bryan. The community became official in 1904 when Zachariah R. Guess opened a post office in his general store.

ZELLA (McMullen): on TX 97, six miles N of Fowlerton. The town was laid out around 1913 and named for the daughter of one of its developers, Colonel Howard Bland.

THE LAND

From Aloe to Woodbine

ALOE (Victoria): on US 59, five miles SW of Victoria. Established in 1889 as a railroad stop and christened for the yucca plants so prominent in the area.

ALPINE (Brewster): at jct US 67 and 90 and TX 118, county seat. The site was developed in 1882 as a water spot for railroad workers and was known as Osborne. The name was changed in 1883 to Murphyville, honoring Daniel Murphy, donor of land for the town site. Eli Nation and his family were the first permanent Anglo settlers in the area, along with the Mexican family of Margareta de Anda. Who designated the current name is unknown, but it was chosen in 1888 by a man, who, while thumbing through the pages of the Postal Guide, came upon the name Alpine, Alabama. He thought that, since this was a mountainous region, the moniker would be appropriate.

CAP ROCK (Crosby): on TX 207, fifteen miles S of Ralls. Ranches in the region were broken up and sold as farmland in 1925. The community was developed at that time and was christened for the Caprock escarpment.

Town (County)

1. Aloe (Victoria)
2. Alpine (Brewster)
3. Cap Rock (Crosby)
4. Chalk Hill (Rusk)
5. Chalk Mountain (Erath)
6. Clifton (Bosque)
7. Coahoma (Howard)
8. Cotton Flat (Midland)
9. Crabapple (Gillespie)
10. Cross Plains (Callahan)

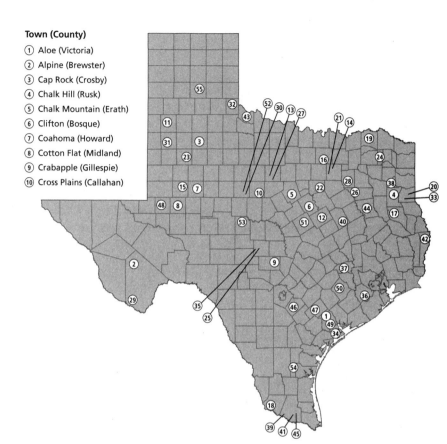

11. Earth (Lamb)
12. Elm Mott (McLennan)
13. Eolian (Stephens)
14. Farmers Branch (Dallas)
15. Flower Grove (Martin)
16. Flower Mound (Denton)
17. Flowery Mountain (Nacogdoches)
18. Fronton (Starr)
19. Glory (Lamar)
20. Grand Bluff (Panola)
21. Grand Prairie (Dallas)
22. Grandview (Johnson)
23. Grassland (Lynn)
24. Grayrock (Franklin)
25. Grit (Mason)

26. Gun Barrel City (Henderson)
27. Gunsight (Stephens)
28. Jiba (Kaufman)
29. Lajitas (Brewster)
30. Lawn (Taylor)
31. Levelland (Hockley)
32. Loco (Childress)
33. Long Branch (Panola)
34. Long Mott (Calhoun)
35. Long Mountain (Mason)
36. Long Point (Fort Bend)
37. Longpoint (Washington)
38. Longview (Gregg)
39. Los Ebanos (Hidalgo)
40. Lost Prairie (Limestone)

41. Madero (Hidalgo)
42. Mayflower (Newton)
43. Medicine Mound (Hardeman)
44. Montalba (Anderson)
45. Monte Alto (Hidalgo)
46. Nockenut (Wilson)
47. Nopal (DeWitt)
48. Notrees (Ector)
49. Nursery (Victoria)
50. Osage (Colorado)
51. Osage (Coryell)
52. Ovalo (Taylor)
53. Paint Rock (Concho)
54. Palito Blanco (Jim Wells)
55. Paloduro (Armstrong)

Town (County)

56 Pandale (Val Verde)
57 Pansy (Crosby)
58 Penitas (Hidalgo)
59 Pilot Grove (Grayson)
60 Pilot Knob (Travis)
61 Pilot Point (Denton)
62 Plainview (Hale)
63 Plainview (Wharton)
64 Plano (Collin)
65 Plantersville (Grimes)

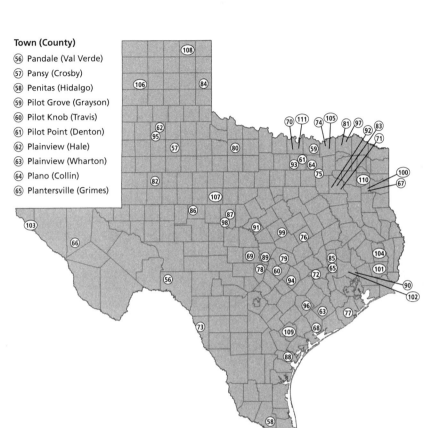

66 Plateau (Culberson)
67 Pleasant Green (Gregg)
68 Point Comfort (Calhoun)
69 Prairie Mountain (Llano)
70 Prairie Point (Cooke)
71 Primrose (Van Zandt)
72 Quarry (Washington)
73 Quemado (Maverick)
74 Ravenna (Fannin)
75 Rockwall (Rockwall)
76 Rosebud (Falls)
77 Rosharon (Brazoria)
78 Round Mountain (Blanco)
79 Round Rock (Williamson)
80 Round Timber (Baylor)
81 Roxton (Lamar)

82 Sand (Dawson)
83 Sand Flat (Van Zandt)
84 Shamrock (Wheeler)
85 Shiro (Grimes)
86 Silver (Coke)
87 Silver Valley (Coleman)
88 Sodville (San Patricio)
89 Spicewood (Burnet)
90 Splendora (Montgomery)
91 Star (Mills)
92 Stone Point (Van Zandt)
93 Stony (Denton)
94 String Prairie (Bastrop)
95 Strip (Hale)
96 Sublime (Lavaca)

97 Sylvan (Lamar)
98 Talpa (Coleman)
99 The Grove (Coryell)
100 The Ridge (Gregg)
101 Thicket (Hardin)
102 Timber (Montgomery)
103 Tornillo (El Paso)
104 Town Bluff (Tyler)
105 Tulip (Fannin)
106 Vega (Oldham)
107 View (Taylor)
108 Waka (Ochiltree)
109 Weesatche (Goliad)
110 West Mountain (Upshur)
111 Woodbine (Cooke)

CHALK HILL (Rusk): eight miles W of Harmony Hill in NE Rusk County. The town was settled around 1875. It takes its name from the white, chalky clay deposits found in the area. This clay is used in all forms of pottery making, including jugs and churns.

CHALK MOUNTAIN (Erath): on US 67, seventeen miles SE of Stephenville. Was part of Somervell County until about 1876, but with resurveying, the site became part of Erath County by 1892. It takes its name from an elevated white rock close by.

CLIFTON (Bosque): at jct TX 6 and FM 219, ten miles S of Meridian. The Samuel Locker, Monroe Locker, Frank Kell, and T. A. McSpadden families settled here in 1852 and 1853, marking the founding of the town site. In 1880, with railroad tracks put down a mile south, residents and businesses moved to be closer to the depot. The hamlet originally carried the name Cliff Town for the limestone cliffs that surround it. Over the years, the two words merged and the current spelling evolved.

COAHOMA (Howard): on IH 20, ten miles NE of Big Spring. The little hamlet began to grow with the coming of the railroad in 1881. The name was probably a reference to Coahoma County, Mississippi, which was named for a Choctaw word meaning "red panther."

COTTON FLAT (Midland): on TX 349, three-and-one-half miles S of Midland. Henry Mayer Halff divided up the Quien Sabe Ranch about 1910 and sold off the land for farms. At the time, the community that emerged was unnamed. Lula Countiss, schoolteacher, and her sister chose Cotton Flat by drawing the name out of a hat.

CRABAPPLE (Gillespie): ten-and-one-half miles N of Fredericksburg. German immigrants settled this site in the mid-1800s. A local stream was called Crabapple Creek for the trees growing along its bank. The town adopted the creek name for its own.

CROSS PLAINS (Callahan): at jct TX 36 and 206, twenty-four miles SE of Baird. Once called Turkey Creek and Schleicher. A post office began operation here in 1877. The town site takes its name from its location, where cattle trails and traders used to cross the West Texas Plains. This was the home of Robert E. Howard, who created the fictional character Conan the Barbarian.

EARTH (Lamb): on US 70 and FM 1055, twelve miles NW of Olton. William H. Halsell developed the community in 1924. It was originally called Fairlawn or Fairleen. There is a thought that O. H. Reeves gave the site its present label because the land was fairly barren and "all that could be seen for miles around was earth." There are those who claim, however, that the name Good Earth was submitted to postal authorities because residents thought their homestead was situated on such productive soil. Postal officials dropped Good. Finally, it is reported that the moniker came from a sandstorm. Even on this, opinions differ. Reeves, serving as postmaster, was chosen to christen the town. While pondering possible options, a sandstorm suddenly appeared, blowing dirt and debris hither and yon. Going one step farther, Reeves supposedly described the storm to postal officials in Washington. He received the comment from them that "The earth seems to move in your country. You will call the post office Earth."

ELM MOTT (McLennan): near int IH 35 and FM 308, eight miles N of Waco. The Battaile, Long, Crabtree, and Christian families settled the region in the early 1870s. It was first called Geneva, but the name had to be changed in 1872 due to duplication. Residents chose Elm Mott for a nearby cluster of elm trees.

EOLIAN (Stephens): on FM 576, eight miles SW of Brackenridge. This site was developed by cattlemen in the 1860s and 1870s. The town received a post office in 1880, which was named by the Post Office Department. The name is from the Latin for the god of winds. Apparently, it is descriptive of the terrain, where the wind blows freely.

FARMERS BRANCH (Dallas): on IH 35 and TX 77, twelve miles N of downtown Dallas. The community was established in 1843 and christened Mustang Branch for the stream where Mustang grapes grew in profusion. William Cochran, landowner, changed the name to Farmers Branch, reflecting the area's rich farmland.

FLOWER GROVE (Martin): on FM 2002 in the NE corner of Martin County. A school district was operating here in 1920. The site honors Hardy Flowers, an early pioneer.

FLOWER MOUND (Denton): at jct FM 1171 and 2499, sixteen miles SE of Denton. The locale was developed shortly after Sam Houston settled a tribal dispute in 1844. This was part of the Peters colony and was christened for a fifty-foot-high mound covered with Indian paintbrush. Native Americans once considered this a holy place.

FLOWERY MOUNTAIN (Nacogdoches): in NW Nacogdoches County. Henry Brewer was granted land here in January 1835. He, his wife, and their six children had traveled from Ohio to settle in Texas. The town was initially known as Brewer's Mountain, but Rev. Washington Wiggins Albritton renamed it for the wildflowers growing around his church.

FRONTON (Starr): on FM 650, five miles W of Roma-Los Saenz. Francisco Guerra first pioneered the region in the late 1700s. At the time, it was designated San Francisco de las Playas by Spanish missionaries. A solid rock bank on the Rio Grande River downstream and across from the site was called La Hacha (Spanish for "axe"), but later became known as Frontón (meaning "pediment" or "bedrock"). The community took its name from the rock.

GLORY (Lamar): on FM 1498, nine miles S of Paris. Established in 1880. Nick Ratliff, store owner, suggested the name Richland, extolling the fertile soil that surrounded the settlement. An official in Washington, upon reading the store owner's glorious description of the countryside, replied, "Only Glory would do your town justice."

GRAND BLUFF (Panola): on FM 2792, eight miles N of Carthage. Developed in the 1840s around a ferry crossing. It is located on a bluff of the Sabine River, and that most likely is the source of its name.

GRAND PRAIRIE (Dallas): on US 80 and 303, IH 20 and 30, and FM 1382, thirteen miles W of downtown Dallas. The community got its beginning in 1863 in a rather unusual fashion. A. M. Dechman, freighter, had a breakdown here on his trip from Jacksonville. He was on his way to Fort Belknap carrying supplies for the Confederate army. Deciding against traveling any farther, Dechman traded his broken wagon, ox team, and two hundred dollars in Confederate currency for 239 acres. It was a natural thing for the settlement to take Dechman's name, sometimes spelled Deckman. The railroad was more influential, however, and in 1877 residents changed the name of the town to coincide with what the railroad had called it since 1873, Grand Prairie. Even that name supposedly came about in a rather unique way. A woman stepped off the train one day and, looking around, said, "What a grand prairie."

GRANDVIEW (Johnson): at jct US 81 and IH 35W, twelve miles SE of Cleburne. F. L. Kirtley developed the town in 1854 when he built a log cabin, connecting to it a blacksmith shop. Kirtley's home/ enterprise was situated on a hill that overlooked an enticing panorama of tall grasses and had an unobstructed view as far as the eye could see. John Whitmire, Kirtley's brother-in-law from Ohio, was visiting and stood gazing out over the breathtaking scene. He said, "What a grand view!" Kirtley liked the expression and adopted it for his store, calling the enterprise Grand View. It remained two words until about 1925, when it evolved into its present form.

GRASSLAND (Lynn): at int FM 212 and 1313, seventeen miles E of Tahoka. This is the oldest settlement in Lynn County and was established as ranch headquarters for Enos and Thomas Seeds in 1888. Enos Seeds was a personal friend of Grover Cleveland, the president of the United States at the time. He christened the site in remembrance of Cleveland's home near Washington, D.C. Some think the name came from the Seeds' plantation, Grasslands.

GRAYROCK (Franklin): on IH 30, six miles SE of Mount Vernon. One of the oldest communities in Franklin County, it had a post office in operation as early as 1848. The village took its moniker from the beautiful gray rock predominant in the region.

GRIT (Mason): on TX 29, six miles NW of Mason. Cotton growers pioneered the region around 1889. Residents wanted to name the community after Major General Frederick Funston, but had to change their minds when a post office was established, as there was already a Funston, Texas. Citizens then tagged the site Grit, apparently for the area's gritty soil.

GUN BARREL CITY (Henderson): on TX 334, twenty-seven miles NW of Athens. Developed after the construction of a reservoir in the mid-1960s. The name came from either an old cattle trail that was reportedly "straight as a gun barrel," or it evolved from the town motto, "We shoot straight with you." Regardless, the town symbol is a rifle.

GUNSIGHT (Stephens): in S Stephens County. Settled in 1879 and coined for a ridge that is as "straight as a gun barrel," with a projecting peak for the sight.

JIBA (Kaufman): near US 175, five miles S of Kaufman. A post office was established here in the late 1800s. In 1900 the town was christened Green, possibly for Eduard H. R. Green, one of the owners of the Texas Midland Railroad. The name was changed to Jiba in 1905. This is a Spanish word, from *giba*, for "hump" and is presumed to refer to a small hill in the vicinity.

LAJITAS (Brewster): on FM 170, twelve miles W of Study Butte. Mexican tribes occupied this area for many years, but were eventually driven off by Apaches. The first Anglos arrived in the region in the mid-1800s, but the site did not begin to grow until 1905 when it became a port of entry from Mexico. The name derives from the Spanish *laja,* for "little flat rocks," and refers to the Boquillas flagstone in the area.

LAWN (Taylor): at int US 84 and FM 604, twenty-four miles S of Abilene. The community of Old Lawn was developed in 1894, but folded when the railroad bypassed it. A new town of Lawn was formed in 1918 at a site that had once been called Jim Ned. There was also once an Old Lawn, no longer in existence. The current community name came from the level terrain and was actually taken from another small village, Oak Lawn.

LEVELLAND (Hockley): on US 385, TX 114, and FM 330. Designated the county seat upon the county's formation in 1921. At first called Hockley City by Charles W. Post, in 1922 the town was renamed to reflect local topography.

LOCO (Childress): at jct FM 1438 and 1034. Settlers were here in the 1880s and a post office was in operation in 1892. This name derives from the Spanish word for "crazy," and the village was christened for the locoweed, which, while not fatal, does make animals act crazy.

LONG BRANCH (Panola): on FM 348, fourteen miles SW of Carthage. A post office was established on the site in 1858, and the place takes its name from a large sandy arm of Murvaul Bayou.

LONG MOTT (Calhoun): at jct of TX 185 and FM 2235, eleven miles SW of Port Lavaca. German immigrants from Indianola arrived here in 1835. They christened the site for the large clump of oak trees in the vicinity.

LONG MOUNTAIN (Mason): one-half mile NW of US 377, some fifteen miles W of Mason. Settlers were in the area prior to the community's development in 1915. The town most likely takes its moniker from an area hill, also called Long Mountain.

LONG POINT (Fort Bend): at int FM 1994 and 361, twenty-four miles SE of Richmond. Homes and a school occupied the hamlet by 1936. Early pioneers reportedly christened the site for a point of timber extending into the prairie near here.

LONGPOINT (Washington): on FM 390, ten miles NW of Brenham. Settled about 1850 on land once owned by Stephen F. Austin. For fifty years or more, the town's name was spelled Long Point. Gideon Lincecum, a botanist, lived on a plantation here from 1848 to 1874 and named it for its position above the Yegua Creek Valley.

LONGVIEW (Gregg): on IH 20 and US 80 and 259; county seat. Founded in the early 1870s with the arrival of the railroad. This place name has many possible origins, all of which have their backers. It could apply to the fact that a person standing on what is sometimes called Methvin Hill could see a long distance. A group was standing on the porch of Dr. Stansbury's house, when one of them, looking out over the vista before them, commented, "What a long view there is from here." "Sure," agreed another, "and what a good name for our new town." R. M. Kelly, who arrived on the scene in 1882, attributes the name to a Mrs. Long, wife of a railroad engineer. One day as she ascended a hill with her husband to look over the new town, she commented, "What a long view there is from here." Her husband replied, "You have just named the new town." Finally, there is tribal lore to add to the sourcebook. Native Americans had been traveling around the present site of Longview from the north to escape a drought. According to legend, the Great Spirit spoke to Chief White Feather, saying, "Ahead lies the land of abundance that thou does gaze upon from a long, long view." Take your pick.

LOS EBANOS (Hidalgo): off FM 886, fourteen miles SW of Mission. Early Mexican pioneers occupied this land and named it for the abundance of ebony trees in the area. Possibly, the site was christened for a 270-year-old ebony tree that once served as a ferry anchor. The site served as a crossing during the Mexican-American War in 1846.

LOST PRAIRIE (Limestone): one mile S of TX 164, three miles SW of Personville. There were families in the area by the 1850s. The settlement took its name from a clear space that was situated in the middle of a timbered region.

MADERO (Hidalgo): off FM 1016, four miles SW of McAllen. A *colonia* also known as Wheel City. A post office opened here in 1915. The site is situated on land granted to Ermenegilda Ochoa by Spain in 1767. The name is Spanish for "timber" and probably refers to the surrounding terrain.

MAYFLOWER (Newton): on TX 87 in W Newton County. William Williams received a grant from the Mexican government for this land in 1834. It was originally known as Surveyville or The Survey, because it was the first known survey conducted in the county. When the site was awarded a post office in the 1890s, citizens learned that there was already a Surveyville in Texas. John Wells suggested the present name for the blooming spring flowers in the vicinity.

MEDICINE MOUND (Hardeman): on FM 1167, twelve miles E of Quanah. Settled by 1908. There are actually four mounds here, but only one is listed as the community name, because just one had a medicinal herb growing on it, which was once used to cure a Native American princess. It is from that incident that the town took its name.

MONTALBA (Anderson): on TX 19, ten miles N of Palestine. Originally called Beaver Valley. The current name was used as early as December 1881 when William J. Hamlett Jr., applied for a post office. Hamlett suggested this derivation of the Spanish for "white mountain" because of the white sand on a mountain to the east.

MONTE ALTO (Hidalgo): off FM 88, sixteen miles N of Weslaco. The Harding and Gill Company developed the site in 1926, the year the railroad came through. First named Rollo, in honor of the son of W. E. Harding, it was replaced by the Spanish term for "high hill," and is probably geographic in nature.

NOCKENUT (Wilson): on FM 1681, twenty miles NE of Floresville. Settled in 1857 by German and Polish immigrants. Henry Hastings chose this unusual name, although he misinterpreted and misspelled the sources. Hastings took the name from two trees, "nockeway" and "hickernut." However, *nockeway* comes from a Native American tribe, the Anaqua. *Hickernut* was Hasting's misspelling of hickory nut.

NOPAL (DeWitt): on FM 108, fifteen miles N of Yorktown. Emil Sasse opened a grocery store at this locale, which then became known as Sasseville. In 1902 the Nopal post office facility in Gonzales County was moved to this site. This word is Spanish for "cactus," and the place name was coined for area vegetation.

NOTREES (Ector): on TX 302, twenty-one miles NW of Odessa. Charlie Brown started his merchandise store here in 1946. He was also the first postmaster and christened the community as such, because when he and his wife first saw the site, there was only one native tree. Later, construction of a large Shell gas plant forced its removal.

NURSERY (Victoria): on US 87, ten miles NW of Victoria. Gilbert Onderdonk opened a nursery here in 1882. His business grew so fast that it was necessary to have a post office. The facility was given the name Nursery, which the village adopted.

OSAGE (Colorado): four miles NE of Weimer. Tom Hubbard and his family arrived from Mississippi in 1851 and settled along Harvey

Creek. The community was named by Dr. Samuel D. McLeary for the abundant bois d'arc, or Osage orange trees, in the area.

OSAGE (Coryell): on FM 185, twelve miles NE of Gatesville. Settlement of the area began around 1860, and the community derives its name from either the Osage (bois d'arc) trees in the region or from the Osage tribe.

OVALO (Taylor): at int FM 614 and US 83, two miles S of Tuscola. Developed in 1909 with arrival of the railroad. It was christened for the oval-shaped valley in which it is located. The word is from the Spanish for "oval."

PAINT ROCK (Concho): at jct RM 380 and US 83, twenty-one miles NE of Eden; county seat. Selected as the site for the county seat in July 1879, it takes its moniker from Native American paintings found on a bluff near the Concho River.

PALITO BLANCO (Jim Wells): off FM 735, fifteen miles SW of Alice. Mexican ranchers settled this vicinity before the 1890s. According to legend the settlers named the town for the hackberry trees in the area.

PALODURO (Armstrong): off FM 2272 on a LR, thirty miles SE of Claude. The town site developed as a side event of Charles Goodnight's setting up the JA Ranch headquarters. It takes its label from the Palo Duro Canyon in which it is located. The name is Spanish for "hardwood" and refers to hardwood trees in the canyon.

PANDALE (Val Verde): on FM 2083 and a LR, some fifty miles NW of Comstock. A post office opened here in 1909. The village takes its name from its location in a valley (dale) shaped like a pan.

PANSY (Crosby): five miles E of Crosbyton. A post office was in operation here in 1894. H. S. Shives, an early pioneer, coined the name Pansy Mills for the flower and two area windmills. It was later changed to its current designation.

PENITAS (Hidalgo): off FM 1427, ten miles NW of McAllen. According to local tradition, José de Escandón led the group that founded this town site in 1749. At one time there was a small hill nearby covered by small pebbles. *Penitas* is from the Spanish for "pebbles." In the early 1900s, the mountain was excavated for use in building roads and railroad beds.

PILOT GROVE (Grayson): on FM 121, sixteen miles SE of Sherman. Settled around 1850 and called Lickskillet. The present moniker comes from James P. Dumas's Pilot Grove Ranch.

PILOT KNOB (Travis): near int US 183 and FM 812, eight miles S of downtown Austin. The site was populated following the Civil War and took its name from a geographical feature believed to be the remains of a volcano.

PILOT POINT (Denton): at jct US 377 and FM 455, eighteen miles N of Denton. The region was occupied as early as 1845, and the town was platted by James Pierson in 1854. The site was christened for the peak of a ridge that could be seen from far off.

PLAINVIEW (Hale): at int IH 27, US 87 and 70, and TX 194; county seat. In 1886 Z. T. Maxwell and his family, along with two thousand head of sheep, moved from Floyd County and set up a farm here. Around the same time Edwin Lowden Lowe of Tennessee settled on land north of Maxwell. The two men joined forces and obtained a post office in March 1887. They suggested the names of Runningwater or Hackberry Grove for the facility. These names were rejected, and Lowe chose Plainview for the vast treeless plain surrounding the post office. The town was chartered under that same name in July 1888 and designated county seat one month later, when Hale County was established.

PLAINVIEW (Wharton): on FM 441 and 1163, five miles SW of El Campo. A community was developed here by at least 1917. Its name derives from the fact that the surrounding land is flat and the town is in "plain view" of the city of El Campo.

PLANO (Collin): on TX 75, twelve miles S of McKinney. William Forman developed the town site, and his family moved here from Kentucky in 1851. The site was on the grant of colonists Joseph Clepper and Sanford Beck. Forman then built a store and other enterprises. Names submitted to postal authorities for the place included Forman and Fillmore, the latter for President Millard Fillmore (1850–1853). Dr. Henry Dye suggested Plano, Spanish for "flat" or "level," for the surrounding terrain. The Post Office Department rejected the two earlier submissions and recorded Dye's suggestion. The site is often called the Balloon [hot air] Capital of Texas.

PLANTERSVILLE (Grimes): at jct TX 105 and FM 1774, fourteen miles SE of Navasota. Anglo settlers from Alabama and Arkansas seem to have been the earliest arrivals, coming in the 1830s. A community did not arise here until around 1840, and a post office wasn't in place until 1856. The facility and the town took their names from a suggestion made by Mrs. J. L. Greene. She recommended the name to honor planters who had settled the site.

PLATEAU (Culberson): on IH 10, sixteen miles E of Van Horn. A railroad section house was constructed here in the early 1880s. The village takes its name from its location on a level (flat) prairie.

PLEASANT GREEN (Gregg): on FM 349, some three miles S of Lakeport. Emancipated slaves developed this site following the Civil War. The origin of the place name is unique. It seems that in the 1880s, another dry spell hit this part of Texas. The peas in nearby Peatown wilted and died out. Those in the neighboring community [here] survived. "It was so pleasant to see the bright green among all the dead growth, it became known as Pleasant Green."

POINT COMFORT (Calhoun): jct FM 1593 and TX 35, two miles E of Port Lavaca. This was part of Jackson County until 1846, when Calhoun County was established. The town was developed in the early 1950s and christened by members of the Mitchell family. They considered the breeze from the Gulf of Mexico to be such a comfort.

PRAIRIE MOUNTAIN (Llano): on FM 2323, twenty miles SW of Llano. In the early 1900s the site was called, at various times, Starks, Putnam, and Hickory. In 1906 it was christened for a nearby mountain, which obtained its label for its location in an area of the Llano Basin surrounded by flat terrain.

PRAIRIE POINT (Cooke): on FM 992, twenty miles SW of Gainesville. A schoolhouse was built here in the mid-1850s. The building was situated on a hill overlooking the prairie.

PRIMROSE (Van Zandt): on FM 314, seventeen miles SE of Canton. Developed in the early 1900s when J. D. Johnson built a store here. He supposedly labeled the village for area wildflowers.

QUARRY (Washington): on TX 36, fourteen miles NW of Brenham. A railroad station was on the site by 1884. The town took its name from stone quarries in the area, which were the source of its economic power in the 1890s.

QUEMADO (Maverick): on US 277, eighteen miles NW of Eagle Pass. The Wipff family started their cattle ranch in the vicinity about 1871. Going back in time, it is believed that the first Catholic mass in Texas was held in the Quemado Valley in 1675 during the Bosque-Larios expedition. The community took its name from the Quemado Valley, which was designated from the Spanish *quemadura*, which means "burn." The early Spanish explorers believed that the region had been scorched by some ancient volcanic eruption.

RAVENNA (Fannin): at jct FM 274 and 1753, five miles NW of Bonham. Colonists began moving into the region prior to 1850. The community was originally called Willow Point, but the name had been changed to its present designation by the 1880s. Tradition has it that the settlement acquired its moniker from the many ravines in the area, especially one that cuts through the middle of the town site.

ROCKWALL (Rockwall): at int TX 66 and 205; county seat. The Boydstun family from Illinois set up house in this vicinity in the late 1840s. A community known as Rockwall was in place by 1854 on land donated by Elijah Elgin. It took its name from the discovery in 1851 of a natural stone wall that lay beneath the surface of the town site.

ROSEBUD (Falls): at int TX 77 and FM 431, twenty-one miles SW of Marlin. Developed by the Texas Townsite Company in 1889 and incorporated in November 1905. It was originally known as Pool's Crossing, then Greer's Horsepen. An American Beauty rosebud growing in the yard of Jennie Mullins inspired the present moniker.

ROSHARON (Brazoria): at int FM 521 and 1462, fourteen miles N of Angleton. Settled before the Civil War. As far as records show, the site had no name until 1859. In that year the railroad built a stop here and called it Masterson's Station for a local plantation owner. Some residents had a nickname for it—Buttermilk Station—because an early resident often treated the train crews to fresh buttermilk. Around 1900 George Wetmore Colles (Collins?) moved onto property in the vicinity. He named his acreage and the nearby town Rose of Sharon Garden Ranch for the Cherokee roses that grew in the region. The community's moniker was later shortened to its present spelling.

ROUND MOUNTAIN (Blanco): at jct US 281 and FM 962, eleven miles N of Johnson City. Joseph Bird built a log cabin in the territory in 1854, becoming the first settler on the scene. A post office was established in 1857 and the name of the facility, as well as the town, relates to a local landmark.

ROUND ROCK (Williamson): on IH 35, sixteen miles N of downtown Austin. Jacob M. Harrell set up a blacksmith shop in 1848 on

Brushy Creek; the site was first named for the stream. The place name was changed in 1854 at the suggestion of Thomas C. Oatts, the first postmaster, and Harrell for an anvil-shaped rock in the creek.

ROUND TIMBER (Baylor): on FM 2374, fifteen miles SE of Seymour. This was the first organized settlement in the county when, in 1874, John W. Stevens built a cabin here. C. C. "Lum" Mills had attempted settlement in the late 1850s or early 1860s; he was driven away by Native Americans, but returned in 1875. The moniker refers to two round clumps of oak trees found in the area.

ROXTON (Lamar): at jct FM 137 and 38, eighteen miles SW of Paris. The first settlement in the vicinity was in 1837 by Eli Shelton and called Fort Shelton. He located it on Cane Creek, some three miles southwest of the present town site. Sometime around 1853 the site became known as Prairie Mount. It officially acquired the handle of Roxton in 1869; the name is thought to derive from either Rockstown or Rockston. The origin goes back to either a prominent white limestone outcropping in the vicinity or to a distinctive rock gate and posts that William Klyce built at his home and store.

SAND (Dawson): on US 180, fifteen miles W of Lamesa. A post office was established in Ebbie Lee's store, and the name came from the hamlet's location in an area once known as Sands of Texas.

SAND FLAT (Van Zandt): on FM 857 and 1255, fourteen miles NE of Canton. A community existed here prior to 1936 and was labeled for its location on level, sandy terrain.

SHAMROCK (Wheeler): at jct IH 40 and US 83, twenty miles S of Wheeler. George Nickel, an Irishman and sheep rancher, suggested this name when he applied for a post office in 1890 because it symbolizes luck and courage. The city did not become a viable community until the train arrived on the scene in 1902.

SHIRO (Grimes): at jct TX 30 and FM 1486, twelve miles NE of Anderson. The first settlers in the region made their homes near Prairie Plains. This was during the 1830s, but no community developed until the railroad came through. Citizens in Prairie Plains moved to Shiro and established a settlement in 1902. Frances Marion Mayfield, postmistress, suggested its current designation, taking the tag from a listing of botanical names in a nursery catalog. The name is supposedly that of a Japanese shrub.

SILVER (Coke): on a LR between FM 1672 and TX 208, sixteen miles NW of Robert Lee. Established in the 1870s as a ranching community. There are a couple of theories associated with the naming of the village. One is that the sandy area had a silvery appearance at certain times of the day due to the sparseness of vegetation. Another view is that there were rumors of area silver exploration in early days.

SILVER VALLEY (Coleman): on US 84, twelve miles NW of Coleman. B. E. Smith and B. R. Brown arrived in the area around 1886. Discussion revolves around whether the site was christened from the settlers' hopes for a silver lode in surrounding hills or because of the fertility of the soil.

SODVILLE (San Patricio): at int of FM 1074 and 1944, seven miles S of Sinton. A number of large ranches here were subdivided and sold as farms in the early 1900s. It is believed that real estate agents were the first to refer to the site as Sodville, an apparent reference to the farming region.

SPICEWOOD (Burnet): one mile N of TX 71, nine miles SE of Marble Falls. A post office opened here in 1889 with James B. Pringle as postmaster. The community most likely took its name from the timber growing on nearby Little Cypress Creek.

SPLENDORA (Montgomery): at jct US 59 and FM 2090, six miles N of New Caney. Charles Cox was influential in having the railroad place a spur here. This was in the late 1800s, and the site acquired the name Cox's Switch. M. S. King, a schoolteacher, as well as the first postmaster, changed the name in 1896, referring to the splendor of the surrounding wildflowers.

STAR (Mills): on US 84 and FM 1047, eighteen miles E of Goldthwaite. Alec Street platted the town site in the mid-1880s and christened it for nearby Star Mountain. The rise supposedly acquired its moniker because, from an aerial view, there is a perfect five-point star at its peak.

STONE POINT (Van Zandt): on TX 243, seven miles W of Canton. First settled in 1878 by families from the Southern states. The site was tagged for its location at the base of a rocky hill.

STONY (Denton): on FM 2622, ten miles W of Denton. Developed in the late 1850s, it takes its moniker from the stony area in which it is situated.

STRING PRAIRIE (Bastrop): on TX 304, twenty miles SW of Bastrop. Developed before the Civil War. In 1886 a String Prairie post office opened with George Zimmerman as postmaster. A long line of mesquite trees in the region probably influenced the moniker.

STRIP (Hale): five miles E of Abernathy in extreme S Hale County. The community was set up in 1904 and there is nothing erotic about its name. The tag simply designates a strip of land some one-and-a-half miles wide and fifteen miles long.

SUBLIME (Lavaca): at int FM 142, 146, 125 and US 90A, eight miles E of Hallettsville. Robert Miller donated land for the town site in the late 1880s. The site was first known as Strune's Store for Diedtrich Strune. The current designation takes its source from the soil's richness in Sudan grass. The region had its own legend for a time, being the home of "Wildman of the Navidad," around 1838.

SYLVAN (Lamar): off FM 2121, seven miles E of Paris. The community took shape around a school that opened for classes in the late 1860s. Henry Campbell christened the site, relating it to the grove of trees in which it was situated.

TALPA (Coleman): at jct TX 67 and FM 2132, twenty miles SW of Coleman. A community existed here prior to 1904 and was developed as a railroad switch. It is believed to have been named for a large catalpa tree in the vicinity.

THE GROVE (Coryell): on FM 1114, sixteen miles SE of Gatesville. Developed around 1859 and first called Morrison Grove, probably for an early settler. Its present title comes from the grove of live oak trees surrounding the site.

THE RIDGE (Gregg): jct FM 449 and 2751, two miles SE of Omega. Also known as Freedman's Ridge, apparently because emancipated slaves colonized the site following the Civil War. The present name comes from the village's location on a small rise.

THICKET (Hardin): at jct FM 787 and 1293, twenty-two miles W of Kountze. Grew up around a railroad flag stop in 1901. Christened for its location in the Big Thicket of East Texas.

TIMBER (Montgomery): eleven miles E of Conroe, near FM 2854. The railroad came through here in 1889, and a post office was established in 1902. Its handle comes from the fact that it developed during a timber bonanza.

TORNILLO (El Paso): on TX 20, thirty-five miles S of El Paso. The Tornillo Townsite Company, owned by several businessmen from El

Paso, laid out the village in 1909. The name supposedly comes from a member of the mesquite family, which was hauled from the site to El Paso for firewood.

TOWN BLUFF (Tyler): at jct TX 92 and FM 1742, sixteen miles E of Woodville. Also known as Townbluff and Fairview. This is one of the oldest settlements in Tyler County. It had a ferry as early as 1833 and was organized as a community in the 1840s. Originally part of the municipality of Liberty, it took its name for its location on and at the foot of a steep incline on the Nueces River. The town is known as the "Natchez on the Nueces."

TULIP (Fannin): on FM 273, twelve miles N of Bonham. Developed in 1836 and originally known as Lexington. Its current moniker came about in 1840 for the Tulip Bend of Red River.

VEGA (Oldham): at jct IH 40 and TX 385; county seat. The area was opened in 1879 for homesteading, and N. J. Whitfield was the first to arrive in the fall of 1899. The name Vega (Spanish for "plains") was bestowed by surveyors A. M. Miller and Howard Trigg.

VIEW (Taylor): at int US 277 and FM 1235, thirteen miles SW of Abilene. The Western Development Company of Sweetwater founded the site in 1910. It was known as Caps Sides at the time. The present name came from the developer and relates to its location on a hill overlooking an expanse of farmland.

WAKA (Ochiltree): on TX 15, twenty-two miles SW of Perrytown. German immigrants colonized the region in 1885 and named it Wawaka. The railroad came in three miles north of the site, so in 1921 the residents moved to be adjacent to the rail line. They named their new community Waka, supposedly a Native American word meaning "marshy."

WEESATCHE (Goliad): on TX 119, thirteen miles N of Goliad. Settled in the late 1840s or early 1850s and called Middletown for its location midway between Goliad and Clinton. This moniker had to be changed in 1860 because it duplicated another Texas town. Residents then chose the present label, christening it for the huisache, or sweet acacia, tree common to the area. The name was misspelled either by the residents or by postal officials.

WEST MOUNTAIN (Upshur): at jct US 271 and FM 276, eight miles SE of Gilmer. The site was founded by Isaac Moody, one of the earliest Anglo settlers in the county, and had a post office in place as early as 1859. The village takes its moniker from a nearby hill.

WOODBINE (Cooke): int FM 678 and 3164, eight miles E of Gainesville. There were pioneers in the region as early as 1845, but R. C. Nelson was the first permanent resident, arriving in 1864. W. H. Mitchell opened the community's first mercantile store, donated land for the town site in 1876, and named the place Mineola. The railroad came through in 1879 and renamed the settlement for the wild woodbine vines in the vicinity.

RELIGION

From Anthony to Weeping Mary

ANTHONY (El Paso): at jct TX 20 and IH 10, sixteen miles NW of downtown El Paso. A Mexican American woman established the community prior to 1884 and built a chapel to St. Anthony of Padua. For a while, after 1885, the site became known as La Tuna (Spanish for "prickly pear") for the local Federal Correctional Institution. In the 1950s the town was officially incorporated as Anthony. This is the home of the Leap Year Capital of the World, a club open to anyone who has a birthday on February 29.

APOLONIA (Grimes): three miles E of Anderson. Founded in the mid-1830s, but as far as is known, did not have an official name. Polish settlers christened it in 1889 for Saint Appolonia. The spelling was altered.

BABYLON (Navarro): seventeen miles SW of Corsicana. Former slaves founded the settlement about 1895. They built a church, which they named for the ancient biblical town. The village took the church's moniker.

BELLS (Grayson): on US 82, ten miles E of Sherman. Originally called Duganville for a pioneering family that arrived in the area in

Town (County)

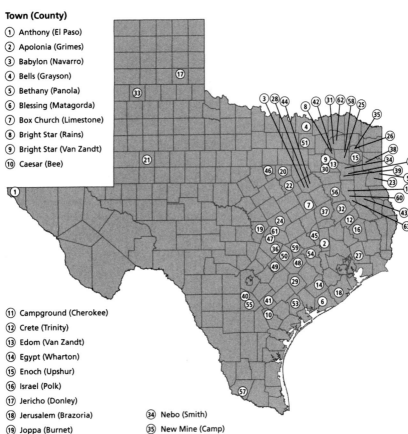

1. Anthony (El Paso)
2. Apolonia (Grimes)
3. Babylon (Navarro)
4. Bells (Grayson)
5. Bethany (Panola)
6. Blessing (Matagorda)
7. Box Church (Limestone)
8. Bright Star (Rains)
9. Bright Star (Van Zandt)
10. Caesar (Bee)
11. Campground (Cherokee)
12. Crete (Trinity)
13. Edom (Van Zandt)
14. Egypt (Wharton)
15. Enoch (Upshur)
16. Israel (Polk)
17. Jericho (Donley)
18. Jerusalem (Brazoria)
19. Joppa (Burnet)
20. Joshua (Johnson)
21. Key (Dawson)
22. Lebanon (Hill)
23. Liberty Chapel (Panola)
24. Little Flock (Bell)
25. Little Hope (Wood)
26. Living Green (Camp)
27. Macedonia (Liberty)
28. Mount Nebo (Navarro)
29. Mount Olive (Lavaca)
30. Mount Pisgah (Van Zandt)
31. Mount Zion (Hopkins)
32. Mount Zion (Houston)
33. Nazareth (Castro)
34. Nebo (Smith)
35. New Mine (Camp)
36. New Sweden (Travis)
37. Nineveh (Leon)
38. Noonday (Harrison)
39. Noonday (Smith)
40. Old Rock Church (Atascosa)
41. Panna Maria (Karnes)
42. Pilgrim Rest (Rains)
43. Pisgah (Nacogdoches)
44. Pisgah (Navarro)
45. Reliance (Brazos)
46. Rock Church (Hood)
47. Rock House (Williamson)
48. St. John (Fayette)
49. St. John Colony (Caldwell)
50. St. Marys Colony (Bastrop)
51. St. Paul (Collin)
52. St. Viola (Smith)
53. Salem (Victoria)
54. Salem (Washington)
55. Sand Branch Church (Atascosa)
56. Sand Flat Church (Anderson)
57. Santa Cruz (Starr)
58. Sharon (Wood)
59. Sweet Home (Lee)
60. Sweet Union (Cherokee)
61. Theon (Williamson)
62. Tira (Hopkins)
63. Weeping Mary (Cherokee)

1835. The name was later changed to Gospel Ridge for the large number of churches located here. Each of the churches had a bell, and when application for a post office was made in 1879, the name Bells was submitted and accepted.

BETHANY (Panola): on US 79, twenty-two miles NE of Carthage. Originally settled about 1840 and known as Vernon. The label was changed to Bethany around 1849 for the religious connotation.

BLESSING (Matagorda): W of jct TX 35 and FM 616, twenty miles W of Bay City. When the railroad established a town on the ranch of Jonathan and Shanghai Pierce in 1903, they wanted to name it Thank God. Postal officials weren't overly fond of that tag, but did christen it in a religious vein—Blessing—anyway.

BOX CHURCH (Limestone): on FM 937, four miles S of Groesbeck. Originally known as Hog Range. A church was founded here in the 1890s and took its name from the fact that it was constructed of "boxing plank" without framing.

BRIGHT STAR (Rains): on FM 2795, six miles SE of Emory. Founded around the time of the Civil War. The site was christened for a primitive Baptist church from earlier days. The church acquired its name, as the story goes, when settlers, resting on a hill, saw a bright star in the night sky.

BRIGHT STAR (Van Zandt): at int FM 47 and 1395, eighteen miles NW of Canton. The place had a school in 1890. The community took its name from a church, which was, in turn, influenced by the biblical star so prominent at the time of the birth of Christ.

CAESAR (Bee): on FM 798, eight miles NW of Pettus. Peter Wolfe colonized the region prior to 1876, and the site became known as Wolfes Neighborhood. In the early 1900s, R. L. Peevy built a store on the spot and applied for a post office. He sent a list of possible names to Washington, all of which came from the Bible. Postal authorities chose Caesar.

CAMPGROUND (Cherokee): on TX 294, twelve miles SW of Rusk. Settled around the time of the Civil War and christened for a church.

CRETE (Trinity): off FM 358, eleven miles N of Groveton. Settlers from De Ridder, Louisiana, founded the community in the 1870s. It was originally known as East Prairie, but the name was changed to Crete in 1902, taking the moniker from a biblical reference to the Mediterranean island. Some residents today refer to the place as Possum Walk.

EDOM (Van Zandt): on FM 279, 314, and 2339, sixteen miles SE of Canton. The original settlement, called Hamburg, was developed in 1849. In 1855 the Hamburg post office moved to a locale one mile south of the present village. It then took the name Edom, the name given Esau in the book of Genesis.

EGYPT (Wharton): on FM 102, eleven miles NW of Wharton. The town was originally in Colorado County, but became part of Wharton County at the formation of the latter in 1846. This is one of the oldest and most historic towns in Wharton County, dating to the year John C. Clark settled on the site in 1822. Eli Mercer came on the scene in 1829, built a plantation, and set up a ferry to traverse the Colorado River. The new settlement quickly acquired the name Mercer's Crossing. Blessed with fertile soil and abundant rain, the community supplied corn to its neighbors during a drought, much as the biblical Joseph (of the multicolored coat) had done for the pharaoh when drought struck other parts of the region. Because of this, the community became known as Egypt. In another version, following the drought of 1827, farmers from Stephen F. Austin's colony came to this region to obtain corn. They referred to the venture as "going down into Egypt," which, of course, came from a biblical reference.

ENOCH (Upshur): on FM 49, two miles W of Gilmer. This is a Mormon settlement founded around 1912. The name relates to the Old Testament patriarch, the father of Methuselah.

ISRAEL (Polk): on FM 1316, NE of Livingston. The religious community was founded in 1895 by a sect known as Israelites. To emphasize their religious belief, a deed is recorded in the Polk County courthouse that shows the citizens deeded their land to the "Lord God of Israel, Creator of Heaven and Earth."

JERICHO (Donley): off IH 40 in N Donley County. Established as a railroad stop in 1902. Judge John Altizer is responsible for the site's moniker, associating it with the biblical Jericho in Palestine.

JERUSALEM (Brazoria): N of FM 2611, sixteen miles SW of Angleton. Developed before 1896 and carries a religious connotation.

JOPPA (Burnet): on FM 210, seven miles NE of Bertram. Settled prior to 1880 and originally known as Pool Branch, after a pool formed by a waterfall in the vicinity. The name was changed in 1891 and relates to the biblical Joppa (Jaffa), today a part of modern Tel Aviv, Israel.

JOSHUA (Johnson): at int TX 174 and FM 917, seven miles SW of Burleson. The village started around 1881 as a railroad stop and was called Caddo Peak. The moniker had to be changed due to duplication. Dr. D. B. McMillan supposedly suggested the current designation, relating it to the biblical Joshua.

KEY (Dawson): at jct US 180 and FM 178, twelve miles E of Lamesa. This village was populated by 1914 and was christened for the Key Baptist Church.

LEBANON (Hill): S of int FM 2114 and 1304, sixteen miles SW of Hillsboro. The Lebanon Methodist Church was founded here in

1872, and the town adopted that name. This is a biblical reference, from the cedars of Lebanon.

LIBERTY CHAPEL (Panola): on US 79, three miles NE of Carthage. Founded following the Civil War and first called Frogpond. The name was later changed to Liberty Chapel for a local house of worship.

LITTLE FLOCK (Bell): three miles E of Temple. The community was settled in the 1860s, and a Baptist church opened in 1884. On the day of the first service, Parson Lancaster commented, "Indeed, this is a little flock," apparently referring to the small attendance. His comment served as inspiration for the community label. Possibly, the name came from Luke 12:32: "Fear not, little flock; for it is your Father's good pleasure to give you the Kingdom."

LITTLE HOPE (Wood): at int FM 154 and 312, ten miles E of Quitman. The area was settled at least by the 1850s. Early residents had little hope for the survival of the Missionary Baptist Church, which was founded in 1881.

LIVING GREEN (Camp): on FM 1519, five miles SW of Pittsburg. The hamlet grew up around the Living Green Baptist Church, an African American chapel organized in 1875.

MACEDONIA (Liberty): five miles NE of jct TX 321 and FM 1008, sixteen miles NW of Liberty. A Chicago, Illinois, syndicate purchased 12,000 acres in this region in 1914. Its aim was to establish a colony of Greek immigrants to work at truck farming. While the colony never materialized, the syndicate coined the name Macedonia for the little village, taking the name of a Baptist church founded in 1845.

MOUNT NEBO (Navarro): seven miles S of Corsicana. Founded prior to 1900 and christened for the biblical peak from which Moses saw the Promised Land.

MOUNT OLIVE (Lavaca): on FM 531, six miles SE of Shiner. The Culpepper family settled here around 1838. The site carries a name relating to a Baptist church founded in 1848.

MOUNT PISGAH (Van Zandt): off FM 2909 between Canton and Martins Mills. A school was in session here at least by 1890. The moniker comes from a mountain range at the north end of the Dead Sea in Israel. Mount Nebo is its highest peak.

MOUNT ZION (Hopkins): on TX 11, fifteen miles NW of Sulphur Springs. The community was settled prior to 1898, and the name is that of ancient Jerusalem.

MOUNT ZION (Houston): off FM 2544, six miles SW of Grapeland. The site developed around a school that had been established in the early 1890s. For the origin of its name, see Mount Zion (Hopkins).

NAZARETH (Castro): at int TX 86 and FM 168, fourteen miles E of Dimmitt. This small hamlet was settled prior to 1902 and has gone by various names: Wynne, Shamrock, and Dimmitt. In 1902, Father Joseph Reisdorff, a Catholic priest, gave it its current designation. The priest "intended to place the parish under invocation and protection of the Holy Family of Nazareth."

NEBO (Smith): off FM 16, two miles E of Lindale. Settled prior to 1903. See Mount Nebo.

NEW MINE (Camp): on FM 1519, three miles SW of Pittsburg. The village developed around the New Mine Baptist Church, which was organized in 1892.

NEW SWEDEN (Travis): on FM 973, five miles NE of Manor. Developed in 1873 and called Knight's Ranch. The New Sweden Lutheran Church was founded in 1886, and the little community changed its name accordingly.

NINEVEH (Leon): on FM 3178, eight miles NW of Malvern. Established in the late 1800s on a stagecoach route. A Miss McCreary suggested the current moniker because "a great deal of squabbling in town brought to mind the biblical Nineveh, the Assyrian capital known as a seat of wickedness."

NOONDAY (Harrison): on FM 450, four miles N of Hallsville. Also known as Shortview. The name was changed in 1876 after a Baptist church was built on the site. A meeting was held to select a name for the church. The meeting convened at high noon.

NOONDAY (Smith): on TX 155, seven miles S of Tyler. The hamlet was occupied by the 1860s, and Captain Edward W. Smith christened the site for the Noonday Baptist Church in his hometown in Georgia.

OLD ROCK CHURCH (Atascosa): E of FM 476, seven miles S of Lytle. Also known as Old Rock Baptist Church. Settlers moved into the region in 1857 and began work on a church. The building was completed in 1872 and apparently takes its name for the material used in constructing the house of worship.

PANNA MARIA (Karnes): jct FM 81 and 2724, four miles N of Karnes City. This is the oldest permanent Polish settlement in America. Settlers led by Father Leopold Moczygemba arrived here in either late 1854 or early 1855 and christened the community for the Virgin Mary.

PILGRIM REST (Rains): on FM 2946, four miles E of Emory. Settlement took place here around the time of the Civil War. In earlier days Marshall, Jefferson, and Shreveport were the trading centers of this area. A church, which later took the name Pilgrim Rest, was where travelers (known as pilgrims) moving between the three marketing centers stopped to rest. There is some speculation that the moniker pays homage to Brother Pilgrim, an early frontier Baptist preacher.

PISGAH (Nacogdoches): on FM 1878, ten miles NE of Nacogdoches. Developed prior to 1900. This is a biblical name and refers to one of the ancient high places of Moab east of the north shore of the Dead Sea. Sacrifices were offered on this holy site, also known as Nebo. See Mount Pisgah.

PISGAH (Navarro): on Pisgah Ridge, seven miles S of Corsicana. Settled in the 1840s. See Mount Pisgah.

RELIANCE (Brazos): on FM 1179, nine miles N of Bryan. Originally known as Little Georgia, referring to the home of the first settlers, who arrived in the 1850s. David Lloyd, having migrated from Mississippi, changed the name in 1873, honoring the Reliance Baptist Church, which he founded.

ROCK CHURCH (Hood): near the Paluxy River in SW Hood County. The first white settlers entered the area in the mid-1800s. The Jesse Caraway family donated land for a church, which became a chapel, school, and community center. The community name denotes the material used in the construction.

ROCK HOUSE (Williamson): on FM 3405, three miles N of Liberty Hill. In earlier days the site was sometimes called Draco for an early Native American village once located here; the word means "favorite place." Development of the region started sometime before 1871. The community took its name from a Baptist house of worship made of rock built by the residents sometime between 1871 and 1878.

ST. JOHN (Fayette): on FM 957, four miles SW of Schulenburg. A Catholic church and the community were officially dedicated in June 1894, the day of the feast of the Nativity of St. John the Baptist.

ST. JOHN COLONY (Caldwell): on FM 672, ten miles NE of Lockhart. In the early 1870s, Rev. John Henry Winn led a group of African American families from Webberville, Texas, to this site. The minister's followers named the place Winn's Colony in honor of their leader. The name was changed in 1873 once the St. John Missionary Baptist Church was founded.

ST. MARYS COLONY (Bastrop): on TX 21, seventeen miles W of Bastrop. George and Mary Doyle donated two thousand acres in this area shortly after the emancipation of slaves in 1865. The site was intended to serve as an African American farming community. The name chosen for the settlement probably came from a local church. It is believed that a preacher known as Meridan selected the name.

ST. PAUL (Collin): on FM 2514, eleven miles S of McKinney. A post office opened here in 1876. The town relates its name to the evangelist Paul.

ST. VIOLA (Smith): at int FM 2767 and 2908, four miles E of Tyler. This was a church community before 1936 and supposedly was christened for an African American house of worship.

SALEM (Victoria): twelve miles NE of Victoria. Four real estate agents including D. G. Musselman founded the hamlet between 1910 and 1911. The men, organizers of the Higginson Colonization Company, christened the place from a biblical point of reference, as Salem is supposedly an ancient name for Jerusalem.

SALEM (Washington): at int CR 32 and 33, three miles SW of Brenham. In 1856 Rev. Johann Georg Ebiner and his congregation organized the Evangelical Lutheran Church of Salem on this spot.

SAND BRANCH CHURCH (Atascosa): on FM 2504, three miles N of TX 173, between Kyote and Rossville. The site was settled about 1870. The name is for a local church founded by a congregation of Baptist pioneers, the name of which came from a local stream.

SAND FLAT CHURCH (Anderson): on FM 2022, sixteen miles SE of Palestine. Also known as Sand Flat. The church was probably christened for the sandy soil in the vicinity.

SANTA CRUZ (Starr): off US 83, four miles E of Rio Grande City. This was once a railroad station known as Dreamland. The present designation is Spanish for "holy cross." Citizens placed a large cross at the top of a hill near the community to give thanks for rain that ended a drought that devastated the region from 1888 to 1894.

SHARON (Wood): on TX 37, five miles S of Winnsboro. Epreham Willingham established the Sharon Baptist Church in 1852. It is said to be the oldest house of worship in Wood County.

SWEET HOME (Lee): on FM 141, eight miles NE of Giddings. African American families from Washington and Fayette counties settled the community prior to 1880. The Sweet Home Church was founded in 1890.

SWEET UNION (Cherokee): on FM 1247, twenty-two miles S of Rusk. Freed slaves settled the site in 1865 and called it Hogjaw. This very unusual moniker came about at the time the settlement was developed. A local man was on trial for stealing a hog. The accused pleaded innocent, but the state produced the hog's head, which supposedly was found under a stump. The accused was found guilty. The sentence is unknown, but the name Hogjaw stuck to the village. In 1899 Nelson Jones erected a building that housed both a church and a school. This gave rise to the community name of Sweet Union.

THEON (Williamson): on FM 1105, NE of Georgetown. Immigrants from Germany, Bohemia, and Moravia arrived here in the late 1800s. Known as Behmville for pioneer H. T. Behrens, then as Leubner for William Leubner, another early settler and merchant. A request for a post office to be called Bernville, an apparent misspelling of Behmville, was submitted in July 1890. Regardless, postal officials did not accept that name. Citizens resubmitted the application, this time suggesting Theon, supposedly from the Greek, meaning "to God." It is believed a local priest made the suggestion.

TIRA (Hopkins): on FM 1536, thirteen miles N of Sulphur Springs. First known as Chapman Arm for Jimmy Chapman, who settled in the area in 1850. The name was changed to Tira, a corruption of the biblical name Tyre, with the opening of the post office in 1858.

WEEPING MARY (Cherokee): off TX 21, eighteen miles W of Rusk. More than likely settled by former slaves following the Civil War. Probably took its name from the religious image of Mary Magdalene weeping at the tomb of Jesus.

WATERWORKS

From Agua Dulce to Wizard Wells

AGUA DULCE (Nueces): at int FM 70 and TX 44, seventeen miles W of Robstown. A settlement had developed here by the 1900s. The name is Spanish for "sweet water," and relates to a nearby creek.

AGUA NUEVA (Jim Hogg): on FM 1017, thirty-five miles S of Hebbronville. Settled sometime before 1900; Sixto Garcia opened a store here in 1903. Since this is Spanish for "new water," the site most likely carries the name of the Spanish land grant, Agua Nueva de Abajo. Some sources, however, offer that it might have been christened for a local spring.

ALUM (Wilson): off TX 123, sixteen miles NE of Floresville. Developed before 1900. The alum content of the water in a local stream gave the creek its name, which carried over to the community.

AQUILLA (Hill): on FM 933, twelve miles SW of Hillsboro. The region was populated in the 1840s. The community was originally called Mudtown, but the name was changed in 1879 and refers to Aquilla Creek. This is supposedly from the Spanish *aquila*, which means "eagle."

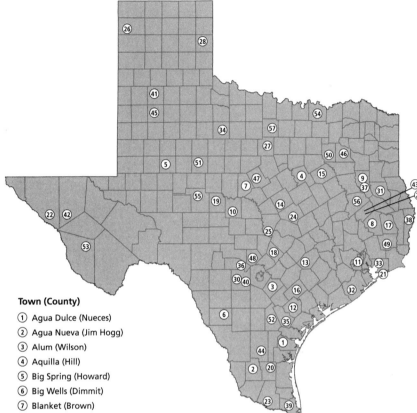

Town (County)

1. Agua Dulce (Nueces)
2. Agua Nueva (Jim Hogg)
3. Alum (Wilson)
4. Aquilla (Hill)
5. Big Spring (Howard)
6. Big Wells (Dimmit)
7. Blanket (Brown)
8. Bold Springs (Polk)
9. Box Creek (Cherokee)
10. Calf Creek (McCulloch)
11. Channelview (Harris)
12. Charco (Goliad)
13. Cistern (Fayette)
14. Copperas Cove (Coryell)
15. Cryer Creek (Navarro)
16. Cuero (DeWitt)
17. Dam B (Tyler)
18. Dripping Springs (Hays)
19. Eola (Concho)
20. Flowella (Brooks)
21. High Island (Galveston)
22. Hot Wells (Hudspeth)
23. La Joya (Hidalgo)
24. Little River Academy (Bell)
25. Marble Falls (Burnet)
26. Middle Water (Hartley)
27. Mineral Wells (Palo Pinto)
28. Mobeetie (Wheeler)
29. Mossy (Trinity)
30. New Fountain (Medina)
31. Oil Springs (Nacogdoches)
32. Old Ocean (Brazoria)
33. Old River-Winfree (Chambers)
34. Paint Creek (Haskell)
35. Papalote (Bee)
36. Pipe Creek (Bandera)
37. Ponta (Cherokee)
38. Quicksand (Newton)
39. Rio Hondo (Cameron)
40. Riomedina (Medina)
41. Runningwater (Hale)
42. Rustler Springs (Culberson)
43. Scrub Creek (Trinity)
44. Sejita (Duval)
45. Shallowater (Lubbock)
46. Silver Lake (Van Zandt)
47. Sipe Springs (Comanche)
48. Sisterdale (Kendall)
49. Sour Lake (Hardin)
50. Styx (Kaufman)
51. Sweetwater (Nolan)
52. Three Rivers (Live Oak)
53. Tinaja (Presidio)
54. Tioga (Grayson)
55. Water Valley (Tom Green)
56. Weches (Houston)
57. Wizard Wells (Jack)

BIG SPRING (Howard): at int IH 20, US 80 and 87, TX 350, and FM 700; county seat. Explorers and settlers have traversed this region since 1849. Derives its moniker from a nearby "big spring" in Sulphur Draw.

BIG WELLS (Dimmit): on TX 85, seventeen miles NE of Carrizo Springs. The Hurst and Brundage Company started a settlement here in 1910 as part of a promotional endeavor. It acquired its tag from artesian wells once found in the vicinity.

BLANKET (Brown): on US 67 and 377, ten miles NE of Brownwood. Settled in the 1860s or 1870s, it took its name from a nearby creek. The stream received its handle in 1852 when a surveying party came across a band of Tonkawas. These Native Americans had been caught in a heavy rain and had spread their blankets on bushes along the creek bank to dry. The sight of the blankets gave inspiration for the name.

BOLD SPRINGS (Polk): on FM 350 and 942, N of Livingston. Established during the 1840s, this was one of a number of small communities in the area known collectively as the Louisiana Settlement. Was christened for the "very large" springs in the area.

BOX CREEK (Cherokee): SE of Rusk in S Cherokee County. Roland W. Box developed the site about 1835. The locale took its name from a local creek that, it would seem, honors the Box family.

CALF CREEK (McCulloch): on FM 1311, twelve miles SW of Brady. This site has had three names in as many different locations. The first settlement was two miles south of the present location in 1874 and was known as Deland for a local family. In 1909 the community shifted about a mile north and became Tucker, honoring a local store owner. In 1915 it moved a mile farther north, to its present location, and again changed its name, this time to Calf Creek. It acquired its moniker from a stream, which was reportedly christened for a lost calf being found in the creek. Another story asserts that the name came from the time the stream was used as a holding area by rustlers for stolen cattle.

CHANNELVIEW (Harris): S of IH 10, eight miles E of Houston. Also known as Channel View. Settled in the early 1900s and christened for its location on the northeastern curve of the Houston Ship Channel.

CHARCO (Goliad): on TX 239, seventeen miles NW of Goliad. A post office opened here in 1855. The site could have taken its name from the Native American word for a petrified tree stump that had served as a marker for early travelers. The word is also Spanish for "puddle" for the many ponds which were found here.

CISTERN (Fayette): on TX 95, twelve miles NW of Flatonia. Arose during the 1850s and was first called Whiteside's Prairie, then Cockrill's Hill, the latter for M. Cockrill, a business entrepreneur. The name was officially changed to Cistern when the well water that had been serving the community suddenly turned up with too much iron and sulphur. This required that each family build an underground water reservoir, or cistern.

COPPERAS COVE (Coryell): at int US 190 and FM 116, twenty-four miles SW of Gatesville. Pioneers settled here from 1845 to 1850. First called Cove, but when a post office was established, the name had to be changed due to duplication. Coperas was added in March 1879. This final designation came about when a Santa Fe engineer drank from the creek and commented, "Egad! Coperas!" The water had an unusual taste, as though it contained copper. The spelling was changed to its present form in 1901.

CRYER CREEK (Navarro): at int FM 2930 and 1126, four miles N of Barry. William Melton settled here in 1845. The town's name comes from the creek, which carries over from an early legend. Settlers thought a waterfall in the stream sounded like a woman crying.

CUERO (DeWitt): at int US 183, 77A, and 87; county seat. Robert J. Kleberg surveyed the site in 1873, and it became the seat of county government in 1876. When the Spanish came through on a surveying and mapping expedition, Native Americans told them that the name of a local creek was "Rawhide," or in Spanish *cuero crudo*. The name came from the practice of killing cattle that got stuck in the muddy creek bed. The Spanish recorded the creek name as such, using their word *cuero*, "leather."

DAM B (Tyler): on US 190 and FM 92, twelve miles NE of Woodville. The settlement date of this community is unknown. Took its handle from the fact that three dams were planned for the area, but only one, designated Dam B, was built on the Neches River.

DRIPPING SPRINGS (Hays): on US 290, twenty miles N of San Marcos. Emerged as a viable community before the Civil War. The site was christened about 1850 by the Moss, Wallace, and Pound families from the descriptive words, "Where the Tonkawa once prowled, the cool, clear waters . . . dripped musically from the limestone overhead."

EOLA (Concho): at jct FM 381 and 765, thirteen miles SW of Paint Rock. A post office was established here in 1901. It was known as Jordan at the time. The name was changed in 1902, supposedly for a local creek called Aeolus, the Greek keeper of the winds.

FLOWELLA (Brooks): at int FM 2191 and TX 285, four miles E of Falfurrias. Burton and Danforth, developers, platted the town site in 1909. It was laid out so that at its center would be a "flowing well."

HIGH ISLAND (Galveston): on TX 124, on Bolivar Peninsula at the eastern end of Galveston County. Anson Jones, the last president of the Republic of Texas (1844–1846), referred to the site as High Island in 1845. Martin Dunman was the first Anglo in the region, arriving in 1845. He settled on a league of land ceded to him for his service in the Texas Revolution. As legend has it, the pirate Jean Laffite roamed this region, and Charles Cronea supposedly put up a house on the site. At thirty-eight feet in elevation, this is the highest point on the Gulf of Mexico between Mobile, Alabama, and the Yucatan Peninsula in Mexico. During hurricanes and floods, residents from the flat area of Bolivar Peninsula and the coastal lowlands seek protection on High Island. At such times, this is often the only point above water.

HOT WELLS (Hudspeth): twenty-four miles SE of Sierra Blanca. A viable community existed here prior to 1912 and carries a name relating to hot springs found in the vicinity.

LA JOYA (Hidalgo): on US 83, sixteen miles W of McAllen. This is an old area, with settlers in the region by 1749. The town is situated on what was known in Spanish days as Los Ejidos de Reynosa Viejo, "shared grazing lands for Old Reynosa." The community was incorporated in 1927 and derives its moniker from a small lake west of the city. The word is Spanish for "jewel" and was apparently applied to the beauty of the lake, which, settlers commented, would shine like a jewel when the sun hit the water.

LITTLE RIVER ACADEMY (Bell): at int TX 95 and FM 436, eight miles S of Temple. The town, situated on Little River, is one of the earliest settlements in Bell County, with pioneers arriving here about 1836. A neighboring community was called Academy for a school. The two communities merged in 1980, thus acquiring the current name.

MARBLE FALLS (Burnet): at int US 281 and FM 1431, thirteen miles SE of Burnet. Adam Rankin laid out the town site in 1886. This locale was familiar to travelers as far back as 1871. The falls on the Colorado River for which the town was named were locally called "the marble falls," which have since been covered by Lake Marble Falls.

MIDDLE WATER (Hartley): on US 54 in W Hartley County. Developed in 1888 as a division of the vast XIT Ranch and coined for nearby Middle Water Creek.

MINERAL WELLS (Palo Pinto): at jct US 180 and 281, twelve miles NE of Palo Pinto. The site was settled by 1877, and a town was platted in 1881. Judge J. W. Lynch built a cabin here and dug a well. The well produced a sufficient supply of water, but it was said to be undrinkable. Despite this, the water soon gained a reputation as having healing qualities for such afflictions as "hysterical mania." People began to come to the site to sample the water, and a health resort soon developed. The city takes its name from the wells.

MOBEETIE (Wheeler): on TX 152, sixteen miles NW of Wheeler. This community started out in 1874 when Charles Rath and Bob Wright built a mercantile store at a buffalo hunters' camp on Sweetwater Creek. The name was then Hidetown, so called because residents used buffalo hides to cover their dwellings. The little village moved in 1878 to be closer to Fort Elliott, then known as Sweetwater. When an application for a post office was presented, residents discovered that there was already a Sweetwater in Texas. They then used the name Mobeetie, possibly because it was a Native American word meaning "sweet water."

MOSSY (Trinity): nine miles NE of Groveton. Settled around the time of the Civil War and first called Ashworth Settlement for the Ashworth family. The site was christened Mossy Creek in 1898, apparently for a local stream, then in time the name was shortened simply to Mossy.

NEW FOUNTAIN (Medina): on FM 2676, four miles NW of Hondo. Settlers first moved here in 1845. In less than a year they were placed in dire straits because their limited good water supply had soaked into the porous limestone creek bed. They discovered that the water resurfaced some four miles downstream. Most of the settlers relocated to that spot and appropriately christened their resettlement New Fountain.

OIL SPRINGS (Nacogdoches): on FM 226, thirteen miles E of Nacogdoches. Native Americans used natural petroleum seepage for medicinal purposes as early as the 1790s. As Spanish and Anglo settlers moved into the region, they also learned to apply the oil when needed. Lyn E. Taliafero Barret began drilling for oil in 1859 and finally hit pay dirt in 1866. The community takes its name from the earlier springs.

OLD OCEAN (Brazoria): on TX 35 and 524, five miles NW of Sweeney. A town site was laid out on the Joseph H. Polley and Samuel Chance land grant of July 1824; it acquired the label Chance's Prairie. The current moniker relates to a nearby oil field, which geologists contend is the bed of an "ancient ocean," and came about after oil was discovered in 1934. The name was changed to its current designation in 1936.

OLD RIVER-WINFREE (Chambers): at jct FM 565 and 1409, twenty miles NW of Anahuac. Robert Wiseman was among the first settlers, arriving in 1827. It is believed that the site carried the name of Archer in the 1830s. The present moniker comes from its location near Old River and from that of an early regional land grantee, a man named Winfree. The town was incorporated as Old River-Winfree in 1979.

PAINT CREEK (Haskell): on FM 600, seven miles E of Haskell. This village came about when five school districts were consolidated: Howard, McConnell, Post, Rose, and Weaver. In 1937 Wayne Perry suggested that the school district be named for Paint Creek, a nearby stream. The creek acquired its tag from the color of the water, caused by the soil over which it flows. It is a true red, and when there is flooding or a heavy run, it colors the Clear Fork into which it flows.

PAPALOTE (Bee): on TX 181, eighteen miles S of Beeville. This is one of the county's oldest communities, stretching back to the arrival of Irish immigrants in 1812. They settled along Papalote Creek, and the town site adopted the same name. The word is Spanish for "kite" and refers to the kite-shaped rocks in the creek bed.

PIPE CREEK (Bandera): on TX 16, nine miles E of Bandera. Founded about 1870 and named for nearby Pipe Creek. There is a legend about how the stream acquired its name. Native Americans were pursuing an Anglo settler in earlier days. In the chase, he dropped his smoking pipe by the creek, stopped to retrieve it, and still made good his escape.

PONTA (Cherokee): E of TX 110, nine miles N of Rusk. Donaho, a small village, had a short life span that began in 1901 and lasted until the railroad bypassed it. Hubbard Guinn surveyed another town site on the line, and it was named Hubb in his honor. In 1903 Robert Montgomery, postmaster, changed the name to Ponta, from the Latin term *pontus* for "bridge," and related the name to the bridges over Mud Creek.

QUICKSAND (Newton): at jct TX 87 and FM 1414, four miles NE of Newton. There was a community here sometime before 1848. It is also known as Quicksand Creek, taking its title from a nearby creek, which was labeled for the quicksand in the stream.

RIO HONDO (Cameron): off FM 508 and 1846, twelve miles NE of Harlingen. The community was developed in 1910 when J. R. George, the first settler, opened a general store that also housed the post office; he was the postmaster. The word is Spanish for "deep river," and the settlement was christened for its location on the Arroyo Colorado.

RIOMEDINA (Medina): on FM 471, six miles N of Castroville. As far as is known, the first business enterprise on this site was a saloon owned and operated by Armin Boehm around 1900. The place name comes from its location between two branches of the Medina River.

RUNNINGWATER (Hale): on FM 1424, twelve miles NW of Plainview. A post office was established here in 1890, and it was for a time known as Wadsworth. For publicity and commendatory purposes, it was renamed in 1891 for the presence of flowing water.

RUSTLER SPRINGS (Culberson): forty-two miles N of Kent in N Culberson County. Also known as Tarver, Lula, and Sulphuria. A sulphur plant has been located here since the early 1900s. In 1969 the village was renamed, taking its moniker from nearby Rustler Hills.

SCRUB CREEK (Trinity): off FM 358, ten miles NE of Groveton. Settled sometime around the Civil War and christened for a nearby creek. The stream was so designated from early days, when on Saturday night this was the central bathing spot for area residents. This, of course, preceded the days of indoor plumbing.

SEJITA (Duval): on FM 3249, twenty-five miles S of Benavides. A post office was in place in 1914. The village name, from the Spanish *ceja* or "eyebrow," relates to a crescent-shaped dam that formed a local watering spot for livestock.

SHALLOWATER (Lubbock): on TX 84, twelve miles NW of Lubbock. The Ripley Townsite Company, named for a Santa Fe Railroad official, platted the settlement in 1909. In this section of the country, wells usually have to be sunk deep to find water. Here, however, it was found at very shallow depths.

SILVER LAKE (Van Zandt): on US 80 and FM 1255, eight miles NE of Canton. John Jordan surveyed and acquired land title to thirty square miles in 1845. This was the official start of the settlement, which was developed in 1873 as a railroad stop located on the salt flats along the Sabine River. The site moniker relates to a small lake in the vicinity. The body of water was named either for its silvery appearance or for the tale that Native Americans or the Mexican army hid silver in the lake sometime between 1832 and 1836 to prevent the Texas Army from capturing it.

SIPE SPRINGS (Comanche): at int FM 1477 and 587, seventeen miles NW of Comanche. Settlers were in the region by about 1870, and the town was laid out around 1873. The place takes its name from a different approach to spelling—or a tongue-in-cheek one. It is from the nearby springs that "seeped" out of rock formations.

SISTERDALE (Kendall): on FM 1376 and 473, thirteen miles N of Boerne. Nicolaus Zink established the community in 1847, and it takes its moniker from its location between two streams known as Sister Creeks.

SOUR LAKE (Hardin): on TX 105 and 326, fifteen miles SW of Hardin. Also known as Sour Lake Springs. This is the oldest continually existing community in the county. Stephen Jackson first settled the site about 1835. It received its designation for area mineral waters that feed into Sour Lake.

STYX (Kaufman): eight miles W of Cedar Creek Reservoir in SC Kaufman County. A post office was opened in 1899. A Dr. Gordon christened the hamlet for the river in the underworld in Greek mythology.

SWEETWATER (Nolan): on IH 20, US 80/84, TX 70, and FM 419; county seat. Texas Rangers named the place in 1874. They were scouting for Native Americans along the creek of the same name, which was spelled as two words until 1918. The "water in a land of bitter streams" was very satisfying and made a strong impression on the lawmen. Natives attribute the freshness of the water to the elm trees and gypsum in the region. The town was designated county seat when the county was established in 1881.

THREE RIVERS (Live Oak): at int TX 72 and US 281, eleven miles N of George West. A railroad depot opened here in 1913 on land owned by Annie T. Hamilton and honored her with the name Hamiltonburg. Mail for this destination was often misrouted to the Texas community of Hamilton, and vice versa. Local residents requested that the name be changed. Charles R. Tips, landowner, suggested that the site be christened for its location near the three rivers: Atascosa, Frio, and Nueces. Postal authorities approved the name on 1 May 1914.

TINAJA (Presidio): two miles NE of San Estahan Lake in N Presidio County. The site was chosen as a railroad station in 1930. The word is

Spanish for "large earthen jar" or "tank." There was a place here that held water and was so called long before the railroad came through.

TIOGA (Grayson): on US 377, twenty miles SW of Sherman. The settlement came into being when the railroad reached the area in 1881. Train crews used water from a local well and called the place Tioga, supposedly a New York Native American word meaning "swift current" or "fair and beautiful." This is the birthplace of Western movie star and sportsman Gene Autry. An unsuccessful effort was made in 1937 to change the town's name to Autry Springs.

WATER VALLEY (Tom Green): on US 87, twenty-two miles NW of San Angelo. Among the early settlers was Captain William Turner in 1878. Two men known as Phelin and Glynn founded the community when they dammed the North Concho River and dug an irrigation ditch. The post office was called, variously, Yandell, Argenta, and Stella between 1885 and 1888. It was also called Rethaville, Mayes Store, or Mayesville in 1888 and 1889. S. S. McCary and J. O. Hanson officially renamed the site in 1889.

WECHES (Houston): at jct TX 21 and FM 3016, twenty-one miles NE of Crockett. T. J. Rennin established the community in about 1847 and named it for the Neches River. It retained this name until a post office opened in 1853, when the spelling was changed to Naches. In 1887, when application for a new post office was submitted, residents discovered that there was already a town by that name in Texas. They simply substituted "We" for the "Na" and came up with the new designation.

WIZARD WELLS (Jack): on FM 1156, thirteen miles E of Jacksboro. Settled in the 1880s. It was first known as Old Vineyard for G. W. Vineyard, who owned the land from which the water, he had discovered, cured ulcers and other ailments. The current moniker was derived from the wells that dispense mineral water with "curative" powers.

BY THE NUMBERS

From Dime Box to Twin Sisters

DIME BOX (Lee): on FM 141, twelve miles NE of Giddings. Organized between 1869 and 1877 when a settler built a sawmill near what is now TX 21. Joseph S. Brown is believed to have been the builder of the mill, and for a time the place was called Brown's Mill. Prior to receipt of a post office, residents placed a mailbox on a spot on the road to San Antonio. Freighters making trips through the vicinity picked up and delivered mail. The service charge for each round-trip was one dime. The settlement grew, and a petition for a post office was submitted. When the post office opened in 1877, authorities believed that Brown's Mill would be too easily confused with Brownsville. A new moniker was needed. To preserve the memory of the community mailbox, resident Dr. R. H. Morgan suggested the name Dime Box.

DOUBLE KNOBBS (Mason): on TX 29, eight miles NW of Mason. The area was settled around 1890 when the Dodd and Clark families arrived on the scene. The site was named for two nearby hills that lie on either side of the highway.

DOUBLE OAK (Denton): on FM 407, ten miles S of Denton. Although there was a school district in the vicinity as early as 1884,

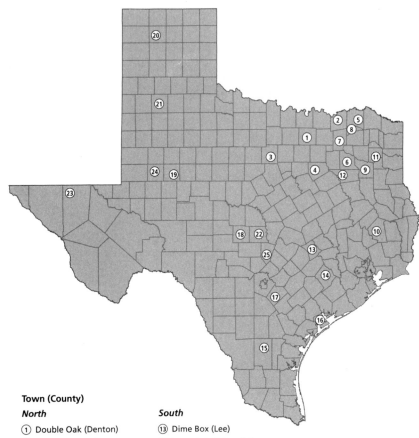

Town (County)

North
① Double Oak (Denton)
② Duplex (Fannin)
③ Lone Camp (Palo Pinto)
④ Lone Elm (Ellis)
⑤ Lone Star (Lamar)

South
⑬ Dime Box (Lee)
⑭ Lone Oak (Colorado)
⑮ Seven Sisters (Duval)
⑯ Six Mile (Calhoun)
⑰ Three Oaks (Wilson)

East
⑥ Four Mile Prairie (Van Zandt)
⑦ Lone Oak (Hunt)
⑧ Lone Star (Delta)
⑨ Pounds (Smith)
⑩ Seven Oaks (Polk)
⑪ Seven Pines (Gregg-Upshur)
⑫ Seven Points (Henderson)

West
⑱ Double Knobbs (Mason)
⑲ Forsan (Howard)
⑳ Four Way (Moore)
㉑ Halfway (Hale)
㉒ Lone Grove (Llano)
㉓ Nickel Creek (Culberson)
㉔ Three League (Martin)
㉕ Twin Sisters (Blanco)

the town itself was not incorporated until 1974. There is a belief that an ordinance published by the town's first council dictated that a minimum of two oak trees should be in every yard. No such law exists today, and it is most likely that the site was named for the old Double Oak School, which was established in 1884. Two (double) oak trees constitute the town logo.

DUPLEX (Fannin): on FM 273, fifteen miles N of Bonham. The community was formed in the early 1880s and named for two of the original settlers. Rather than carry their names, residents chose this dual designation.

FORSAN (Howard): on FM 461, twelve miles SE of Big Spring. Clayton Stewart, the first settler in the region, donated land for a town site in 1928. The community was labeled for the "four" oil "sands" believed to be located in the vicinity. Their estimation was slightly off: there were actually five sands, if not more.

FOUR MILE PRAIRIE (Van Zandt): on FM 90, twelve miles SW of Canton. Norwegian immigrants who moved from Henderson County formed the site in 1847. The name is a geographical one, from a sandy prairie ten miles long, the boundaries of which are two streams, Cedar Creek on the west and Lacy Fork on the east, that are four miles apart.

FOUR WAY (Moore): four miles N of Masterson in southern Moore County. The site was formed in the late 1920s following the discovery of natural gas. It acquired its moniker from its position where US 87 crosses the road linking Stinnett and Channing.

HALFWAY (Hale): at int US 70 and FM 179, fourteen miles W of Plainview. The community was developed in 1909 and named for its location between the county seat of Plainview and the city of Olton, in Camp County.

LONE CAMP (Palo Pinto): on FM 4, eight miles N of Santo. There were settlers in the region as early as the 1870s, but it wasn't until

1904 that a ranch was divided up and sold to farmers. A Mr. Spencer was appointed to build and petition for a post office. At the time his family had gone off to visit relatives, and he was living in a tent. There was no one else in the area, and he thought to himself how lonely the place was. Thus, the name.

LONE ELM (Ellis): on FM 875, five miles W of Waxahachie. The Jones, Delk, and Johnson families had moved into the area and established homes by 1885. The community name supposedly is from an elm tree from which horse thieves were hanged.

LONE GROVE (Llano): on FM 2241, nine miles NE of Llano. The first village was established as a post office in 1876 with John R. Coggin as postmaster and was located on the west bank of the Little Llano River in a small grove of pecan trees. This was inspiration for the community's label.

LONE OAK (Colorado): on FM 1291, thirteen miles N of Columbus. In the 1880s the place was known as Pisek and, at times, was also called Sandy Point. The name was changed to Lone Oak in 1941. A large, single oak tree grew in the middle of the intersection of the two main roads running through the settlement.

LONE OAK (Hunt): at int US 69 and FM 513 and 1567, ten miles SE of Greenville. The area was host to settlers as early as the late 1850s. The hamlet took its moniker from an oak tree landmark that stood alone on the grass-covered prairie.

LONE STAR (Delta): one mile E of Jot Em Down in W Delta County. First known as Barton and then Volney. In 1878 three men from Kentucky set up a school here. A lone star painted on a barn was inspiration for the school and later the community name.

LONE STAR (Lamar): on FM 906, twelve miles N of Blossom. A school was organized at the site as early as 1896. The settlement adopted the state nickname for its label.

NICKEL CREEK (Culberson): on US 62/180, five miles NE of Pine Springs. Also known as Nickel Creek Station. The community was probably founded in the late 1940s and christened for a nearby stream.

POUNDS (Smith): on TX 64, two miles W of Tyler Loop 323. Settlers were most likely in the region by the 1840s. The community name relates to a prominent businessman, W. A. Pounds.

SEVEN OAKS (Polk): on US 59, fifteen miles N of Livingston. Completion of the railroad through the vicinity in 1880 led to the establishment of numerous sawmills. An early settler named the locale Seven Oaks for his ancestral estate in England.

SEVEN PINES (Gregg-Upshur): on TX 300, one mile N of Longview. The village was developed around 1900 and tagged for seven large pine trees in the vicinity.

SEVEN POINTS (Henderson): on TX 274, twenty miles NW of Athens. The community was born in the 1960s after construction of Cedar Creek Reservoir. The town's name for the intersection of seven roads at a single point was foreseen by a longtime resident, who stated that he was riding a horse through the area with a friend hired by the state to report on creek levels in the region. The friend was quoted as saying, "Some day there's going to be a city here, and I'll bet they name it after these roads." His prediction was accurate.

SEVEN SISTERS (Duval): on FM 2359, ten miles NE of Freer. The community was established after oil was discovered in the vicinity in 1935. Some believe the site was named for the Seven Sisters Oil Field, which surveyors tagged for seven small mounds that looked alike. There is another contention that the name related to the seven attractive daughters of an important landowner named Don Refugio Serna.

SIX MILE (Calhoun): on FM 1090, six miles N of Port Lavaca. The town site sits on land that was part of a grant ceded to Valentine Garcia.

The village was originally called Markeville, then Royal. The current moniker was chosen for its location six miles north of Port Lavaca.

THREE LEAGUE (Martin): in NC Martin County. The Three Leagues Gin existed in 1925. It was so designated because three leagues (numbers 251, 253, 254) made up the district.

THREE OAKS (Wilson): on FM 1344, eleven miles S of Floresville. The community was formed when Tom Dewees started selling off a portion of his ranch in 1901 to German and Czech farmers. At the time, the community had no name. One day a traveler sitting in the local store asked the name of the village. When advised that it had none, he immediately suggested that it be christened for the three large oak trees situated near the store.

TWIN SISTERS (Blanco): on US 281, seven miles S of Blanco. Tennessean Joel Cherry homesteaded the region in 1854. The site was christened for two mountains identical in size and form.

9

EDIBLES AND DRINKABLES

From Banquete to Teacup

BANQUETE (Nueces): at int TX 44 and FM 666, nine miles S of San Patricio. A post office began operation here in 1859. The word is Spanish for "banquet." One belief is that the name came from a feast held to celebrate a new road between the Nueces River and the Rio Grande. Another theory contends that the moniker came about from a feast put on by Mexicans when they welcomed Irish settlers to the area in 1832.

BEANS PLACE (Jasper): W of TX 63, twelve miles NW of Jasper. Also known as Beans, Cross, and Horger. Ira S. Bean put in a mercantile business here in 1903. He established a post office and named it Horger for James M. Horger, president of the W. H. Ford Male and Female College at nearby Newton from 1893 to 1897. Horger and Borger, another Texas city, looked and sounded too similar, and postal authorities requested that the former change its name. Residents went back to the early settler and businessman to come up with the current designation.

BEANS PRAIRIE (Cherokee): W of Alto in S Cherokee County. Also known as Bean's Creek. Peter Ellis Bean settled here around 1839.

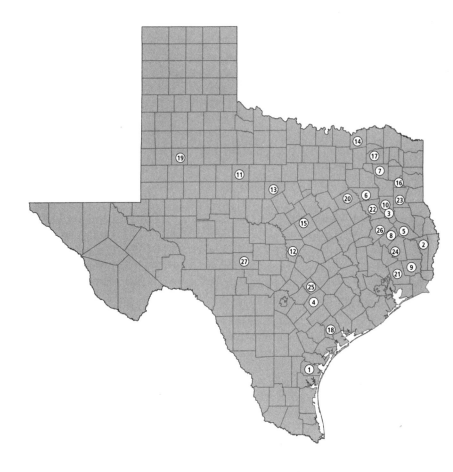

Town (County)

- ① Banquete (Nueces)
- ② Beans Place (Jasper)
- ③ Beans Prairie (Cherokee)
- ④ Bebe (Gonzales)
- ⑤ Cheeseland (Angelina)
- ⑥ Coffee City (Henderson)
- ⑦ Coke (Wood)
- ⑧ Crib Creek (Trinity)
- ⑨ Honey Island (Hardin)
- ⑩ Java (Cherokee)
- ⑪ Noodle (Jones)
- ⑫ Oatmeal (Burnet)
- ⑬ Okra (Eastland)
- ⑭ Orangeville (Fannin)
- ⑮ Pancake (Coryell)
- ⑯ Peatown (Gregg)
- ⑰ Peerless (Hopkins)
- ⑱ Raisin (Victoria)
- ⑲ Redwine (Lynn)
- ⑳ Rice (Navarro)
- ㉑ Rye (Liberty)
- ㉒ Salmon (Anderson)
- ㉓ Short Pone (Rusk)
- ㉔ Soda (Polk)
- ㉕ Soda Springs (Caldwell)
- ㉖ Sorghumville (Houston)
- ㉗ Teacup (Kimble)

BEBE (Gonzales): on TX 97, some sixteen miles SW of Gonzales. Community first called Stroman for the co-owner of a mercantile store. A post office was opened in 1900, and the name had to be changed, probably due to duplication. The current label supposedly comes from B. B. Baking Powder signs that lined the roads leading to the village.

CHEESELAND (Angelina): N Angelina County. Jacob Ferguson Humphrey moved to the site in 1844 and built a home and fortification for his family. Wenzel Hillenkamp and his family moved here before the Civil War and settled on thirty acres given them by Humphrey. They started a large business enterprise consisting of not only their personal home, but also a coach station, post office, and general store. His wife must have been famous for her cheeses. Not only did Hillenkamp sell the product in his store, but in 1884, when the community was organized, it took the name Cheeseland. There is some contention, though, that the first cheese producer was from somewhere up north.

COFFEE CITY (Henderson): off TX 155, twenty miles SE of Athens. Lake Palestine was developed in the early 1960s. This community grew up by the lake, and the name is purportedly that of a local family.

COKE (Wood): on FM 515 and 69, ten miles N of Quitman. While there were settlers in the region as early as the 1850s, a community did not emerge until after coal was discovered nearby. The current designation has no relation to the popular soft drink; instead, it refers to Richard Coke, governor of Texas (1874–1876). On the other hand, since there was a source of coal in the vicinity, possibly the name is from the coal by-product.

CRIB CREEK (Trinity): off FM 357 in N Trinity County. The community was founded before the Civil War, and the moniker relates to a small corncrib built by members of the Caddo tribes.

HONEY ISLAND (Hardin): at jct FM 1003 and 1293, eight miles W of Kountze. The site sits on a rise between Cypress and Flat creeks. When the two streams flood, it isolates the village, making it a virtual island. Rumor has it that during the Civil War Jayhawkers congregated in the region and existed mostly on honey from a multitude of beehives. A railroad station was established here in 1901 and was dubbed Matile. By 1907 the Honey Island post office was in operation, and the little hamlet took its name from that facility.

JAVA (Cherokee): eleven miles W of Rusk. This is little more than a ghost town today. Migrants from Alabama and Tennessee settled the region from 1840 to 1850. A community did not emerge until the 1890s when prisoners from Texas State Penitentiary in Rusk were brought in to mine coal for state-owned iron furnaces. The origin of the name is more unusual than the name itself. It seems that at a dance, a young lass felt her petticoat slip from around her waist to the floor. Onlookers were given a clear view of the name on the garment: Java. The underwear had been made from a coffee sack, and Java was the brand name.

NOODLE (Jones): on FM 1812, ten miles N of Merkel. Settlers were in the region by 1882. The community moniker comes from a creek, so named because it twists and turns like a noodle. Alternatively, according to folklore, noodle meant "nothing," signifying a dry creek bed.

OATMEAL (Burnet): on FM 243, eight miles SE of Burnet. This is the second oldest community in Burnet County. A German family, reportedly named Habermill, came to the region in 1849 and settled on what is now Oatmeal Creek. Some believe the name of the stream, and ultimately the settlement, came from that of Othneil, a mill owner, or a supposed translation of the name Habermill (*haber* is a German dialect word for *hafer*, "oats"). There is also a general feeling that the name comes from that of an early family, Oatmeal.

OKRA (Eastland): on FM 1027, twenty-two miles S of Eastland. A settlement began here in 1880 and took its name from the local farm crop.

ORANGEVILLE (Fannin): on FM 151, ten miles SW of Bonham. Although settlers were in the vicinity by mid-1836, a community was not organized until 1858. A Mr. Parmelee, store owner in nearby Valley Creek, had a growth of "oversized oranges" adjacent to his place of business. Travelers from New York were impressed by the size of the fruit. Actually, as local residents knew, they were bois d'arc apples, but the citizens were so amused by the comments from the New Englanders that they christened their home Orangeville.

PANCAKE (Coryell): at int FM 2955 and 217, thirteen miles NW of Gatesville. A post office was in operation here as early as 1884. Another one of those "breakfast food" communities, this one honors J. R. Pancake, postmaster.

PEATOWN (Gregg): on FM 2011, two miles W of Gregg County Airport. Developed in the 1840s and known as Edwardsville for Haden Harrison Edwards, settler. A bad farming season caused the change in names, because the only successful crop that year was peas.

PEERLESS (Hopkins): on FM 71, eleven miles NW of Sulphur Springs. Eli Lindley moved to this vicinity in 1842. Eight years later a small village developed and was called Gay's Mills for a water-powered flour mill operated by John D. Gay. In the 1870s, it was called Hilldale, probably for its location. Then, in 1880, it went by the name of Fairyland (Fairy Land). This latter, unique label is said to have come about from the view, probably of the menfolk, that the young ladies attending dances looked like fairies and that the surrounding hilly terrain made the community look like a fairyland. In about 1891, the moniker was changed to its current designation. While the name itself isn't really that unusual, the story behind it is. A farming family by the name of Cotton planted a brand of potatoes called Peerless. Heavy rains prevented harvesting the crop when it was time, and the overripe spuds began to rot. Naturally, this gave off an odor quite unpleasing to the entire populace. Consequently, this brought on a redesignation of the place name.

RAISIN (Victoria): on US 59, eight miles SW of Victoria. Developed in 1889 as a railroad stop and was known as Lucy. When a post office was approved, the name had to be changed because of its similarity to some other Texas town names. Several recommendations were submitted to postal officials, but all were rejected. One day some men were gathered in a store owned by J. Riemenschneider when in walked J. K. Reeves from a nearby settlement. Reeves had a bunch of grapes, and one of the men noted that the grapes should make fine raisins. Another man made the tongue-in-cheek comment that maybe they ought to name their community Raisin. On the other hand, there is the remote possibility that Reeves's efforts to grow raisins brought on the moniker.

REDWINE (Lynn): at int FM 1054 and 3332, three miles NW of Stewart Lake. M. M. Redwine and his family, from Georgia, settled in the area in 1903.

RICE (Navarro): on IH 45 and US 287, ten miles N of Corsicana. Settled in the late 1860s. The railroad line came through here in 1872, and the town was named for William Marsh Rice, a partner in the rail line company.

RYE (Liberty): at jct FM 787 and TX 146, twenty-four miles NE of Cleveland. The region was populated as early as the 1850s. The community carries the name of M. C. Rye, who settled here in 1902.

SALMON (Anderson): on US 287, fourteen miles SE of Palestine. A post office opened for business in 1902; the hamlet honors S. D. Salmon, the first postmaster.

SHORT PONE (Rusk): between US 79 and FM 839, six miles SW of Henderson. Also called Pone. Times were hard in the South during Reconstruction, and this little village was known for making very "short" corn bread (pone).

SODA (Polk): on US 190, W of Livingston. Founded around the time of the Civil War and called Bluff Creek for a stream in the vicinity. The name had to be changed in 1898, probably due to duplication. Four names were sent to postal officials, who didn't particularly care for any of them. By using the first letters of each of the four names, however, they came up with Soda.

SODA SPRINGS (Caldwell): on FM 1322, NE of Luling. The place had a post office in 1857 and went by the name Sour Springs. The current moniker comes from the local springs, which had an unusual taste caused by their high sodium carbonate content.

SORGHUMVILLE (Houston): off FM 230, six miles SW of Lovelady. Believed to have been a viable community around 1900 and most likely takes its name from a species of natural grass.

TEACUP (Kimble): on US 377, eight miles NE of Junction. The site was official at least by 1933. It took its moniker from a geographical feature, a nearby mountain so named because it resembles an upside-down teacup.

PERSONAL NAMES

From Addran to Zipperlandville

ADDRAN (Hopkins): near TX 19 and 154, ten miles N of Sulphur Springs. In the late 1850s, a minister who had attended Add-Ran College (one of the root colleges of what would later become Texas Christian University in Fort Worth) settled in the vicinity.

AD HALL (Milam): on FM 466, six miles W of Cameron. A post office was opened here in 1874, and the community name relates to *Ad*am J. *Hall*, an early settler.

ALANREED (Gray): on IH 40 and US 66, seven miles W of McLean. Development started in the 1880s, and the town became known variously as Springtown or Spring Tank, the latter for a large spring-fed tank. It has also been known as Prairie Dog Town and Gouge Eye for a saloon fight. A railroad surveyor platted the current town site in 1900, and the moniker supposedly comes from that of a contracting firm, Alan and Reed.

ANGLETON (Brazoria): on TX 288 and 35/207; county seat. In early 1890 Lewis R. Bryan Sr. and Faustino Kiber bought the land where the town site is presently located. They christened the town in

Town (County)

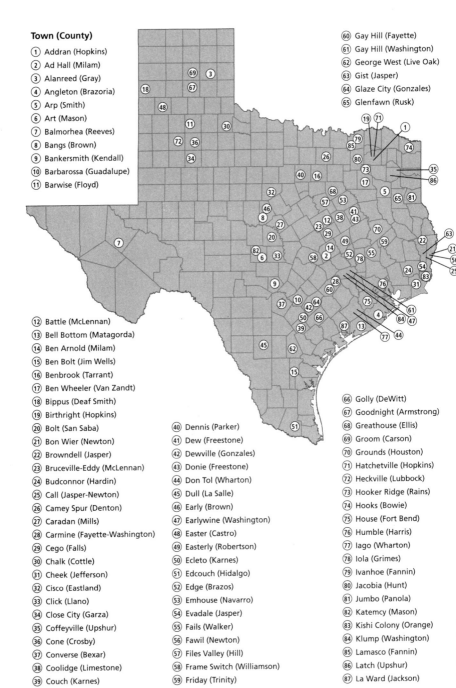

1. Addran (Hopkins)
2. Ad Hall (Milam)
3. Alanreed (Gray)
4. Angleton (Brazoria)
5. Arp (Smith)
6. Art (Mason)
7. Balmorhea (Reeves)
8. Bangs (Brown)
9. Bankersmith (Kendall)
10. Barbarossa (Guadalupe)
11. Barwise (Floyd)

12. Battle (McLennan)
13. Bell Bottom (Matagorda)
14. Ben Arnold (Milam)
15. Ben Bolt (Jim Wells)
16. Benbrook (Tarrant)
17. Ben Wheeler (Van Zandt)
18. Bippus (Deaf Smith)
19. Birthright (Hopkins)
20. Bolt (San Saba)
21. Bon Wier (Newton)
22. Browndell (Jasper)
23. Bruceville-Eddy (McLennan)
24. Budconnor (Hardin)
25. Call (Jasper-Newton)
26. Camey Spur (Denton)
27. Caradan (Mills)
28. Carmine (Fayette-Washington)
29. Cego (Falls)
30. Chalk (Cottle)
31. Cheek (Jefferson)
32. Cisco (Eastland)
33. Click (Llano)
34. Close City (Garza)
35. Coffeyville (Upshur)
36. Cone (Crosby)
37. Converse (Bexar)
38. Coolidge (Limestone)
39. Couch (Karnes)

40. Dennis (Parker)
41. Dew (Freestone)
42. Dewville (Gonzales)
43. Donie (Freestone)
44. Don Tol (Wharton)
45. Dull (La Salle)
46. Early (Brown)
47. Earlywine (Washington)
48. Easter (Castro)
49. Easterly (Robertson)
50. Ecleto (Karnes)
51. Edcouch (Hidalgo)
52. Edge (Brazos)
53. Emhouse (Navarro)
54. Evadale (Jasper)
55. Fails (Walker)
56. Fawil (Newton)
57. Files Valley (Hill)
58. Frame Switch (Williamson)
59. Friday (Trinity)

60. Gay Hill (Fayette)
61. Gay Hill (Washington)
62. George West (Live Oak)
63. Gist (Jasper)
64. Glaze City (Gonzales)
65. Glenfawn (Rusk)
66. Golly (DeWitt)
67. Goodnight (Armstrong)
68. Greathouse (Ellis)
69. Groom (Carson)
70. Grounds (Houston)
71. Hatchetville (Hopkins)
72. Heckville (Lubbock)
73. Hooker Ridge (Rains)
74. Hooks (Bowie)
75. House (Fort Bend)
76. Humble (Harris)
77. Iago (Wharton)
78. Iola (Grimes)
79. Ivanhoe (Fannin)
80. Jacobia (Hunt)
81. Jumbo (Panola)
82. Katemcy (Mason)
83. Kishi Colony (Orange)
84. Klump (Washington)
85. Lamasco (Fannin)
86. Latch (Upshur)
87. La Ward (Jackson)

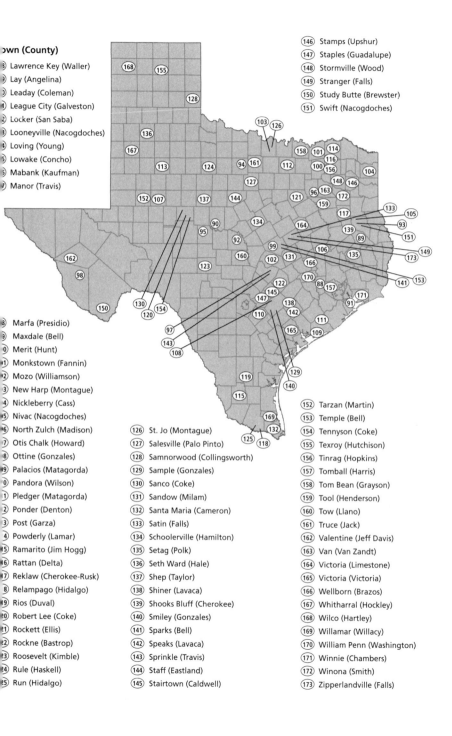

honor of Mrs. George W. Angle, whose husband had been the prime mover in obtaining a deepwater port at Velasco.

ARP (Smith): on TX 135, eighteen miles SE of Tyler. John G. and Eliza Sartain settled here prior to 1868. In 1872 the village went by the moniker Jarvis Switch. A post office opened in 1898 under the name Strawberry. It was officially designated in 1899, remembering a popular newspaper editor, William Arp.

ART (Mason): on TX 29, seven miles E of Mason. This is one of the oldest communities in the county, being settled about 1856, when five German families moved into the vicinity. It was first called Willow Creek for the stream. In 1886 Otto Plehwe became the first postmaster and named the place Plehweville. Postal officials requested the name be simplified, preferably to a three-letter word. Residents chose Art, the general consensus being that there was no significance to the selection. Some believe, however, that the moniker was taken from the last three letters of the name of the postmaster at the time, Eli Dech*art*.

BALMORHEA (Reeves): on FM 1215 and US 290, one mile SW of Brogardo. Land promoters platted the town site in 1906, and it was christened for three real estate men, *Bal*colm, *Mo*row, and *Rhea*.

BANGS (Brown): on US 67 and 84, six miles W of Brownwood. A post office opened in 1886, and the site honors Samuel Bangs, who owned the land on which the town sits.

BANKERSMITH (Kendall): on a LR, thirteen miles NE of Comfort. The community came into being with the arrival of the railroad in 1913. Temple Doswell Smith founded the first bank in the city of Fredericksburg and was most popularly known as Banker Smith.

BARBAROSSA (Guadalupe): on FM 758, ten miles N of Seguin. German immigrants arrived here shortly after the Civil War. Some believe the place carries the name of Holy Roman Emperor Frederick Barbarossa (Frederick I, 1152–1190).

BARWISE (Floyd): on FM 784, eleven miles W of Floydada. The town was platted following the arrival of the railroad in 1928. At first called String for J. W. Stringer, probably an early settler, the name had to be changed because of duplication. The present name remembers the Joseph Hodson Barwise family of Wichita Falls.

BATTLE (McLennan): between TX 164 and FM 2957, three miles NW of Mart. The community was founded around 1880 and was at first called Battle Institute, most likely for a local school. The current designation, as well as the former, pays homage to Nicholas William Battle, who donated land for a school and two churches.

BELL BOTTOM (Matagorda): sixteen miles SE of Bay City. A. C. Bell bought acreage in the late 1800s in what was called "bottom" land.

BEN ARNOLD (Milam): on US 77, seven miles N of Cameron. Also spelled Benarnold. The town began in 1890 as a railway stop and was named for Bennie Arnold, the three-year-old daughter of B. I. Arnold. The little girl served as mascot on the first train to arrive at the new station.

BEN BOLT (Jim Wells): on FM 2508, off US 281, seven miles S of Alice. The town was platted in 1904 and the origin of its moniker is associated with music. L. B. Collins christened the town from a popular song, "Ben Bolt," which begins with the words "Don't you remember sweet Alice, Ben Bolt?"

BENBROOK (Tarrant): at int IH 20 and US 377, ten miles SW of Fort Worth. Laid out around 1857 and called Miranda. A short time later it was renamed for James M. Benbrook, a migrant from Indiana, who arrived in the region about 1874. Benbrook was instrumental in persuading officials of the Texas and Pacific Railway to build a line through the settlement.

BEN WHEELER (Van Zandt): on TX 64 and FM 279 and 858, twelve miles SE of Canton. Was originally part of Henderson County. Probably emerged in the 1840s and was named for Kentuckian Benjamin Wheeler, who received a land grant of 640 acres in the region.

BIPPUS (Deaf Smith): on a LR in NW Deaf Smith County. The area was populated in about 1910 on land that once belonged to the XIT Ranch. The village remembers George Bippus, who donated land for a school.

BIRTHRIGHT (Hopkins): on FM 71, ten miles NE of Sulphur Springs. Also known as Lone Star. In 1870 a store was situated in the ranch house owned by E. C. Birthright.

BOLT (San Saba): on Lower Simpson Creek in E San Saba County. Settled prior to 1854 and christened for William James Bolt, saloon and store owner.

BON WIER (Newton): at jct FM 1416 and 363 and US 190, ten miles SE of Newton. Platted in 1905 and relates to B. F. *Bon*ner and R. W. *Wier,* manager and surgeon, respectively, of the Kirby Lumber Company.

BROWNDELL (Jasper): at jct FM 1007 and US 96, twelve miles N of Jasper. Founded in 1903 and named for Dell Brown, wife of an official of the Maryland Trust Company.

BRUCEVILLE-EDDY (McLennan): on IH 35, eighteen miles SW of Waco. This site was originally two separate communities, each of which became railroad stations in 1882. Bruceville honors Lucien N. *Bruce,* who donated land for the station. Eddy was called Martin until a post office was opened in 1882. The site was christened for Everett

B. Eddy, a railroad superintendent. The two communities were incorporated as one in the mid-1970s.

BUDCONNOR (Hardin): in SW Hardin County. Laid out as a logging camp around 1903 and named for a claim agent employed by the Beaumont, Sour Lake, and Western Railroad.

CALL (Jasper-Newton): at int FM 1004 and 1013, twenty miles SE of Jasper. Sister city of Call Junction. George Adams Sr. founded the town in 1895 and named it for his business associate, Dennis Call.

CAMEY SPUR (Denton): on TX 121, sixteen miles SE of Denton. Platted around 1852 as a rail spur, it remembers Captain William McKamy, with an alteration in spelling.

CARADAN (Mills): on FM 575, nine miles NE of Goldthwaite. Founded in the 1880s and relates to early pioneers Samuel *Cara*way and *Dan* T. Bush.

CARMINE (Fayette-Washington): on US 290 at the Fayette-Washington county line. Dr. B. J. Thigpen and his family arrived prior to the end of 1885. The site was originally known as Sylvan, but the name was changed to Carmine in 1892 to pay tribute to Newton Carmean, the first postmaster. The change in spelling was probably made by either the post office or somewhere in transition.

CEGO (Falls): on FM 1950, seven miles SW of Chilton. German American farmers settled here in the 1880s and called the place Pleasant Valley. When a post office was approved for the site in 1895, residents discovered that there was another Pleasant Valley in the state. They chose Cego as the new moniker, relating the name to a cotton picker who had toiled on several farms in the area.

CHALK (Cottle): on FM 1278, fourteen miles S of Paducah. The community is located on land that once was part of W. Q. Richards's

3D Ranch. Several economic factors forced Richards to establish a settlement here from 1905 to 1907. At the time it was called Richards Colony, then later known as Dutch. The name was changed in 1908 to honor James M. Chalk, first postmaster.

CHEEK (Jefferson): on TX 124, seven miles SW of Beaumont. J. R. Cheek platted the town site in 1907.

CISCO (Eastland): at int US 183 and IH 20, ten miles W of Eastland. Rev. C. G. Stevens was the first permanent settler, arriving in the late 1870s. He called the place Red Gap. The label was changed to Cisco about 1884, honoring John A. Cisco, a New York financier credited with having the Houston and Texas Central Railroad come through this region. Conrad Hilton, the world famous hotelman, started his empire here.

CLICK (Llano): fifteen miles SE of Llano. A post office opened here in 1880. The village was christened for either Malachi Click, an early settler, or for George Washington Click.

CLOSE CITY (Garza): on RM 399, two miles N of US 380, eleven miles W of Post. Charles William Post, cereal magnate, purchased land in this region, on which he planned to establish a settlement. This site was within the boundaries of that initial purchase. The first residents of the little community used mostly tents for their homes. This brought on snide remarks by outsiders, who referred to the place as Ragtown. This name became even more popular after a severe storm tore up many of the tents, leaving only rags tied to tent posts. Officially, though, the current designation is for E. B. Close, Post's son-in-law.

COFFEYVILLE (Upshur): S of TX 155, five miles W of Lake O' The Pines. Farmers from the Old South settled this region between 1845 and 1866, making this one of the oldest communities in East Texas. Some say that an early traveler spilled green coffee beans along the trail he was traveling and the beans took root and grew. Another thought is that, in the early days, this was nothing more than a camping site, and the smell of brewing coffee influenced the moniker. The historical origin of the community's name is the Coffee family, early settlers in the vicinity.

CONE (Crosby): on US 62, ten miles N of Crosbyton. The village was settled in 1901 and christened for James Stanton Cone, early-day mailman.

CONVERSE (Bexar): on FM 1976, thirteen miles NE of downtown San Antonio. In 1877, a Major Converse, chief engineer of the Southern Pacific Railroad, purchased land in this area, which included the future town site.

COOLIDGE (Limestone): at int of TX 171 and 73, eleven miles NW of Mexia. The little village was developed with the arrival of the rail line in 1903. It was named for a stockholder of the railway company. The original spelling of the name was "Cooledge," which was corrected in 1930.

COUCH (Karnes): off TX 239, seven miles SE of Kenedy. Once known as Oklahoma Settlement. D. F. Couch was influential in developing this region by bringing in settlers from Oklahoma Territory in the early 1890s.

DENNIS (Parker): on FM 1543, fifteen miles SW of Weatherford. Judge N. M. Dennis founded the little community around 1892, following construction of a bridge across the Brazos River.

DEW (Freestone): at jct TX 75 and FM 489, nine miles S of Fairfield. Settled in the 1850s and called Avant or Avant Prairie, probably for early settlers. In 1870 the community took the name Sunshine for the Sunshine Methodist Church. In 1885, residents wanted to pay homage to one of their own, a man named Drew. Postal officials in Washington misread the name and recorded it as Dew.

DEWVILLE (Gonzales): at int of a LR and FM 1117, twenty-five miles SW of Gonzales. The Dew brothers, Frank and Thomas, opened a steam-powered gin here in 1885.

DONIE (Freestone): on TX 164, eleven miles S of Teague. The original community is believed to have been established in the 1880s. An application for a post office was made in 1898, with residents wanting to honor their own with the name Douie, an early settler. This was misread in Washington, and the current spelling is the result. In 1907 the townspeople moved the entire community two miles east to have access to the newly laid railroad tracks.

DON TOL (Wharton): on FM 1301, twelve miles SE of Wharton. Two Taylor brothers, William Toliver and Solomon, joined with Green Duncan following the Civil War and developed this area. Being ambitious, they did most anything to gain income: farming, freighting, and the like. Laborers employed by the trio referred to William Toliver as *Don* (Spanish for "Mr.") Tol. The Don Tol Plantation home is still in existence.

DULL (La Salle): three-and-one-half miles SE of Los Angeles. The community was settled in the early 1900s and at first called Nettavilla. The origin of the current moniker comes from the Dull Ranch. A. J. and J. J. Dull, of Harrisburg, Pennsylvania, were ceded a vast territory by the state of Texas in exchange for steel with which to build railroads. The author O. Henry (William S. Porter), who left his native North Carolina for health reasons, was employed on the Dull Ranch for a short period of time.

EARLY (Brown): at int US 67 and 84, three miles E of Brownwood. Developed in the early 1850s and christened for Walter Early, who donated land for a school and the first Baptist church.

EARLYWINE (Washington): on TX 105, six miles from Brenham. A post office was opened here in the 1800s, and the first postmaster was John W. Earlywine.

EASTER (Castro): on FM 2397, fourteen miles NW of Dimmitt. The William Frank Easter family settled here in 1905.

EASTERLY (Robertson): on US 79, twelve miles NE of Franklin. Founded in the 1870s and known as Acorn. Easterly became its official name after 1881 for twin brothers Dan J. and John Easterly. The former was the first postmaster.

ECLETO (Karnes): on FM 627, ten miles NE of Helena. In 1921 Walter Riedel and associates opened a store and cotton gin here. Some historians claim that the site was once known as Cleto for a local Native American. The Spanish wrote it as *El Cleto*, and Anglos, as they often did, simply changed the spelling to its present form.

EDCOUCH (Hidalgo): at int TX 107 and FM 1015, eighteen miles NE of McAllen. Founded in 1927, it honors *Ed*ward *Couch*, landowner and banker.

EDGE (Brazos): on FM 974, fourteen miles N of Bryan. Dr. John Edge developed the little community in the 1870s.

EMHOUSE (Navarro): at jct FM 1126, 1839, and 3383, eight miles NW of Corsicana. Platted in 1906 and first called Lyford. When a post office was opened, duplication with another town name was discovered. The citizens renamed the site, saluting Colonel E. M. House, superintendent of the Bayou Valley Railroad.

EVADALE (Jasper): at jct US 96 and FM 105 and 1131, thirty-five miles SW of Jasper. From 1830 to 1840 this locale was called Richardson Bluff for Benjamin Richardson, early settler. After Richardson's death in 1849, the site became known as Ford's Bluff, most likely for Charles T. Ford, businessman. John Henry Kirby rebuilt a tramline running from Ford's Bluff eight miles outside the town. Kirby then christened the site for Miss Eva Dale, schoolteacher.

FAILS (Walker): on TX 75, ten miles NW of Huntsville. A community existed here by 1911 and was christened for Joe Fails, who donated land for a school.

FAWIL (Newton): on FM 363, five miles W of Bon Wier. This was part of a land grant from the Texas Revolution of 1836. Fonzo A. Wilson brought in a sawmill in the early 1900s. When he erected a sign for his place of business, he only had room to paint his initials, *F. A.,* and the beginning of his last name, *Wilson.*

FILES VALLEY (Hill): on FM 66, fourteen miles NE of Hillsboro. Also known as Files. The site was originally called Eureka Valley, but was renamed in November 1879 for David Sidney Files, who built the first house in the vicinity.

FRAME SWITCH (Williamson): on US 79, three miles W of Taylor. Sheepman Soloman George Yakey settled the site as early as 1882. The village became a switching station for the International-Great Northern Railroad. It takes its moniker from the combination of *Switch* and the surname of David *Frame,* the father of Mattie Frame, wife of Solomon Yakey.

FRIDAY (Trinity): on FM 1280, nine miles NW of Groveton. Founded about the time of the Civil War and called Ellis Prairie for Benjamin B. Ellis, early settler. Today's designation honors another settler, Fred Friday.

GAY HILL (Fayette): on TX 71, six miles SE of La Grange. Developed in the 1830s and relates to James Gay, whose brother Thomas had established a Gay Hill community in Washington County.

GAY HILL (Washington): on FM 390, twelve miles NW of Brenham. Originally known as Chriesman Settlement. Rev. Hugh Wilson founded the second Presbyterian church in Texas on this spot in 1839. When a post office was opened in 1840, the community took the name from the owners of a general store, Thomas *Gay* and William C. J. *Hill.*

GEORGE WEST (Live Oak): at int US 281 and 59; county seat. George Washington West founded a ranch in the county in the early 1900s. He also donated land for a town site and railroad right-of-way.

GIST (Jasper): on TX 62, thirty-eight miles S of Jasper. Developed by 1902. While this word normally refers to the heart of a matter, the town was christened for J. P. Gist, developer.

GLAZE CITY (Gonzales): on RM 443, some fourteen miles E of Gonzales. Named for the man instrumental in promoting settlement of the community in 1926.

GLENFAWN (Rusk): on FM 2753, sixteen miles SW of Henderson. This region was occupied before the Civil War. The question is still unanswered: Did Ellis Glen or Glen Garland kill a fawn? Regardless, it is believed that plantation owner Julien Sidney Devereux christened the site.

GOLLY (DeWitt): twelve miles S of Cuero. A school opened here in 1884, and the village honors Anton Golly, a school board trustee.

GOODNIGHT (Armstrong): on US 287, twelve miles SE of Claude. Colonel Charles Goodnight settled on a ranch near here in 1887. Goodnight was a trailblazer, cattleman, and rancher, just to mention a few of his exploits.

GREATHOUSE (Ellis): ten miles SW of Waxahachie. The place was laid out by the 1930s and honors Archibald Greathouse, settler.

GROOM (Carson): on IH 40, sixteen miles E of Conway. The community was founded around 1902 and named for B. B. Groom, rancher.

GROUNDS (Houston): on FM 2022, nine miles NE of Crockett. Was known as Jones School House in the late 1850s, but the present designation is for John Grounds, settler.

HATCHETVILLE (Hopkins): on FM 3236, nine miles NE of Sulphur Springs. The name remembers E. L. Hatchet, who opened a store here in 1908.

HECKVILLE (Lubbock): on FM 400, seven miles N of Idalou. Henry Heck put up a gin here around 1948.

HOOKER RIDGE (Rains): on FM 513, twelve miles NW of Emory. Platted prior to 1904, it remembers the Hooker family, early settlers in this area.

HOOKS (Bowie): on US 82, nine miles E of Boston. The community grew up in the late 1830s around a plantation owned by Warren Hooks.

HOUSE (Fort Bend): twenty miles SE of Richmond. This was a railroad stop in 1885 and had a post office in 1909. It was tagged for the Thomas House Plantation.

HUMBLE (Harris): on US 59, eighteen miles NE of Houston. This was a settlement by 1870 and salutes Pleasant S. Humble, settler and ferry operator, who was in the region before the Civil War.

IAGO (Wharton): at int FM 1301 and 1096, twelve miles E of Wharton. The village was platted prior to the Civil War. In one version of the origin of the moniker, a Dr. Reilford suggested the name because of its shortness and the fact that it contained three vowels. A more romantic rendition is that C. W. Kemp and M. D. Taylor coined the name for the villain in Shakespeare's *Othello,* who planted seeds of distrust in Othello of his wife, Desdemona.

IOLA (Grimes): on FM 39, twenty miles NW of Anderson. The thought is that the community was named (with a variance in spelling) for Edward Ar*iola,* who was one of Stephen F. Austin's colonists. Ariola settled in the region in 1836.

IVANHOE (Fannin): on FM 273, ten miles N of Bonham. Laid out in 1885 and known as Hawkins Prairie for Strother Hawkins, an early settler. When a post office was opened, citizens wanted a more attention-getting name. Captain Joe Dupree suggested Ivanhoe, one of his favorite fictional heroes.

JACOBIA (Hunt): on FM 118, six miles NE of Greenville. A community was established in the 1850s and called Jacob's Prairie for an early settler. The name had evolved to its current spelling by 1887.

JUMBO (Panola): off TX 315, seventeen miles SW of Carthage. Farmers were here before the Civil War. The place relates to a sheepherder who was known as "Jumbo" for his size.

KATEMCY (Mason): on FM 1222, one mile E of US 87, sixteen miles N of Mason. The community was founded in the 1870s, and among the early pioneers were the families of Elbert Watts, Andy Coots, and William Turner. It is possible the place temporarily went by the name Coatsville. The site was named Hammerville early on for the noise made while Elias and Alfred Cowan were building the first home in the vicinity. When a post office was opened, officials rejected Hammerville because there were already too many "villes" in Texas. Ketemoczy, a Comanche chief, often wintered near a local creek and his name was submitted to the Post Office Department. Officials in Washington shortened it to Katemcy.

KISHI COLONY (Orange): in C Orange County. Kichimatsu Kishi founded this community in 1907, which was one of at least three small Japanese settlements established at the time.

KLUMP (Washington): on FM 389, eight miles SW of Brenham. A post office was in operation here prior to 1899 and remembers the Klump family, early settlers.

LAMASCO (Fannin): on FM 1396, eight miles NE of Bonham. Established around 1850, the town derived its moniker from three early settlers, *La*w, *Ma*son, and *Sco*tt.

LATCH (Upshur): on FM 1795, eight miles W of Gilmer. Founded in the late 1880s and called Know. The name was changed in 1894 to remember lumberman L. A. "Daddy" Latch.

LA WARD (Jackson): on TX 172, fourteen miles S of Ganado. Platted in 1904 and named for *La*fayette *Ward*, rancher.

LAWRENCE KEY (Waller): near FM 1736, two miles E of TX 6, and six miles NE of Hempstead. In February 1891, J. M. and Mamie A. Key deeded six acres to the Methodist Episcopal church "to be used only for Divine and School purposes under forfeit." The first part of the community moniker comes from Simon Lawrence, an active member of the church.

LAY (Angelina): twelve miles S of Lufkin. The region was pioneered prior to the Civil War, but the post office didn't open here until 1898. The community was named for William C. Lay, the first postmaster.

LEADAY (Coleman): on FM 2134 in SW Coleman County. Rick Coffey founded the community in 1861. Coffey's enterprises—general store, saloon, post office—were washed away by a flood, and a new community known as Trigger was established on the opposite side of the Colorado River. William H. Day owned a ranch in the region in 1876 that included the acreage on which Trigger was situated. The current community came about when Day sold off part of his ranchland to farmers. The town carries the name of the ranch owners, J. C. *Lea* and his wife Mable, who had been Mrs. William H. *Day*.

LEAGUE CITY (Galveston): on TX 3 and US 75, between Houston and Galveston. This locale was previously known as Butlers Ranch or Clear Creek. In 1893, J. C. League acquired the property and established the town site on the railroad line.

LOCKER (San Saba): on RM 500, seventeen miles NW of San Saba. A settlement began here in the 1870s and was known as Knob, then

Mount Pleasant. J. Monroe Locker and his family arrived in the area in the 1890s and put up the first general store and cotton gin.

LOONEYVILLE (Nacogdoches): near jct FM 225 and 343, six miles NW of Nacogdoches. The community is situated near a creek called Loco or Crazy Creek for the wild course it follows in its flow. The site itself, however, honors John Looney, who opened a store here in the early 1870s.

LOVING (Young): on TX 114, eighteen miles SE of Olney. Laid out prior to 1910. This was once part of the Lost Valley Loving Ranch on the Goodnight-Loving Trail. The town was christened for the Oliver Loving family.

LOWAKE (Concho): on RM 1929 and 381, nine miles NW of Paint Rock. The community was developed in 1909 with the arrival of the railroad. It was christened for two farmers, *Lowe* and Sch*lake*.

MABANK (Kaufman): on US 175 and FM 90, sixteen miles SE of Kaufman. Lorenzo D. Stover was the region's first settler, arriving in 1846. John R. Jones named this site Lawn City in 1887 for a popular dress material that he carried in his store. For some reason, it was changed to Lawndale later that year. G. W. Mason and Thomas Eubank set aside a square mile tract in 1900 near the railroad tracks. They derived the label for the site from their names, *Ma*son and E*ubank*.

MANOR (Travis): on US 290, twelve miles NE of downtown Austin. A post office named Grassdale opened here in 1859 with James Manor, a landowner from Tennessee, serving as postmaster. Manor later donated land for the railroad so the town was renamed in his honor.

MARFA (Presidio): at jct US 90 and 67; county seat. This was developed as a railroad stop in 1883. The wife of a railroad executive selected this name, taking it from that of a servant girl in Fyodor Dostoevsky's novel *The Brothers Karamazov*.

MAXDALE (Bell): eight miles SW of Killeen. Developed prior to 1883. In the early days of its existence, it was known as Pleasant Grove for a grove of live oak trees in the vicinity. Frank McBryde Sr. applied for a post office, but was advised that there was already a Pleasant Grove in Texas. Permission was given to change the moniker to Mc's Dale, after the McBrydes, but when the post office opened in June 1883, the name was changed to Maxdale.

MERIT (Hunt): on FM 36, fifteen miles NW of Greenville. Settlers were in the region in the late 1860s or early 1870s. The community acquired its handle through compromise. Some residents wanted it named for Judge Merritt; others objected to having the place carry an individual's name. Merit was the compromise, apparently still derived from the judge's name.

MONKSTOWN (Fannin): on FM 273, sixteen miles NE of Bonham. Probably developed around the 1870s. At first it was called Blue Prairie for reasons unknown, but the current moniker remembers James Monk.

MOZO (Williamson): on FM 971, nine miles NE of Georgetown. The Mazoch family built a gin here around 1909. It is believed that the current designation is a corruption of Mazoch.

NEW HARP (Montague): off FM 1655, sixteen miles SE of Montague. Known as Harp Town until about 1900; thereafter it was called Harp. Both names refer to Nixon P. Harp, store owner.

NICKLEBERRY (Cass): on FM 1399, two miles SE of Marietta. More than likely this community was platted in the early 1920s. It was christened for the son of one of the first settlers, whose last name was Berry. The first name of the son is no longer known, and only this nickname survives. On the other hand, it is possible that the community remembers the Tip Nickleberry family.

NIVAC (Nacogdoches): on FM 204, one-and-one-half miles E of Cushing. Developed about 1903 as a logging settlement. George Cavin put in a sawmill and planer, and the site was named for him, only spelled backward.

NORTH ZULCH (Madison): at int TX 21 and US 190, thirteen miles W of Madisonville. The original site was founded by and named for Dr. Julius Zulch in 1907. Sometime later, the town moved a mile northward to be near the Trinity and Brazos Valley Railroad line. Consequently, residents changed the name to its present designation.

OTIS CHALK (Howard): on FM 821, twenty-two miles SE of Big Spring. The town grew up in the 1920s with the discovery of oil. It was named for the rancher on whose land oil was found. There are some accounts that the post office was opened in February 1939 when the site was called Chalkton. Regardless, in June 1939 the name was changed to its present form.

OTTINE (Gonzales): on PR 11, nine miles NW of Gonzales. Originally known as Otto's Station, the name was officially recorded in 1879 with the combining of names of the community founders: Adolph *Otto* and his wife Chris*tine*.

PALACIOS (Matagorda): on TX 35, twelve miles S of Blessing. The community is situated on Tres Palacios Bay, after which it was named. The name is Spanish for "three palaces," and therein lies a bit of folklore. It seems that sailors from a Spanish ship that wrecked in Matagorda Bay thought they saw palaces on the shore. As they neared land, the vision disappeared. Moving from lore to more reasonable claims, some believe that the bay and the Tres Palacios River were actually named for Jose Felix Trespalacios. The town of Tres Palacios was platted in 1902, but since there was already a community by that name in the state, residents changed the name by dropping the first word.

PANDORA (Wilson): at jct US 87 and FM 1107, twenty miles NE of Floresville. This was set as a railroad stop in the 1890s. The community acquired its moniker in a tongue-in-cheek manner. In earlier days, two prominent families lived here, the Montgomerys and the Skyeses. As is often the case in small towns, these families had their names on virtually every business and piece of property. When the railroad came through, bringing with it some prominence, the question arose as to whether to call the place Montgomeryville or Skyestown. Realizing what a bucket of worms would be uncapped, and thinking of how one of the families would react should its name not be selected, a railroad employee commented, "We've opened the box. We'll call it 'Pandora.'" This name refers to the mythical figure who opened a forbidden box and unleashed a horde of evils upon the world.

PLEDGER (Matagorda): at jct FM 1301 and 1728, nineteen miles N of Bay City. Stephen F. Austin led the first pioneers to this area in 1824 and 1827. A post office was opened in 1880. Postmaster John Walton Brown named the community in remembrance of his deceased wife, Narcissa Pledger.

PONDER (Denton): at int FM 156 and 2249. Settlers were here by the 1850s, and a railroad community called Gerald was on the site. The name was changed in 1889 because of duplication and honors W. A. Ponder, landowner and banker.

POST (Garza): at jct US 84 and 380; county seat. First called Post City. Charles William Post, cereal magnate, founded the town in 1907 and owned some 200,000 acres in the region.

POWDERLY (Lamar): on US 271, eleven miles N of Paris. Founded around the time of the Civil War. First known as Lenoir, the name was changed in the 1880s. The name now pays homage to Terence V. Powderly, commissioner of immigration during the McKinley administration.

RAMARITO (Jim Hogg): E of TX 1017, thirty-eight miles S of Hebbronville. The area was originally settled in the late 1700s. It wasn't until the 1880s, though, that a permanent settlement was realized, when A. Ramirez established his ranch headquarters in the vicinity. When a town was laid out it was named Ramarito instead of Ramirez, because a community by the latter name already existed in Texas.

RATTAN (Delta): at int FM 1530 and 3388, three miles SE of Pecan Gap. There were pioneers in this region as early as the 1820s. One of the first was a man by the name of Blue. A post office opened here in 1893 and was named for C. V. Rattan, postmaster at nearby Cooper, who greatly assisted the local community in acquiring a postal facility.

REKLAW (Cherokee-Rusk): at jct US 84 and TX 204, ten miles NE of Rusk. Natural resources around nearby Iron Mountain had attracted miners and prospectors as far back as the short-lived Republic of Texas, but the coming of the railroad in 1902 led to the birth of this little hamlet. Residents wanted to honor one of their own, Margaret Walker, landowner. Duplication once more stepped in to necessitate a change. They simply took her last name and spelled it backward.

RELAMPAGO (Hidalgo): off US 281, ten miles SE of Weslaco. This was originally part of the Spanish Llano Grande land grant ceded to Juan José Ballí in May 1790. The land was divided among his heirs in 1848, and by 1852 there was a viable community on land inherited by Cirildo Hinojosa. *Relámpago* is Spanish for "lightning flash." It is thought that the community received its name from an early settler who was a go-getter, always on the move, and earned this as his nickname. The more logical explanation, however, is that it was christened to remember an electrical storm of the 1880s.

RIOS (Duval): on FM 1329, thirteen miles SE of Benavides. Developed some time before 1938, the town is believed to have been named for Calletonio Rios, who platted the region in 1896.

ROBERT LEE (Coke): at jct TX 158 and 208; county seat. R. E. Cartledge and his father-in-law, L. B. Harris, laid out the community prior to 1891 and christened it for the Civil War Confederate general.

ROCKETT (Ellis): on FM 813, five miles NW of Waxahachie. Developed in 1846 and first called Liberty. The site was renamed in 1852, recognizing John Rockett, an early settler.

ROCKNE (Bastrop): on FM 535, twelve miles SW of Bastrop. The area had a settlement called Meuth for Andrew Meuth by 1846. Around 1892 a little hamlet occupied what is today the site of Rockne. It was at first called Walnut Creek, then Lehman or Lehmanville for the family that donated land for a church. William Hilbig and his family arrived in 1922 and opened a store; the site soon acquired the handle of Hilbigville. Knute Rockne, famous football coach at Notre Dame University, died in March 1931. Soon after, schoolchildren, backed by other residents, particularly those of Norwegian ancestry like Rockne, petitioned for a name change. Father Strobel suggested the new name at a town meeting, and it was passed.

ROOSEVELT (Kimble): on RM 291, sixteen miles W of Junction. A post office opened here in 1898, and W. B. Wagoner, village founder, christened it for Theodore Roosevelt.

RULE (Haskell): at int US 380 and TX 6, thirteen miles W of Haskell. A post office was in operation here in 1903, and the town name refers to William A. Rule Sr., railroad official.

RUN (Hidalgo): on US 281, seven miles S of Donna. George Ruthven built a store here in 1903. The town moniker was derived from his name, *Ru*thven.

ST. JO (Montague): at int US 83 and TX 59, fifteen miles E of Montague. Ithane and Prince Singletary founded this community in 1849. It was first known as Head of Elm for its location near the headwaters of the Elm Fork of the Trinity River. It took its present moniker in 1873 when the town was developed, relating the name to the absentee landlord, Joseph A. Howell, land promoter.

SALESVILLE (Palo Pinto): on FM 2270, eight miles N of Mineral Wells. Christened in 1880 for Theopalus Sale, store owner.

SAMNORWOOD (Collingsworth): W of US 83 on FM 1036, sixteen miles N of Wellington. The community was developed in 1931 with the arrival of the railroad and takes the name of Sam W. Norwood, early pioneer.

SAMPLE (Gonzales): on US 87, twenty-four miles S of Gonzales. A. H. and Jim Sample were early settlers, arriving in the 1870s.

SANCO (Coke): on a LR E of TX 208, seven miles N of Robert Lee. This was part of Tom Green County when ranchers settled here in the 1880s. The site carries the name of Sanaco, with a variance in spelling, a Comanche chief who used to camp in the vicinity.

SANDOW (Milam): on FM 1786, eight miles SW of Rockdale. Mule drivers used this place as a stop in early days and called it Freezeout. A post office opened in 1873 and was called Millerton for Emil Miller, who donated land for a school. The McAlester Fuel Company set up shop in 1922 and renamed the community Sandow, after a famous strongman being promoted by showman Florenz Ziegfeld.

SANTA MARIA (Cameron): at jct US 281 and FM 2556, twelve miles SW of Harlingen. José de Escandón and his followers settled the region in the mid-1750s. Spain eventually ceded the land to Rosa María Hinojosa de Ballí in 1777. When a post office opened here in 1878, it derived its name from Maria Ballí.

SATIN (Falls): on FM 134, four miles from Chilton. In 1872 a man named J. H. Robertson opened a sawmill on nearby Cow Creek. The population shifted to the current location when the railroad came through in the 1890s. The town was originally named Laguna because of a large lake nearby, and then Cedar Point for the native cedars which were harvested here. Satin, supposedly relating to a railroad employee, had become the town's official designation by 1917.

SCHOOLERVILLE (Hamilton): on US 281, six miles SW of Hamilton. Christened for J. L. Schooler, an early settler who arrived here in 1870.

SETAG (Polk): in NC Polk County. This was a mining site settled prior to 1917. The moniker was derived from the name of James T. Gates, miner, by reversing the spelling of his last name, probably to avoid duplication.

SETH WARD (Hale): at int FM 1767 and 400, two miles NE of Plainview. The Central Plains College and Conservatory of Music was established here in 1907. In 1910 the school name changed to Seth Ward College, honoring a Methodist bishop. The community assumed the school's new name.

SHEP (Taylor): on FM 1086, five miles NW of Happy Valley. John Crayton was the first arrival in the area, coming in the 1870s. The community assumed its present moniker from Andrew Martin *Shep*-pard, an early settler who owned a store, a ranch, and was also the postmaster.

SHINER (Lavaca): at int US 90A and TX 95, fourteen miles W of Hallettsville. First called Half Moon, then New Half Moon, but the label was changed in 1888 to Shiner for H. B. Shiner, settler and donor of land for a railroad right-of-way.

SHOOKS BLUFF (Cherokee): in S Cherokee County. The hamlet was named for Jefferson Shook, a native of Missouri who opened a mercantile business here in the 1850s, and for its location on a bluff overlooking the Neches River.

SMILEY (Gonzales): at int US 87 and FM 3234 and 108, twenty-one miles S of Gonzales. John Smiley's arrival in the early 1870s marked the settlement of the village. He was a trader and sheepherder and placed his homesite beside a long narrow lake that quickly took the name Smiley's, Smileys, or Smiley Lake.

SPARKS (Bell): on FM 95, eleven miles SE of Belton. The community grew up around a railroad station in the late 1800s and was most likely christened for the Sparks family.

SPEAKS (Lavaca): on FM 530, twenty miles SE of Hallettsville. The town site is on land ceded in 1835 to Archibald S. White. A settlement called Speaksville for a store owner was up and running. Later, the community became known as Boxville. In 1928 the little hamlet was officially designated Speaks.

SPRINKLE (Travis): nine miles NE of Austin. Erasmus Frederick Sprinkle brought his family from Virginia to this region in the 1870s.

STAFF (Eastland): off FM 2214, some eight miles SE of Eastland. When the Round Mountain Baptist Church was established here in 1896, it marked the birth of the town. Sometime after 1897 Ferdinando S. Taylor built a store that also housed the post office. He christened the site after Professor Staff, a close friend who lived in Carlton, Texas. A biblical reference from the Twenty-third Psalm has also been attributed to the origin: "Thy rod and thy staff, they comfort me."

STAIRTOWN (Caldwell): at int TX 80 and FM 671, six miles NW of Luling. This started as an oil boomtown in the 1920s with the discovery of black gold at the nearby Luling oil field. The site honors a Mr. Stair, landowner.

STAMPS (Upshur): on FM 1649, ten miles NE of Gilmer. Laid out sometime after 1900, the town honors W. O. Stamps, local entrepreneur.

STAPLES (Guadalupe): at int TX 621 and CR 1977, twenty miles NE of Seguin. The area contained settlers as early as 1852 and was labeled in 1871 for John D. Staples, store owner.

STORMVILLE (Wood): on FM 2225, seven miles N of Quitman. A post office was in operation here by 1878, and the site was known as Stormville. The name most likely related to W. Storm, who once owned a flour mill and a gin here.

STRANGER (Falls): off TX 7, ten miles E of Marlin. Settled in the late 1840s and known as Upper or North Blue Ridge. Citizens were searching for a new name, as they were not too happy with their present one, when a stagecoach pulled into town. A man disembarked and introduced himself as Stranger. The county tax rolls of 1870 list a man named Strangere, so it is possible the two were one and the same. Whether this is the case has little bearing, because the townspeople liked the idea of their settlement being called Stranger. There is another theory, which holds that a post office representative asked the local blacksmith, a recent arrival, to suggest a name for the site. The blacksmith declined, saying he was a "stranger" to the town.

STUDY BUTTE (Brewster): on TX 118, five miles E of Terlingua. The town was laid out in the early 1900s with the interest in regional mercury mining. The village was christened for Will Study, manager of the Big Bend Mercury Mine.

SWIFT (Nacogdoches): at jct TX 7 and FM 2713, ten miles E of Nacogdoches. Developed in 1838, the town remembers W. H. Swift Jr., the first postmaster.

TARZAN (Martin): on TX 176, five miles W of Lenorah. This town was viable before 1925. Tant Lindsay, store owner, sent a list of names to Washington. Postal authorities selected Tarzan from the list and appointed Lindsay as postmaster. It is believed that Lindsay took the name from the character in the popular comic strip.

TEMPLE (Bell): at int IH 35 and US 53 and 95, six miles NE of Belton. Jonathan E. Moore sold 187 acres in 1880 to the Gulf, Colorado, and Santa Fe Railway. The railroad established a construction camp and called it Temple Junction, honoring Bernard Moore Temple, chief engineer of the railway. Local residents referred to the site as Mud Town or Tanglefoot. In 1881 a post office opened for business, and the city assumed the name Temple.

TENNYSON (Coke): on US 277, ten miles S of Bronte. Samuel and J. W. Sayner, from England, settled in the vicinity in 1882. It was they who suggested the name in tribute to English poet Alfred Lord Tennyson.

TEXROY (Hutchison): five miles SE of Borger. Platted in the late 1920s at the apex of the area oil boom. The town moniker pays tribute to S. D. *"Tex"* Mcil*roy*, founder of the Dixon Creek Oil and Refinery Company.

TINRAG (Hopkins): on TX 11, six miles W of Sulphur Springs. Started as a railroad stop sometime before 1900. The moniker remembers the Garnit family, with the name spelled backward for some unknown reason.

TOMBALL (Harris): on FM 2920, thirty miles N of Houston. Prior to 1850, the area was the site of a farming community on a land grant given in 1838 to the heirs of William Hurd. The settlement was called Peck for a well-known engineer. The town was renamed in 1907, remembering *Thom*as Henry *Ball*, who was the moving force behind having the railroad routed through the vicinity.

TOM BEAN (Grayson): on TX 11 and FM 902 and 2729, ten miles SE of Sherman. Platted in 1888 as a railroad station. Tom Bean, a surveyor from Bonham, donated fifty acres for a town site and the railroad right-of-way.

TOOL (Henderson): on TX 274, twenty-three miles NW of Athens. Settled as early as 1835 and originally known as Hog Fork. It was christened in 1905 for George Tool, merchant.

TOW (Llano): on FM 2241, twenty miles NE of Llano. This is the oldest community in the county, starting when the Cowan family arrived from Tennessee in 1852. The moniker honors William Tow, who settled here with his family in 1853.

TRUCE (Jack): on TX 59, fifteen miles NE of Jacksboro. A post office opened here in 1893 and was named for a local family.

VALENTINE (Jeff Davis): on US 90, thirty-six miles W of Fort Davis. Established and christened on 14 February 1882 with the arrival of the railroad. The smaller of the county's two towns, it is thought the place name came from a Longfellow poem; others believe it honors the president of the Wells Fargo Company. Then there are those who feel it was christened to remember the first day a train ran through town, which was Saint Valentine's Day.

VAN (Van Zandt): on FM 314, TX 110, and IH 20, fourteen miles E of Canton. Settled prior to the Civil War and called Ratty Towns, or Who'd A Thought It, when a man named Ratty Towns tried to open a store here. Why he didn't isn't known. The place was renamed Swindall for George Swindall, landowner. Its present designation came from a schoolteacher, Henry *Vance*, who opened a post office and honored himself as well as *Van*nie Tunnel.

VICTORIA (Limestone): on a mail route from Mart, fourteen miles W of Groesbeck. The town had a school as early as 1898. The site is named in honor of England's Queen Victoria.

VICTORIA (Victoria): jct US 59, 77, and 87; county seat. One of the oldest cities in Texas. Established in 1824 by Martín de León and christened Guadalupe Victoria for the first president of the Republic of Mexico. The Mexican settlers fled to Mexico following the Battle of San Jacinto, and Anglos resettled the site. It then became known as Victoria.

WELLBORN (Brazos): on FM 2154, four miles E of College Station. Emerged in 1867 as a railroad construction camp. There are at least three sources for the origin of this community name: it was named for a well used by workers at the construction camp, or for E. W. Wellborn, or it is a derivative of W. W. Wilburn. Take your pick.

WHITHARRAL (Hockley): on US 385, ten miles N of Levelland. The Littlefield Ranch broke up some of its holdings in 1924 and sold them off as farms. The community was christened for Dr. *Whit*field *Harral*, donor of land for a school and cemetery.

WILCO (Hartley): on FM 2577 in extreme NE Hartley County. Brothers James Edward and Frank B. Wilson founded the town in 1909, and it was originally called Wilcoe. The present moniker is believed to have come from the personal name of the brothers, along with the businesses they established in the vicinity.

WILLAMAR (Willacy): on FM 490 and 1420, ten miles SE of Raymondville. The town was founded in 1921 and pays homage to *Will* Harding and *Lamar* Gill, founders of the community. The town site is situated on land that was once part of the Spanish grant ceded to José Narciso Cavazos.

WILLIAM PENN (Washington): on FM 390, twelve miles NE of Brenham. This site was originally part of a Mexican land grant ceded to Isaac Jackson, one of the Old Three Hundred settlers. John G. Pitts, another Old Three Hundred pioneer, bought the site in 1839.

John C. Eldridge, from Virginia, settled the community in 1849 and christened it for the steamboat *William Penn*.

WINNIE (Chambers): at jct TX 124 and IH 10, eighteen miles NW of Anahuac. Laid out in 1895 by railroad officials E. Dee Normandie and L. P. Featherstone. The community name refers to Fox Winnie, a contractor employed by the railroad.

WINONA (Smith): at int FM 16 and TX 155, three miles N of Owentown. The Tyler Tap Railroad developed the site in 1877 as a station and christened it for the daughter of railroad president James P. Douglas.

ZIPPERLANDVILLE (Falls): on TX 53, five miles W of Rosebud. Also known as Zipperlen or Zipperlenville. Settled in the 1870s by German, Yugoslav, and Czech migrants. The name honors the Zipperlen family, early merchants in the community, with a deviation in spelling.

FARAWAY PLACES

From Africa to Yorktown

AFRICA (Shelby): three miles SE of Center, near US 96. Freed slaves founded this predominantly African American settlement soon after the Civil War, which probably accounts for its name.

ALABAMA (Trinity): on FM 357, sixteen miles NE of Groveton. Founded around 1865 and refers to the Alabama tribe, who migrated from Mississippi in the 1820s.

ALBANY (Shackelford): at int TX 6 and US 283; county seat. Founded in 1874 on land donated by Sheriff Henry C. Jacobs. William Cruger christened the town for his former home in Georgia. This is the site of the Fort Griffin Fandangle, a jamboree that has taken place annually since 1938.

AMSTERDAM (Brazoria): on Chocolate Bayou, ten miles W of Angleton. A community was in place by the 1890s. The original designation was Gothland, but when Dutch settlers moved in sometime after 1890, they changed the name to Amsterdam, apparently for their previous homeland.

Town (County)

1. Africa (Shelby)
2. Alabama (Trinity)
3. Albany (Shackelford)
4. Amsterdam (Brazoria)
5. Argenta (Live Oak)
6. Argyle (Denton)
7. Athens (Henderson)
8. Atlanta (Cass)
9. Belgrade (Newton)
10. Berlin (Washington)

44. Fresno (Fort Bend)
45. Frisco (Collin)
46. Geneva (Sabine)
47. Georgia (Lamar)
48. Germany (Houston)
49. Goshen (Walker)

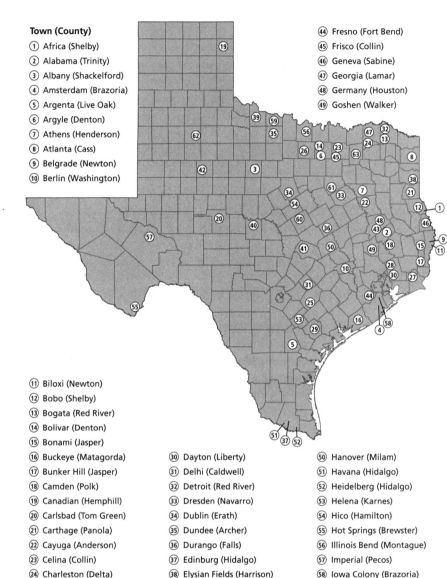

11. Biloxi (Newton)
12. Bobo (Shelby)
13. Bogata (Red River)
14. Bolivar (Denton)
15. Bonami (Jasper)
16. Buckeye (Matagorda)
17. Bunker Hill (Jasper)
18. Camden (Polk)
19. Canadian (Hemphill)
20. Carlsbad (Tom Green)
21. Carthage (Panola)
22. Cayuga (Anderson)
23. Celina (Collin)
24. Charleston (Delta)
25. Cheapside (Gonzales)
26. Chico (Wise)
27. China (Jefferson)
28. Cleveland (Liberty)
29. Cologne (Goliad)

30. Dayton (Liberty)
31. Delhi (Caldwell)
32. Detroit (Red River)
33. Dresden (Navarro)
34. Dublin (Erath)
35. Dundee (Archer)
36. Durango (Falls)
37. Edinburg (Hidalgo)
38. Elysian Fields (Harrison)
39. Fargo (Wilbarger)
40. Fife (McCulloch)
41. Florence (Williamson)
42. Fluvanna (Scurry)
43. Fodice (Houston)

50. Hanover (Milam)
51. Havana (Hidalgo)
52. Heidelberg (Hidalgo)
53. Helena (Karnes)
54. Hico (Hamilton)
55. Hot Springs (Brewster)
56. Illinois Bend (Montague)
57. Imperial (Pecos)
58. Iowa Colony (Brazoria)
59. Iowa Park (Wichita)
60. Ireland (Coryell)
61. Italy (Ellis)
62. Kalgary (Crosby)
63. Kingston (Hunt)

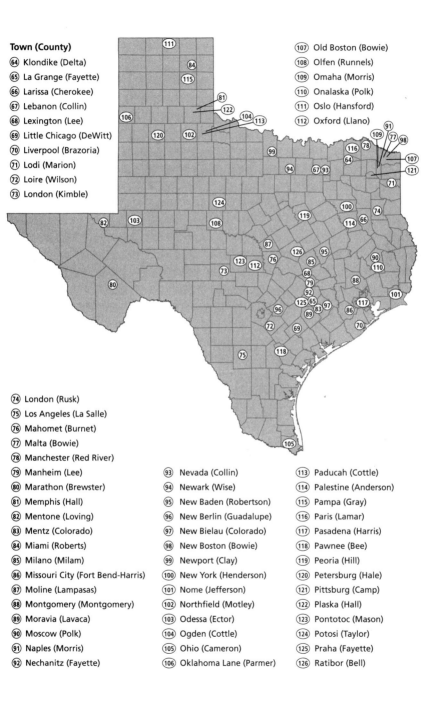

Town (County)
- 64 Klondike (Delta)
- 65 La Grange (Fayette)
- 66 Larissa (Cherokee)
- 67 Lebanon (Collin)
- 68 Lexington (Lee)
- 69 Little Chicago (DeWitt)
- 70 Liverpool (Brazoria)
- 71 Lodi (Marion)
- 72 Loire (Wilson)
- 73 London (Kimble)

- 107 Old Boston (Bowie)
- 108 Olfen (Runnels)
- 109 Omaha (Morris)
- 110 Onalaska (Polk)
- 111 Oslo (Hansford)
- 112 Oxford (Llano)

- 74 London (Rusk)
- 75 Los Angeles (La Salle)
- 76 Mahomet (Burnet)
- 77 Malta (Bowie)
- 78 Manchester (Red River)
- 79 Manheim (Lee)
- 80 Marathon (Brewster)
- 81 Memphis (Hall)
- 82 Mentone (Loving)
- 83 Mentz (Colorado)
- 84 Miami (Roberts)
- 85 Milano (Milam)
- 86 Missouri City (Fort Bend-Harris)
- 87 Moline (Lampasas)
- 88 Montgomery (Montgomery)
- 89 Moravia (Lavaca)
- 90 Moscow (Polk)
- 91 Naples (Morris)
- 92 Nechanitz (Fayette)

- 93 Nevada (Collin)
- 94 Newark (Wise)
- 95 New Baden (Robertson)
- 96 New Berlin (Guadalupe)
- 97 New Bielau (Colorado)
- 98 New Boston (Bowie)
- 99 Newport (Clay)
- 100 New York (Henderson)
- 101 Nome (Jefferson)
- 102 Northfield (Motley)
- 103 Odessa (Ector)
- 104 Ogden (Cottle)
- 105 Ohio (Cameron)
- 106 Oklahoma Lane (Parmer)

- 113 Paducah (Cottle)
- 114 Palestine (Anderson)
- 115 Pampa (Gray)
- 116 Paris (Lamar)
- 117 Pasadena (Harris)
- 118 Pawnee (Bee)
- 119 Peoria (Hill)
- 120 Petersburg (Hale)
- 121 Pittsburg (Camp)
- 122 Plaska (Hall)
- 123 Pontotoc (Mason)
- 124 Potosi (Taylor)
- 125 Praha (Fayette)
- 126 Ratibor (Bell)

Town (County)

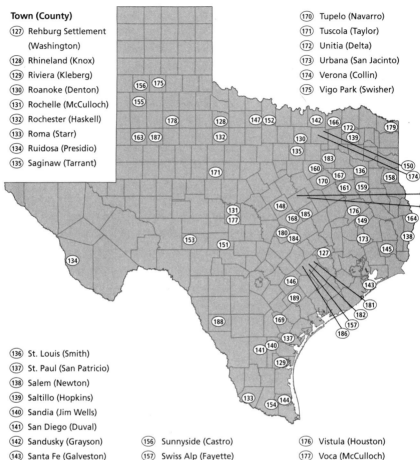

127. Rehburg Settlement (Washington)
128. Rhineland (Knox)
129. Riviera (Kleberg)
130. Roanoke (Denton)
131. Rochelle (McCulloch)
132. Rochester (Haskell)
133. Roma (Starr)
134. Ruidosa (Presidio)
135. Saginaw (Tarrant)

170. Tupelo (Navarro)
171. Tuscola (Taylor)
172. Unitia (Delta)
173. Urbana (San Jacinto)
174. Verona (Collin)
175. Vigo Park (Swisher)

136. St. Louis (Smith)
137. St. Paul (San Patricio)
138. Salem (Newton)
139. Saltillo (Hopkins)
140. Sandia (Jim Wells)
141. San Diego (Duval)
142. Sandusky (Grayson)
143. Santa Fe (Galveston)
144. Santa Monica (Willacy)
145. Saratoga (Hardin)
146. Saturn (Gonzales)
147. Scotland (Archer)
148. Seattle (Coryell)
149. Sebastapol (Trinity)
150. Sedalia (Collin)
151. Segovia (Kimble)
152. Shannon (Clay)
153. Sonora (Sutton)
154. Stockholm (Hidalgo)
155. Sudan (Lamb)

156. Sunnyside (Castro)
157. Swiss Alp (Fayette)
158. Tacoma (Panola)
159. Talladega (Cherokee)
160. Tellico (Ellis)
161. Tennessee Colony (Anderson)
162. Tokio (McLennan)
163. Tokio (Terry)
164. Toledo (Newton)
165. Tours (McLennan)
166. Trenton (Fannin)
167. Trinidad (Henderson)
168. Troy (Bell)
169. Tulsita (Bee)

176. Vistula (Houston)
177. Voca (McCulloch)
178. Wake (Crosby)
179. Wake Village (Bowie)
180. Walburg (Williamson)
181. Walhalla (Fayette)
182. Warda (Fayette)
183. Warsaw (Kaufman)
184. Waterloo (Williamson)
185. Westphalia (Falls)
186. West Point (Fayette)
187. West Point (Lynn)
188. Winter Haven (Dimmit)
189. Yorktown (DeWitt)

ARGENTA (Live Oak): on FM 88, nineteen miles SE of George West. Richard Bethel Bomar was the first settler of record in the vicinity, coming from Oklahoma in 1903. By 1907 the little village was called Ego. Many residents thought that name too pretentious and desired a change. Argenta was chosen because it was the name of the former home of several citizens who had moved here from Arkansas.

ARGYLE (Denton): on US 377, six miles SW of Denton. Fourteen families, led by the Peters colony, settled in the area between 1850 and 1867. The site was then called either Pilot Knob or Waintown. The community was finally platted in November 1881 and christened by a railroad engineer for a garden in France.

ATHENS (Henderson): on TX 19 and 31 and US 175; county seat. In earlier times, was called Buffalo, then Centerville. E. J. Thompson and Joab McManus settled in the region by early 1850. Matthew Cartwright donated land for the county seat. Dulcina A. Holland recommended the current label in 1850 because she hoped the town would become a cultural center.

ATLANTA (Cass): at jct US 59 and TX 43 and 77, fourteen miles NE of Linden. Founded in 1871 with the arrival of the railroad and christened for the Georgia home of many of the settlers.

BELGRADE (Newton): on FM 1416, ten miles SE of Newton. Once called Biloxi by early Native Americans. William McFarland developed the town site in 1837 and named it for the famous river port capital of Serbia. This was the first organized town in the county.

BERLIN (Washington): on CR 30, three miles S of Brenham. The Valentine Hoffman family, immigrants from Hesse, Germany, settled here in 1848. The village was called Pesch from 1881 to 1902 for a family that operated a general store. The present designation is for the German capital city.

BILOXI (Newton): at jct FM 1416 and 2460, eighteen miles SE of Newton. Native Americans were settled here prior to 1822 and called the site Biloxi, either for the tribe name or for the Mississippi community. In 1829 Lorenzo de Zavala received this region as part of a land grant from the Mexican government. Anglo settlers migrated to the vicinity in the 1830s.

BOBO (Shelby): on US 84, twelve miles NW of Center. The site emerged in the mid-1880s as a railroad stop. The origin of the community name is suspect. It seems that Emmett Burns, from Teneha, enlisted in the National Guard in 1903 with other young men from the area. While stationed in a place called Timpson, they would chant the names of their hometowns while marching. The calls would resound with "Teneha, Timpson, Bobo, and Blair." The chant evolved into a marching step and words were added: "Let me off just any ol' where." While there remain questions as to whether this is the true origin of the name, another possibility is that the locale was christened for Bobo, Mississippi. There is no backing for another claim that the moniker gained prominence shortly before World War I. Soldiers, just before shipping out, often held crap and other dice games. As a shooter started to roll the dice, one called out "Tennyhaw!" The next shooter yelled, "Bobo!" and so forth. As the soldiers spread to the far reaches of the United States and Europe, these "dice calls" went with them and were picked up by others.

BOGATA (Red River): jct US 271, TX 37, and FM 909, sixteen miles SW of Clarksville. William and Mary Humphries were early settlers in the region, arriving around 1836. At the time the place was called Maple Springs. The current designation was suggested by James E. Horner, postmaster, because he had followed the Latin American rebellion against Spain. He particularly admired Simon Bolivar. Some believe that Horner actually wanted the site labeled in Bolivar's honor, but the name was confused in some manner and was recorded as Bogata.

BOLIVAR (Denton): at int FM 2450 and 455, fourteen miles NW of Denton. William Crawford apparently platted the site in 1859 and ultimately sold the town site to Hiram Daily, a Methodist minister and doctor. Daily christened the spot New Prospect. Ben Brown moved to the community in 1861 and went about persuading residents to rename the place for his former hometown, Bolivar, Tennessee.

BONAMI (Jasper): in EC Jasper County. The community came to life in 1901 when the Lee-Irvine Lumber Company built a sawmill on the rail line that ran through the area. It was initially known as Leeton for D. J. Lee, a partner in the sawmill. For some reason, R. J. Cooper, postmaster, in 1902 renamed the place for a town in Louisiana.

BUCKEYE (Matagorda): on FM 1468, nine miles SW of Bay City. In 1909 J. W. Stoddard and A. A. Plotner bought land in the vicinity from Wylie W. Kuykendall and installed the Plotner-Stoddard Irrigation Canal headquarters on the site. The two men were from Ohio, which is known as the Buckeye State for the native tree.

BUNKER HILL (Jasper): on TX 62 in SE Jasper County. The town was laid out in 1902 and tagged in 1910 for the Massachusetts hill that will be forever famous from the American Revolutionary War.

CAMDEN (Polk): at jct FM 62 and 942, twenty-seven miles NW of Livingston. A lumber company carrying the name W. T. Carter and Brother opened here in 1898. A surveyor is thought to have christened the town site for his former home, Camden, New Jersey.

CANADIAN (Hemphill): on US 60 and 83. E. P. Purcell and O. H. Nelson platted the site as county seat in 1887. It was variously known as Hogtown or Desperado City. Its location on the Canadian River is believed to be the source of its moniker.

CARLSBAD (Tom Green): on US 87, fifteen miles NW of San Angelo. In 1907 T. J. Clegg, Ed Perry, and others acting as the Concho Land Company purchased the vast Hughes Ranch. They sold off lots and laid out a town site, which was called Karlsbad. This tag was levied by the company directors for a spa in Bohemia, a section of the Czech Republic. The moniker eventually evolved into Carlsbad..

CARTHAGE (Panola): at int US 59 and 70; county seat. A post office opened here in 1849. Spearman Holland named the town site for Carthage, Mississippi. This is the birthplace of Tex Ritter, Western movie star and singer, and country music great Jim Reeves.

CAYUGA (Anderson): at int US 287 and FM 59, twenty-five miles NW of Palestine. Settlers from Tennessee were present in the region in the 1840s. Originally known as Cat Bluff, taking its name from the time a Native American woman, while washing clothes in the Trinity River, was attacked by a wildcat. After some struggle, she managed to grab the cat and hold it underwater until it drowned. In another Native American legend, it seems that a wildcat killed a chief's son at this locale. In 1894, a post office opened, and W. A. Davenport, the postmaster, suggested the site be christened for his former hometown, Cayuga, New York.

CELINA (Collin): on TX 289 and FM 455, fifteen miles N of McKinney. Town site founded in 1879 and named by John T. Mulkey for his hometown, Celina, Tennessee.

CHARLESTON (Delta): on FM 895, nine miles E of Cooper. The community was part of Hopkins County until 1870, when Delta County was organized. Settlers arrived here in 1854, having traveled from Charleston, South Carolina.

CHEAPSIDE (Gonzales): on RM 2067, twenty-one miles SE of Gonzales. Thomas Baker moved here from Mississippi in 1857 and became the first permanent settler when he built a log cabin. Sometime later, Dr. E. R. Henry, a local physician whose ancestors came from England, named the settlement for his place of birth, Cheapside, Virginia.

CHICO (Wise): at int TX 101 and FM 1810, five miles N of Bridgeport. Colonel J. T. Brown, who hailed from Chico, California, founded the town in 1875.

CHINA (Jefferson): on US 90, ten miles W of Beaumont. A railroad water stop was set up here in 1860 with the arrival of the Texas and New Orleans Railroad. The stop was situated in a grove of chinaberry trees, which resulted in the site being called China Grove. When a post office was established in 1893, the name was shortened.

CLEVELAND (Liberty): on US 59, twenty-seven miles NW of Liberty. There were settlers in the region following the Texas Revolution in 1836. In 1878 Charles Lander Cleveland deeded 63.6 acres to the Houston, East and West Texas Railroad. His request was that the station be named for him.

COLOGNE (Goliad): on US 59, in E Goliad County. Jim Smith and George Washington, two former slaves, founded this community in the late 1860s. It was originally known as Colony, Perdido Community, Centerville (for its location halfway between Goliad and Victoria), and finally Ira Station, a designation levied by the railroad. The official name of Cologne, given tongue in cheek, emerged in 1898, taken from the abattoirs (slaughterhouses) that made the village such a "sweet smelling place."

DAYTON (Liberty): on US 90, three miles W of Liberty. Founded in 1831 and called West Liberty. It was situated on land that was part of the old Municipality of Santísina Trinidad de la Libertad. Around 1854 the place became known as Day's Town for I. C. Day, landowner. When a post office opened in 1877, it used the name Dayton. In the 1870s the Texas-New Orleans Railroad came through and the site officially became Dayton, a derivation of its original moniker.

DELHI (Caldwell): on FM 304, nineteen miles SE of Lockhart. There was a post office here as early as 1873. Legend has it that the site was christened for a medicine man that hung around here for several months in the late 1800s.

DETROIT (Red River): on US 82, fifteen miles NW of Clarksville. Platted in the early 1870s and first called Bennett. J. M. Stephens, railroad agent, renamed the site in 1887 for his former home in Michigan.

DRESDEN (Navarro): at jct FM 744 and 55, fifteen miles W of Corsicana. Jacob Hartzell had a trading post in the vicinity as early as 1836. The site was first called Spanky, but the name was changed to Melton in 1846. The current designation is believed to refer to the city in Germany.

DUBLIN (Erath): on US 67 and 377, twelve miles SW of Stephenville. A. H. Dobkins laid out the community in 1854. In 1860 it was supposedly christened for two reasons: for a warning cry during Native American raids of "double in" and for the capital of Ireland. There is a third choice, which relates to the double log cabins built by early settlers. This is the birthplace of golfing great Ben Hogan.

DUNDEE (Archer): on US 82 and 277, twelve miles SW of Holliday. The region was well populated prior to the founding of the village in 1890. It is thought that the president of the Wichita Valley Railway Company coined the name for the city in Scotland.

DURANGO (Falls): on FM 935, fifteen miles SW of Marlin. A post office was operating here in 1871, and the site was first known as West Falls. Local lore has the name being changed in 1883 when a drunken cowboy, who had recently returned from south of the border, believed he was still in Durango, Mexico.

EDINBURG (Hidalgo): on US 281 and TX 107; county seat. First called Chapin for Dennis B. Chapin, land promoter. The namesake ran afoul of the law, becoming involved in a homicide, and residents decided they favored a change of monikers. In 1911 they adopted the current name, honoring Edinburgh, Scotland, the birthplace of John McAllen and John Young, early settlers.

ELYSIAN FIELDS (Harrison): at jct FM 31 and 451, eighteen miles SE of Marshall. The name of the town originated in a dinner conversation in New Orleans in 1817. Captain Edward Smith had recently traversed a section of a Caddo village in East Texas known as Biff Springs. He was very impressed with the region and gave glowing reports of its beauty and other attractions. One of the listeners said that it sounded like the Elysian Fields, fabled in Greek mythology. The Native Americans were gone from the area by 1837, when Smith returned with his family. He established one of the first stores in the region and, remembering the earlier conversation in New Orleans, christened the site Elysian Fields.

FARGO (Wilbarger): on FM 924, ten miles N of Vernon. This was set up as a stage stop around 1883, then grew to become a stage depot later that year. A post office was opened in 1891, and James Stafford, postmaster, recommended the name Fargo. Some believe the moniker is whimsical in nature: "Maybe that was as 'far' as they could 'go.'"

FIFE (McCulloch): at int US 283 and FM 765, eighteen miles N of Brady. Robert Kay Finlay's mother named the site in 1882 for her native Fifeshire, Scotland.

FLORENCE (Williamson): on FM 195, twenty-two miles NW of Georgetown. Laid out in the early 1850s and known as Brooksville. The name was changed to its present designation by 1857. The moniker came either from the former Alabama home of the first postmaster, or it might honor Florence Brooks, daughter of the town's first merchant.

FLUVANNA (Scurry): at jct FM 612, 1267, and 2350, twenty-four miles NW of Snyder. Land promoters founded the village in 1908, anticipating the arrival of the railroad. The site was coined for a surveyor's home county in Virginia.

FODICE (Houston): off US 287, four miles W of Pennington. The community was up and running shortly after the Civil War. John O'Neil is believed to be the first settler in the area, soon followed by others from Fordyce, Arkansas. Their former home served as inspiration for the naming by residents. However, there is one thought that the moniker comes from "four dice," a game favored by early settlers.

FRESNO (Fort Bend): on FM 521, twenty miles NE of Richmond. The town site is situated on a land grant dating back to 1824. A post office opened here in 1910. An early settler compared the weather and terrain of the area to that of Fresno, California, where he once resided.

FRISCO (Collin): on TX 289 and FM 720, fourteen miles SW of McKinney. First known as Emerson for Francis Emerson who owned the land on which the town site was situated. The name Emerson too closely resembled that of Emberson in Lamar County and was changed to Frisco City for the St. Louis, San Francisco, and Texas Railway Company. This outfit was popularly known as the Frisco system, so when a post office was opened in 1902, the name was shortened to Frisco.

GENEVA (Sabine): at jct TX 21 and FM 330, ten miles NW of Hemphill. This community is considered one of the oldest continually occupied settlements in East Texas. Antonio Gil Ibarvo established a ranch here in the mid-1700s. A settlement started in the 1850s and was thought to have been called Shawnee Village, then Jimtown, after Jim Halbert and Jim Willis, two early settlers. A post office opened in 1884, and Willis changed the name of the place to Geneva, simply because he liked that moniker.

GEORGIA (Lamar): on FM 2352, four miles S of Direct. Prior to the 1860s, this site was known as Hineman Chapel and Needmore. In August 1860 Robert and Mary Wilkerson donated land for a school, church, and cemetery. The community was christened for the former home of the benefactors.

GERMANY (Houston): off TX 21, ten miles NE of Crockett. This is one of the oldest settlements in the region. Jacob Masters Sr. in about 1820 brought his family and slaves to settle here. Masters and his son received land grants from the Mexican impresario David G. Burnet in February 1835. The town site moniker apparently came from reference made by the freedmen to a family named Grounds, originally from Germany, who settled in the vicinity a few years after Masters.

GOSHEN (Walker): N of jct FM 3179 and 1791, twelve miles SW of Huntsville. Had a post office prior to 1854 and was christened for Goshen, Tennessee, previous home of many of the settlers.

HANOVER (Milam): at int FM 2095 and 3242, ten miles SE of Cameron. Some local historians claim that in 1880 this was the site of the Swenenborg Settlers colony, a communal living experiment that failed. Ed Authifer coined the place name in 1890 for his former home in Germany.

HAVANA (Hidalgo): off US 83, eighteen miles NW of McAllen. This is located on part of the Spanish grant given Don José Matís Tijerina in 1767. The plot was known as Porcion 46, and Tijerina named the settlement for Havana, Cuba, which he had once visited.

HEIDELBERG (Hidalgo): on FM 1425, five miles NE of Mercedes. A German immigrant named Groshauser, land speculator, founded the community in 1921 and supposedly christened it for the city in Germany.

HELENA (Karnes): TX 80, eight miles NE of Karnes City. This is an old city, founded early as a Mexican trading post known as Alamita. It is situated on what was once the busiest road between San Antonio and Goliad. The village was renamed in 1852 to honor Helen, the wife of Dr. Lewis S. Owing, cofounder of the site with Thomas Ruckman. This was the birthplace of the dreaded, bloody "Helena Duel." In this match of mayhem, the left hands of two combatants were tied together. Each fighter was then armed with a knife with a small (three-inch), deadly sharp blade. Blood spilling was expected—and delivered.

HICO (Hamilton): at jct US 281 and TX 6 and 220. A settlement was in place by the mid-1850s and was originally situated on nearby Honey Creek. Dr. John R. Alford, community founder, named the town for his previous place of residence, Hico, Kentucky.

HOT SPRINGS (Brewster): in Big Bend National Park, where Tornillo Creek enters the Rio Grande. There were two major springs known as Boquillas Hot Springs. *Boquilla* is Spanish for "nozzle" or "small opening" and refers to the many springs in the region. The name was changed to its present designation in the early 1900s when the springs became a medicinal attraction.

ILLINOIS BEND (Montague): on FM 677, twenty miles NE of Montague. This community used to be known as Wardville for C. M. Ward, the first store owner in the vicinity. When a post office was approved for the location, the name Wardville was not acceptable, probably due to duplication. Maxville was then submitted, in honor of Max McAmos, an early settler. That was also rejected, probably for the same reason. A third name was suggested, Illinois Bend, and postal officials approved it in 1877. This name related to four families who came to the region from Illinois in 1862.

IMPERIAL (Pecos): at int FM 1053 and 11, twenty-eight miles NE of Fort Stockton. Once known as Redlands, it was settled prior to 1908, but was renamed in 1910 for the Imperial Valley of California. Interestingly enough, Redlands is also the name of a large city in the West Coast state.

IOWA COLONY (Brazoria): on TX 288, S of Manvel. The Immigration Land Company of Des Moines, Iowa, platted the town site in 1908, and Iowans G. I. Hoffman and Robert Beard christened it.

IOWA PARK (Wichita): on TX 370, five miles W of Wichita Falls. A. J. and D. C. Kolp founded the community in 1888, and it was, for a while, known as Daggett Switch. Soon thereafter, the Texas Panhandle Company brought in a number of immigrants by rail from Iowa.

IRELAND (Coryell): on FM 932, sixteen miles NW of Gatesville. Originally called Hamco for its location on the Hamilton-Coryell county line, it was renamed in 1911 in honor of Governor John Ireland (1883–1887).

ITALY (Ellis): at jct US 77 and TX 34, fifteen miles S of Waxahachie. The area was populated by 1860, but the Aycock brothers should be considered developers of the town. They moved here in 1879 and set up homes, a grocery store, and a post office. Citizens wanted to name the site Houston Creek for Sam Houston. This was rejected because of duplication. The postmaster in nearby Waxahachie suggested the name Italy, because he thought the area was much like that found in "sunny Italy."

KALGARY (Crosby): on FM 261, twenty miles SE of Crosbyton. Platted about 1905 and called Spur. E. P. Swensen, owner of the huge SMS Ranch, started selling off sections of his ranch as farmland, and this site became known as Watson for Richard Watson Self, settler. The name had to be changed in 1927, when Watson proved to be a duplication of another Texas community name. Around this time, Canada was prominent in the news because the Royal Canadian Mounted Police were searching for a lost trooper near the town of Calgary. Mrs. Sallie Reed, a resident of Watson, suggested Kalgary, changing the C to K.

KINGSTON (Hunt): on US 69 and FM 3427, ten miles NW of Greenville. The site was developed in 1880. Nick Hodges, Civil War veteran and donor of land for the place, gave it its current designation, reportedly because he surrendered with his Confederate comrades at Kingston, Georgia.

KLONDIKE (Delta): at jct FM 1528 and 2890, three miles SW of Cooper. Also, at one time or another, called Pleasant Grove, Old Pleasant Grove, New Prospect, and Kate. John Hunt donated land for a cemetery, which marked the beginning of the community. In 1897 it was officially dubbed for the Alaskan Klondike.

LA GRANGE (Fayette): on TX 71 and US 77; county seat. Aylett C. Buckner pioneered the region as early as 1819, but it wasn't until John Moore arrived seven years later that any semblance of a community emerged. Moore built a twin blockhouse on the site in 1825 and labeled it Moore's Fort. A little settlement had grown up around the fort by 1831, and the town was platted in 1837. That same year, the county became its own entity and was named for American Revolutionary War hero the Marquis de Lafayette. The county seat took the name of the marquis's château outside Paris, France.

LARISSA (Cherokee): off FM 855, twenty miles NW of Rusk. Isaac Killough and members of his family settled in the vicinity in 1837; they migrated from Talladega County, Alabama. A Native American war party attacked the settlers in 1838 and either killed or kidnapped most of the people. It was another eight years before resettlement would be attempted. In 1846 Thomas H. McKee from Tennessee led a group to the region. It was called McKee Colony, but the following year, McKee's son, T. N. McKee, changed the name to its current designation. As the story goes, McKee (apparently the father) was a Presbyterian minister and wanted to separate his community from that of Talladega because the latter had a saloon. McKee supposedly took the current name from an ancient city of learning in Greece. Today Larisa (one "s") is still a viable city situated some 150 miles northwest of Athens, Greece.

LEBANON (Collin): W of TX 289, three miles SE of Frisco. Settled in 1840 and known as Shahan's Prairie for a local rancher. Settlers from Lebanon, Tennessee, tagged the community with this marker around 1845.

LEXINGTON (Lee): on TX 77, sixteen miles N of Giddings. James Shaw laid out the site in the 1830s when it was called String Prairie. The name was changed in 1850 to Lexington for the Massachusetts town of Revolutionary fame.

LITTLE CHICAGO (DeWitt): near FM 108, N of Yorktown. George Langley opened a mercantile store here around 1890, marking the founding of the town site. He christened the locale for the Illinois metropolis.

LIVERPOOL (Brazoria): on a LR, fifteen miles NE of Angleton. This started out as a trading post around 1827. As recorded, some believe that a Commander Nelson named it for the seaport in England.

LODI (Marion): at int FM 2683 and 248, nine miles NE of Jefferson. Probably came about as a railroad station in the mid-1870s. J. Lopresto christened the site when a post office opened here in 1876. He was an early settler in the region and labeled it for his former home in Italy.

LOIRE (Wilson): on FM 536, fifteen miles W of Floresville. Settled in the 1890s. J. M. Swindler, the first postmaster, is thought to have given the locale its name. He moved to the region with a group of settlers from the Loire River valley of central France.

LONDON (Kimble): on US 377, eighteen miles NE of Junction. Also known as London Town. Len L. Lewis developed the community in either the late 1870s or early 1880s. Whether the name relates to the city in England or the one in Kentucky is up for debate. Several settlers came here from England; John Pearl and his family came from the Kentucky city.

LONDON (Rusk): at jct TX 42 and 323, ten miles NW of Henderson. Also called Old London. The community is thought to have been laid out about 1850, but did not acquire its moniker until around 1890 from English settlers.

LOS ANGELES (La Salle): on TX 97, thirteen miles E of Cotulla. The F. Z. Bishop Land Company of San Antonio founded the village in 1923. It was so named to compare the locale with the mild, temperate climate of the California city.

MAHOMET (Burnet): on FM 243, two miles NE of Bertram. George Ater settled the hamlet in 1853 and named it for Mahomet, Illinois. In 1882 the railroad bypassed Mahomet and established the community of Bertram, two miles to the southeast. The Mahomet post office was moved to a site called Sycamore Springs, situated some ten miles northeast of Bertram. The community soon changed the name Sycamore Springs to Mahomet.

MALTA (Bowie): on US 82, six miles W of New Boston. Had a post office by 1896. Lynn Tucker, an early settler, named the site for Malta, Illinois.

MANCHESTER (Red River): at jct FM 195 and 2118, seven miles NW of Clarksville. Although there were settlers in the region by the antebellum period in Texas, the community was not developed until after the Civil War. It was originally known as Taylor. In 1880 the name was changed to Manchester at the request of the postmaster Joseph E. Srygley to honor his ancestral home in Illinois.

MANHEIM (Lee): on TX 21, six miles NW of Giddings. A post office opened here in 1900. German immigrants mainly settled the region; they probably named the community after Mannheim, Germany, with an alteration in the spelling.

MARATHON (Brewster): at int US 90 and 385, twenty-six miles SE of Alpine. Founded in 1881. Albion E. Shepherd, a sea captain, swapped—sight unseen—his interest in some freighters on the Great

Lakes for the Iron Mountain ranch near the present-day settlement. Shepherd named the place Marathon because the terrain reminded him of Marathon, Greece. Marathon became county seat of Buchel County when it, along with Brewster and Foley counties, was organized in 1887. A decade later Foley and Buchel were disenfranchised and became part of Brewster County.

MEMPHIS (Hall): at jct US 287, TX 256, and FM 1547; county seat. J. C. Montgomery donated land for the settlement in 1889. Although many names for the community were submitted, postal authorities rejected them all. As the story goes, Rev. J. W. Brice, while in Austin, happened to notice a letter addressed erroneously to Memphis, Texas, rather than to Memphis, Tennessee. The mail clerk had written across the face of the envelope, "No such town in Texas." And so a community name was born, being officially recorded as such in September 1890.

MENTONE (Loving): on TX 302; county seat. Oil prospectors James J. Wheat Sr. and Bladen Ramsey laid out the community in 1925. It was first called Ramsey, but had to be changed when postal officials refused that name, probably because of duplication elsewhere. The current moniker came from a French surveyor from Menton, France.

MENTZ (Colorado): on a LR, ten miles NE of Columbus. Occupied about 1846 primarily by German Catholics from Büdesheim, Hesse. A number of these pioneers were from the Diocese of Mainz, and for a while the settlement was called New Mainz. The current spelling eventually evolved.

MIAMI (Roberts): on US 60; county seat. The earliest known settler was Marion Armstrong, who arrived here about 1879, but the community wasn't developed until 1887. B. H. Eldridge laid out the town to follow the proposed rail line. The village name supposedly derives from a Native American word meaning "sweetheart." The town is called "the last real cow town in the Panhandle."

MILANO (Milam): at int US 79 and TX 36, twelve miles SE of Cameron. The place saw the light of day when the railroad made its way here around 1874. The community name is said to relate to a sister city in Italy because of a similarity of climate. Others believe the moniker was supposed to have been Milam, but postal authorities either intentionally or mistakenly changed the spelling, possibly because of duplication with another Texas community.

MISSOURI CITY (Fort Bend-Harris): on US 90A and TX 6, fifteen miles E of Richmond, Fort Bend County. R. M. Cash and L. E. Luckie, Houston real estate developers, organized the city in 1890, spreading much advertising in Missouri newspapers. A large number of settlers from that state came to the vicinity.

MOLINE (Lampasas): on RM 1047, two miles NW of Castle Peak. Settlers put down roots in 1884 near Bennett Creek. Some of these early settlers supposedly named the site for their previous home, Moline, Illinois. Some claim that the handle came from the brand name of a plow in the local blacksmith shop.

MONTGOMERY (Montgomery): at jct TX 105 and FM 149, fifteen miles W of Conroe. Andrew J. Montgomery built a trading post near here in 1823. He migrated from Tennessee, through Alabama, on his way to Texas. This site became the first county seat in 1837. The shifting of fortunes over time and the founding of Conroe along the railway caused the latter to be chosen as the new county seat in 1889.

MORAVIA (Lavaca): on FM 957, twelve miles NW of Hallettsville. The region was occupied in the 1850s, but the community did not emerge until 1881. Several Czech-Moravian settlers moved into the vicinity in the early 1870s. In the 1880s, Ignac Jalufka, a Czech-Moravian settler, coined the name.

MOSCOW (Polk): at jct US 59 and FM 350, twenty miles N of Livingston. Founded in 1844 by David G. Green and known as Greens.

When a post office was approved for the site, a petition was submitted to change the name to Greenville. This was rejected because there was already a Greenville in the state. "Send in Moscow," one citizen supposedly said. "That town is far enough away, there will be no objections." While this theory has some validity, by coincidence, Moscow, Tennessee, was the hometown of David Green.

NAPLES (Morris): on US 67, twelve miles NE of Daingerfield. A railroad station was built here in 1880, and the community grew up around the station. It was first called Belden and then, in 1882, became Station Belden. Postal authorities didn't like the latter, fearing it would be confused with Belton, Bell County. In 1895 residents sent in a list of names for post office authorities to consider. Officials recorded Naples from the list.

NECHANITZ (Fayette): at jct FM 3011 and 2145, eleven miles N of La Grange. Wenzel Matejowsky settled in the vicinity by 1853. The earliest settlers were from Bohemia, in southern Europe, and were the first to enter Fayette County. The hamlet was christened for Matejowsky's former home in Bohemia.

NEVADA (Collin): on FM 1138, twelve miles S of Farmersville. John McMinn and his family settled here in 1835, and the site became known as McMinn Chapel. Granville Stinebaugh purchased 160 acres in 1861 at three dollars an acre and labeled the town to honor the Nevada Territory. Stinebaugh had traversed that region while on his way to search for gold in California in 1849.

NEWARK (Wise): on FM 718, twenty-two miles S of Decatur. Developed in the mid-1850s and known as Caddo Village for the several Native American camps in the vicinity. Benjamin B. Haney is considered the first settler. Later it became Huff Valley for the Huff family; Sueville for Sue Gray, an early settler; and Ragtown, a sarcastic name coined by railroad crews for the rows of raggedy tents that lined the streets of the small settlement. It was renamed Newark in 1893 for the city in New Jersey. The designator of this name could have been G. K. Foster, surveyor and civil engineer, who was originally from New Jersey. The conductor of the Rock Island Railroad might have been the person responsible—indirectly—for the moniker. It seems the site carried the name New Ark, an unofficial usage levied by residents because they had found a "new ark" of security and happiness here. The conductor apparently had a habit of pronouncing the designation as one word, "Newark."

NEW BADEN (Robertson): on US 79, four miles E of Franklin. J. G. Meyer, Matern Leber, and A. B. Langerman, German immigrants, developed the town in 1881 and labeled it for the city in Germany.

NEW BERLIN (Guadalupe): on FM 2538, eleven miles SW of Seguin. A large number of the early settlers to this region were from Germany. They arrived in the 1870s and named their home for the capital city in Germany, thinking that they were setting in motion a new city that might match the achievements of that metropolis. Those dreams never came to fruition.

NEW BIELAU (Colorado): near jct FM 155 and 2144, three miles S of Weimer. Shortly before the Civil War, a group of German families moved from the Industry, Texas, area to this site. By the 1870s, the community they started was going by the moniker New Bielau, after Bielau, Germany.

NEW BOSTON (Bowie): on US 82, twenty-one miles W of Texarkana. There was a community known as Boston near here in earlier times. In the summer of 1876 a railroad laid tracks through a section some four miles distant. It didn't take long for the businessmen of Boston (today known as Old Boston) to realize that they were going to suffer economically when bypassed by the rail line. In a meeting with railroad officials, it was agreed that the railroad would locate a depot at the nearest point to the original settlement of Boston. Once this was established, and since most of the people involved in the endeavor were from Boston, they christened this site New Boston.

NEWPORT (Clay): on FM 1288, twenty-four miles SE of Henrietta. L. Hancock developed the community in 1872. About this time the site was called Bear Hill from the fact that a bear was killed on a hill near the home of J. H. Hardy. There is a tongue-in-cheek explanation for the current place name. Legend has it that one of the first settlers had been a sailor who had sailed all over the world. When he arrived here, he considered it a "new port." The real basis for the name, however, comes from the record of the number of local people whose names were used to form the community moniker: Newton, Ezell, Portwood, Owsley, Regis, and Turner.

NEW YORK (Henderson): on FM 604 and 607, eleven miles E of Athens. James C. Wacker and others settled the community about 1856. The village received its moniker either as a joke by T. B. Herndon for its small size or as a hoped-for future by Davis Reynolds.

NOME (Jefferson): at int US 90, TX 326, and FM 365, twenty miles W of Beaumont. Known in early days variously as Wolf Point, Tiger Point, Petry Woods, and Carter's Woods. The name was changed to Nome following the discovery of oil at Sour Lake in 1900. There are several accounts of the origin of this place name. One is that a train stopped here one morning, and a lady queried of a man standing on the platform if she had arrived in Liberty. The man, being of southern gentility, replied in fashion, "No'm." The label of Nome could have related to the "yellow" gold of the Alaskan city versus the "black" gold of East Texas. And, finally, the site had no name when maps and plats were being drawn up for the region. One cartographer supposedly wrote on his map, "Name?" and printers read the community name as "Nome." This last explanation has to be taken with a grain of salt, since that is exactly the way Nome, Alaska, acquired its moniker.

NORTHFIELD (Motley): on FM 94 and 656, twenty-seven miles NE of Matador. Once known as Bitter Lake. In 1890, D. Cook moved to the site and opened a general store, then became postmaster. He christened the village for his former home in Minnesota, which was infamous for a bank robbery by Jesse James and Cole Younger.

ODESSA (Ector): on US 80, 385, and IH 20; county seat. The town was founded in 1881 with the arrival of the railroad. A legend credits the name to a Native American princess who wandered into the camp of the Texas and Pacific Railway. More than likely the name comes from the Odessa situated on the Russian plains, a region that West Texas is said to resemble.

OGDEN (Cottle): on FM 2532, two miles N of US 70, twelve miles NE of Paducah. The region was populated in the 1880s, and a post office was opened in April 1894. The site was called Blanche for Blanche McAdams. The name was changed to Ogden in 1909 for Alfred Ogden, a landowner who moved to the area from Massachusetts.

OHIO (Cameron): two miles N of US 281 in SW Cameron County. Pioneers from Ohio moved to the vicinity in the early 1900s.

OKLAHOMA LANE (Parmer): on FM 1731, six miles E of Farwell. This was originally part of the vast XIT Ranch. In 1916 Ed McGuire, John Scribner, T. Hooser, and brothers Jim and Joe Johnson bought land from the XIT and settled their families on it. These early settlers and their families were from Oklahoma.

OLD BOSTON (Bowie): at int FM 2149 and TX 8, three miles S of New Boston. W. J. Boston opened the first store here in the 1830s, and the community was named for him. When the railroad bypassed the hamlet in 1876, several businessmen and others moved to the new site to be closer to the rail line. Those who moved christened their new home New Boston, leading the older settlement to assume the moniker of Old Boston.

OLFEN (Runnels): on FM 1874, twelve miles S of Ballinger. Bernard Matthiesen and his family moved here in 1893, and for some reason the place assumed the moniker Fussy Creek. As time passed, it became known as Maas, then, finally, as Olfen for Olfen, Westphalia.

OMAHA (Morris): on US 67, ten miles N of Daingerfield. Thompson Morris laid out the village in the 1880s, and it was known as Morristown. The post office was called Gravette, however, which caused debate between the residents. In 1886 they decided it was time for an official change of the place name. Seven of the early settlers, each from Alabama, placed the name of their former hometowns in a hat. Hugh Ellis had recommended the name Omaha.

ONALASKA (Polk): at int FM 356 and US 190, fifteen miles W of Livingston. While the settlement was viable during the Republic of Texas era, it was not developed until around 1905 when William Carlisle opened a mill here. He named the site for a mill he also operated in Onalaska, Arkansas.

OSLO (Hansford): NW corner of Hansford County. Anders L. Mordt founded the locale in 1908. He migrated from Norway and christened the community after Oslo, Norway's capital city.

OXFORD (Llano): on TX 16, fifteen miles S of Llano. A. J. Johnson moved to this site in 1880 and developed the community. He named it for his former hometown, Oxford, Mississippi.

PADUCAH (Cottle): at int US 70 and 83, and FM 2876; county seat. R. Potts moved here from Paducah, Kentucky, in the mid-1800s. Potts offered free land to settlers if they agreed to name the new community for his former Kentucky home. Also, he pushed to have the site declared the county seat. He achieved both aims.

PALESTINE (Anderson): at int US 79 and 287; county seat. The community was born when the county was founded in 1846. The city was named for Daniel Parker's former hometown, Palestine, Illinois.

PAMPA (Gray): at jct US 60 and TX 70, 152, and 273; county seat. Founded as a railroad station in 1887 and for a time called Glasgow, then Sutton. The latter name was often confused with Sutton County, so George Tyng, manager of the White Deer Land Company, had the name changed to Pampa, because he thought the surrounding terrain resembled the pampas of Argentina, which he once visited. The town site was developed in 1902, which coincided with the date the county was organized.

PARIS (Lamar): on US 271 and 82; county seat. Settled around 1826 and once known as Pinhook. George W. Wright was a local merchant, and one of his employees, Thomas Poteet, suggested the name Paris for the French capital.

PASADENA (Harris): off TX 225, between Houston and Deer Park. John H. Burnett laid out the town in 1893 and named it for Pasadena, California, the "Land of Flowers."

PAWNEE (Bee): at int FM 673 and 798, twenty-two miles NW of Beeville. The first family to move into this area, that of Fred Hoff, arrived around 1890. The present moniker is said to have come from a homesick traveler. He supposedly burned the name of the county he called home in Kansas into a piece of wood and nailed it to a tree. There is another opinion, that Native American arrowheads were found in Sulphur Creek and that the Pawnees might once have camped here or had a settlement on the spot.

PEORIA (Hill): at int TX 22 and FM 1947, six miles SW of Hillsboro. Settled during the 1840s, this is one of the oldest communities in Hill County. It started out as a travelers' rest stop and place for drovers to let their cattle graze and take on water. B. F. Stewart, one of the transients, named the spot for his home, Peoria, Illinois.

PETERSBURG (Hale): at jct FM 54 and 789, thirty-five miles SE of Plainview. Started out in 1891 as a post office in Floyd County. The site was christened in honor of Zach Peters and his wife, Margaret, who was the postmistress. Ed M. White opened a general store at the present town site, which was laid out in 1909, and moved the post office five miles southwest into Hale County.

PITTSBURG (Camp): at jct US 271 and TX 11; county seat. Oldest town in the county, with settlers in the region in the 1830s. Major William Harrison Pitts moved to the area in 1854 and donated land for the town site. It was originally spelled Pittsburgh, but was changed to its present form in 1893.

PLASKA (Hall): at jct FM 1041 and 2472, fourteen miles SW of Memphis. Community situated on land once owned by J. L. Pyle, a popular Baptist circuit rider. The site was known as Lodge when the post office was closed in 1909. Citizens petitioned in 1920 to have the office reopened. Postal authorities agreed, but advised that there was another town of Lodge in Texas. A local resident, M. N. Orr, suggested the name of his hometown in Tennessee, Pulaski, but Washington misspelled the entry, and it was recorded as Plaska.

PONTOTOC (Mason): at jct TX 71 and FM 501, twenty-eight miles NE of Mason. Settlers showed up in the vicinity in the 1850s. Benjamin J. Willis and several other families arrived less than a decade later, and by 1878 a viable community existed. M. Robert Kidd is credited with christening the settlement, influenced by his former home, Pontotoc, Mississippi.

POTOSI (Taylor): on FM 1750, nine miles SE of Abilene. The R. A. Pollard family was in place in the 1870s, and in 1893 named the site for Potosi, Mexico.

PRAHA (Fayette): on FM 1295, three miles E of Flatonia. The site was first called Mulberry, then Hottentot. The latter name came from the Bushmen and Bantus of southern Africa and referred to a band of outlaws. James C. Duff and William and Leroy Criswell settled the vicinity probably in the early 1850s. Bohemian pioneers had been arriving in the region since the mid-1850s, and this group was responsible for naming the community, honoring Prague, the capital of their homeland.

RATIBOR (Bell): W of int FM 2086 and 2904, seven miles E of Temple. Czech migrants settled here about 1900 and named the site for the town of Ratibor in what is now the Czech Republic.

REHBURG SETTLEMENT (Washington): on FM 1948, twelve miles NW of Brenham. Developed by German immigrants in 1847 and christened for Rehburg, Hanover, Germany, the hometown of Ludwig Heine, early settler.

RHINELAND (Knox): at int FM 2534 and 267, fifteen miles SE of Benjamin. In 1895 Father Joseph R. Reisdorff and Hugo Herchenbach enticed J. C. League to cede 12,000 acres for the establishment of a German Catholic colony. This was done, and the site acquired the name Rhineland, relating the moniker to a section of Germany.

RIVIERA (Kleberg): on US 77, fifteen miles S of Kingsville. In 1907 Theodore F. Koch, land promoter from St. Paul, Minnesota, purchased a large section of land from Henrietta King of the King Ranch family and divided it into acreage. It was Koch who founded the town site and coined the name Riviera, because the climate seemed to him to evoke fond memories of the famous French coastline.

ROANOKE (Denton): at int US 377 and TX 114, seventeen miles SW of Denton. There was a community here by 1847 that was called Garden Center or Garden Valley. The present name relates to the city in Virginia.

ROCHELLE (McCulloch): on US 190, ten miles NE of Brady. A post office opened here in 1879 when the place was first called Crewville, then Crothers, both names derived from those of early settlers. A French settler from La Rochelle, France, recommended the present moniker.

ROCHESTER (Haskell): at jct TX 6 and FM 617, sixteen miles NW of Haskell. A. B. Carothers donated land for a railroad right-of-way in 1906, as well as acreage for a town site. He named the place for Rochester, New York.

ROMA (Starr): on US 83, fifteen miles W of Rio Grande City. This is part of the incorporated community known as Roma-Los Saenz. Ranching members of the Saenz family, followers of the José de Escandón expedition, founded the village of Corrales de Saenz in the mid-1760s. As a result of the outcome of the Mexican-American War, this section became property of the United States. The name was then changed to Roma, as proposed by the Oblates of Mary Immaculate. The hilly terrain, much like that of the Italian capital city, is believed to have influenced the place name.

RUIDOSA (Presidio): at jct FM 170 and a LR, sixty miles SW of Marfa. The first official settlement in the vicinity was Vado Piedra ("stone ford"), a Mexican penal colony established around 1824. The prison was short-lived, having to be abandoned when the Mexican militia was slain by Comanches. Almost half a century later, in 1872, William Russell dug irrigation ditches to aid in farming. This began settlement of the region. Ruidosa is from the Spanish *mirloso,* and means "loud" or "noisy." This refers to either the wind that blows here most of the time or to the sound of water as it flows over the dam constructed to irrigate farm crops.

SAGINAW (Tarrant): on TX 496, ten miles NW of Fort Worth. Occupied before the Civil War and known as Dido. It was renamed for the Michigan hometown of J. J. Green, landowner.

ST. LOUIS (Smith): N of int TX 155 and Loop 323, SW of Tyler. Occupied in early 1880s and named for St. Louis, Missouri.

ST. PAUL (San Patricio): at int US 181 and FM 3089, seven miles NW of Sinton. Settlers from the Midwest were in place in the early 1900s, and the town was platted in 1910. There is no religious icon involved in this name since it refers to the nickname given George H. Paul, an entrepreneur of some worth: land agent, lumber dealer, storekeeper, and gin operator.

SALEM (Newton): on FM 2829, some twenty miles S of Newton. Seth Swift settled the area in 1835 and named the community for his birthplace in Massachusetts.

SALTILLO (Hopkins): at jct US 67 and FM 900, sixteen miles E of Sulphur Springs. John Arthur opened a store, mill, and gin here about 1850. He coined the site for Saltillo, Mexico.

SANDIA (Jim Wells): on TX 359, twenty-two miles NE of Alice. The town is situated on part of the 1807 Spanish grant Casa Blanca, issued to Juan José de la Garza Montemayor. John L. Wade purchased the land in 1896 and developed the Wade Ranch. When he passed away, one of his heirs sold his share of the estate to Joseph B. Dibrell. The latter passed development of the vicinity on to Fennell Dibrell and Max Starcke, who laid out the town site in 1907. They chose the name, which in Spanish means "watermelon," for the large number of melons grown in the region.

SAN DIEGO (Duval): at int TX 44 and 359 and FM 1329; county seat. This was a familiar region to travelers in the 1700s. In about 1800 the Spanish government gave two large grants totaling eight leagues. The grants were known as San Diego de Arriba and San Diego de Abajo; Julian Flores and his son Ventura were the benefactors of these grants. The community that emerged here in 1848 was called Perezville for Pablo Perez, landowner. In 1852 the name was changed to relate back to the original grants of San Diego.

SANDUSKY (Grayson): on US 377, seventeen miles NW of Sherman. Populated around 1870 and might have taken its name from

Sandusky, Ohio, reportedly the source of some local cotton ginning machinery.

SANTA FE (Galveston): on TX 6, sixteen miles NW of Galveston. The Gulf, Colorado, and Santa Fe Railway laid tracks through the region in 1877.

SANTA MONICA (Willacy): on FM 1018 and 1420, fourteen miles SE of Raymondville. This was a ranching region as far back as the early 1800s. Clarence Ayers, president of American Life Insurance Company, named the community in 1925 for Santa Monica, California. It was the American Life Insurance Company that paid for development of the area.

SARATOGA (Hardin): at jct TX 105 and FM 770, sixteen miles SW of Kountze. The region was occupied by the 1850s when J. F. Cotton discovered the springs. It has been called New Sour Lake or Friendship. P. S. Watts renamed the town in the 1880s after the spa in New York; he based his promotion as a developer on local springs as having medicinal value.

SATURN (Gonzales): on TX 97, NE of Gonzales. A post office opened here in 1902, and the community was once known as Possum Trot. Local legend relates that this unique moniker came about from the joke made by a young resident. The family was large and the lane on which they were walking was narrow, forcing the family to follow behind the father in single file. The local boy commented that the family "Looks like a bunch of little possums trotting along." The earliest general accepted name for the site was more than likely Nash's Mill for John G. Nash, a pioneer on the scene in 1874 and operator of a gin and a mill. When a post office was approved for the place, five names were submitted by the residents: Mars, Apollo, Saturn, Jupiter, and Io; Saturn was chosen.

SCOTLAND (Archer): at jct US 281 and FM 172, fourteen miles NW of Archer City. The town was founded around 1907 by, and christened for, Henry J. Scott of Toronto, Canada.

SEATTLE (Coryell): some sixteen miles S of Gatesville. A post office was granted in 1899. W. A. Umberhagen, a storekeeper, is believed to have named the site, simply because he liked the sound of Seattle.

SEBASTAPOL (Trinity): on FM 355 and 356, fourteen miles SW of Groveton. Also called Bartholomew. Laid out in either the late 1840s or early 1850s. By the mid-1850s, several Russian merchants had become businessmen here and renamed the community for the Russian Black Sea port.

SEDALIA (Collin): two miles NW of Westminster in extreme N Collin County. A post office in business in January 1889 went by the name Yakima. Its present moniker could have come from the U.S. man-of-war *Sedalia,* but more than likely relates to a city in another state, probably Missouri.

SEGOVIA (Kimble): on IH 10, eleven miles SE of Junction. Platted around the time of the Civil War and named for the city in Spain.

SHANNON (Clay): on FM 175, twenty miles SW of Henrietta. Developed about 1878 around Rachel D. Ivie's general store and called Stampede Springs. The current moniker relates to the home of an early pioneering family that came here from Ireland's Shannon Valley.

SONORA (Sutton): off IH 10 on US 277; county seat. Charles G. Adams, merchant and rancher, settled the site around 1855. In 1887 he named it to remember a family servant from Sonora, Mexico.

STOCKHOLM (Hidalgo): on FM 491, four miles SE of Delta Lake. Swedish immigrants laid out the community around 1912.

SUDAN (Lamb): at jct US 84, FM 298, 303, and 1843, eighteen miles NW of Littlefield. This was once part of the huge 77 Ranch. The community was developed in 1917 and 1918, when ranch owners S. B. Wilson and Wilson Furneaux donated land for a town site. The name of Janes for the site was submitted, but rejected by postal officials, probably because of duplication. It could also have been too much like James, Texas. The present moniker came about in 1918 because two boxcars loaded with Sudan grass were on a railroad siding at the time a name was chosen for the place. P. E. Boesen, a surveyor and land agent, was the person who recommended the name.

SUNNYSIDE (Castro): on US 385, fifteen miles S of Dimmitt. Founded in 1912 following the merger of two rural schools into a central location. Jeff Gilbreath was the instigator of the place name, from the fact that he once lived near Sunnyside, Tennessee. He also felt the local climate was a factor in the selection.

SWISS ALP (Fayette): on US 77, eleven miles S of La Grange. German Lutheran settlers occupied this area around the end of the Civil War. While there is no definitive proof as to the origin of the community name, it is said that H. Seeberger recommended it because he was homesick for his homeland. There is another opinion that it was christened for its rolling hills and scenery.

TACOMA (Panola): at jct FM 1186 and 1794, twelve miles NE of Carthage. J. H. Wooten and his son opened a store and sawmill here in the 1890s and named it for Tacoma, Washington.

TALLADEGA (Cherokee): off FM 855, twenty miles NW of Rusk. Isaac Killough, his wife, and other family members settled here in 1837. They migrated from Talladega County, Alabama. See Larissa.

TELLICO (Ellis): on FM 1181, five miles E of Ennis. Founded sometime before 1856. Since it is situated near the Trinity River, it was originally known as Trinity City. By the mid-1850s the hamlet was going by a new name, which relates to Tellico, North Carolina.

TENNESSEE COLONY (Anderson): off FM 321, fourteen miles NW of Palestine. A large group of settlers from Tennessee and

Alabama developed the community in 1847. Most of the migrants were from Tennessee.

TOKIO (McLennan): at int FM 1858 and 3149, five miles SW of West. Joseph Thomas Rogers purchased 1,200 acres in this region in 1868, and the settlement that emerged became known as the Tokio railroad stop in 1882. Due to patriotic fervor during World War II, the name was changed to Wiggins. Even after the war the name remained changed, but eventually Tokio was once again the official designation.

TOKIO (Terry): at int US 82/380 and a LR, seventeen miles W of Brownfield. Developed about 1908. Mrs. H. L. Ware is believed to have christened the site, deriving the name from the Japanese capital.

TOLEDO (Newton): on Toledo Bend Reservoir and a bend of the Sabine River, in NE Newton County. Had a post office as early as 1873. The name derives from one of four sources: (1) early settlers were from Ohio and named it for the Ohio city; (2) it was named for a Native American chief; (3) it was named for the Spanish city Toledo, which is also on a river bend; or (4) it remembers José Álvarez Toledo y Dubois, a filibuster against New Spain.

TOURS (McLennan): on FM 3149, seventeen miles NE of Waco. A wagon train from Illinois arrived at this spot in November 1874 on the feast day of St. Martin of Tours. These early settlers were mostly of German stock, and they named their new community St. Martinville. Residents petitioned for a post office in 1891 and discovered that the name St. Martinville had been used elsewhere. They renamed their city Tours, after the French city where St. Martin was bishop in the fourth century.

TRENTON (Fannin): on TX 121, US 69, and FM 151, 814, and 815, twelve miles SW of Bonham. Settlers from Tennessee were in the region as early as 1852 when the area was called Wild Cat Thicket.

The community came to life in 1881 and residents named it for the New Jersey city.

TRINIDAD (Henderson): on FM 1667, fifteen miles W of Athens. O. M. Airhart erected a ferry on this site prior to 1840. The conveyance not only provided a crossing for the Trinity River (at that time called the Trinidad), it also marked the beginning of a small village that soon became a part of the landscape. The site later became known as Trinity Switch when the railroad came through in 1880. Later that year, the name was changed to Trinidad, because the earlier name was too often confused with another town called Trinity Switch.

TROY (Bell): on IH 35, seven miles N of Temple. This spot was originally known as Big Elm (pronounced "Ellum") and as New Troy. The little hamlet developed around a railroad station sometime after 1882, replacing a previous community called Troy that was situated some two miles north of Elm Creek. When a post office was opened, postal officials refused Big Elm because it could be confused with Big Allum in south Texas. The residents then agreed on Troy for Troy, New York.

TULSITA (Bee): on US 181 and FM 798, two miles N of Pettus. J. L. Courtney bought 340 acres from George A. Kerr in 1917. Courtney wanted the land for oil development. About thirteen years later, around 1930, he coined the site Tulsa for his earlier home in Oklahoma. Unfortunately, there was already a Tulsa, Texas, so he designated his site Tulsita.

TUPELO (Navarro): on FM 1603, seven miles NE of Corsicana. Laid out about the time of the Civil War and christened for Tupelo, Mississippi.

TUSCOLA (Taylor): at jct USB 83 and FM 613, nineteen miles S of Abilene. The original town site, referred to as "the Flat" by residents, was situated some three miles west of the present location. The place was occupied by 1884 and was named by Clarence M. Cash, one of the town founders, for his previous home in Illinois.

UNITIA (Delta): W of FM 1742, one mile NE of Enloe. Settled by 1878, but not developed until around 1884 upon arrival of the railroad. John Costeen coined the site for his old hometown in Tennessee.

URBANA (San Jacinto): on US 59, in SE San Jacinto County. This was a viable settlement as early as 1908, having grown up after the arrival of the railroad. S. P. Coughlan christened it for his hometown of Urbana, Ohio.

VERONA (Collin): eight miles NE of McKinney. In late 1872 A. R. Womble put up a general store here, which marked the beginning of the community. The site was first called Mississippi when a post office opened in 1883. It was renamed for the daughter of Womble.

VIGO PARK (Swisher): on FM 146, twenty-six miles NE of Tulia. This was the result of real estate development in the early 1900s, with the town site being founded in 1906. It was coined from Vigo and Parke counties in Indiana.

VISTULA (Houston): off FM 3470, seven miles NE of Weldon. Developed around 1900 and believed to have been christened for the Vistula River, an important waterway in Poland.

VOCA (McCulloch): on TX 71 and FM 1851, twelve miles SE of Brady. Settlers were in the region during the period from 1850 to 1860. John and W. C. Deans named the settlement for Avoca, Arkansas.

WAKE (Crosby): on FM 28, in NE Crosby County. In 1902 William Andrew Jackson Jones donated land and the lumber for construction of a post office. The community relates to the Pacific dot of land called Wake Island.

WAKE VILLAGE (Bowie): on US 67, on the W edge of the Texarkana city limits. The community was developed in either 1944 or 1945 to serve as a housing development for employees of nearby Red River Army Depot and the Lone Star Ammunition Plant. The site apparently acquired its label in the same way as Wake.

WALBURG (Williamson): at int FM 972 and 1105, twelve miles NE of Georgetown. Henry Doering began the community when he moved here in 1881 and opened a store the following year. The site was first called Concordia, but in 1886 Doering renamed it for his former home of Walburg, Germany.

WALHALLA (Fayette): at int FM 1291 and CR 209, fourteen miles N of La Grange. Settled in 1830s by German immigrants. The settlers were so pleased with their new home that they took the name from the ancient Norse Valhalla of their Teutonic ancestors, considered an Eden for warriors slain in battle.

WARDA (Fayette): on US 77, ten miles N of La Grange. A. E. Falke, a Wendish immigrant, sparked settlement in what had been a sparsely populated region when he started buying land in 1867. Several years later, in 1874, he opened a general store. Either Falke christened the town or it was chosen to honor him, because the place name is derived from Wartha, Saxony, Germany, the former home of Falke.

WARSAW (Kaufman): on FM 148, seven miles SW of Kaufman. The area was occupied prior to 1840 and known as Warsaw Prairie. It is said that this name was taken from a Native American word meaning "water," rather than the capital city of Poland.

WATERLOO (Williamson): on FM 619, four miles NE of Taylor. Josiah W. Rainwater opened a store here around 1890, starting the village. A post office opened in 1893, and it and the community were named for Rainwater's earlier home in Kentucky.

WESTPHALIA (Falls): on TX 320, eighteen miles SW of Marlin. In 1879 migrants from the province of Westphalia in Germany, who had been residing in Freisburg, Texas, moved to this region.

WEST POINT (Fayette): N of TX 71, twelve miles W of La Grange. Grew up in the 1880s close to a railroad crossing. A post office opened in 1894. William Young christened the hamlet for his former home, West Point, Mississippi.

WEST POINT (Lynn): on US 380 and FM 179, seventeen miles W of Tahoka. A school was in session here as early as 1904. The community is thought to have received its tag for its location on the western point of Lynn County.

WINTER HAVEN (Dimmit): on FM 1407, five miles N of Carrizo Springs. Settlers from Florida put down roots here in 1911 and named it for their former home in the Sunshine State.

YORKTOWN (DeWitt): on TX 72, sixteen miles SW of Cuero. Captain John York moved to Coleto Creek, near the present town site in 1846. Charles Eckert was instrumental in developing the community, which was chartered in 1854. The name pays homage to its early settler, rather than to the Indiana site.

THERE ARE SUCH PLACES

From Admiral to Zephyr

ADMIRAL (Callahan): on FM 2228, thirteen miles SE of Baird. Founded in 1890. German settler Henry L. Buchen, the first postmaster, seems to have been fond of military tradition when he coined this place name.

AIRVILLE (Bell): at int FM 2904 and 437, eleven miles E of Temple. The community developed in 1908 when June Lugo built a store on the site. The settlement name probably comes from its location on Air Line Road between Temple and Rosebud.

ALBA (Wood): at int US 69 and FM 17, ten miles W of Quitman. Also known as Simpkins Prairie and Albia. Joseph Simpkins, a gunsmith, and his family were probably the first settlers in the vicinity; they migrated from Missouri in 1843. The town site was laid out by 1882. There is some evidence that the community name came from the fact that it was originally intended only for white settlers. Another source seems to think the name was for the son of a railroad official. Actually, *alba* is Spanish for "dawn," and the village could have taken the moniker as an indication of their arrival at a new home or some such meaning.

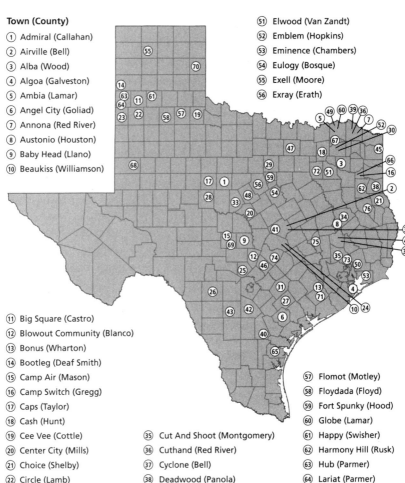

Town (County)

1. Admiral (Callahan)
2. Airville (Bell)
3. Alba (Wood)
4. Algoa (Galveston)
5. Ambia (Lamar)
6. Angel City (Goliad)
7. Annona (Red River)
8. Austonio (Houston)
9. Baby Head (Llano)
10. Beaukiss (Williamson)

51. Elwood (Van Zandt)
52. Emblem (Hopkins)
53. Eminence (Chambers)
54. Eulogy (Bosque)
55. Exell (Moore)
56. Exray (Erath)

11. Big Square (Castro)
12. Blowout Community (Blanco)
13. Bonus (Wharton)
14. Bootleg (Deaf Smith)
15. Camp Air (Mason)
16. Camp Switch (Gregg)
17. Caps (Taylor)
18. Cash (Hunt)
19. Cee Vee (Cottle)
20. Center City (Mills)
21. Choice (Shelby)
22. Circle (Lamb)
23. Circle Back (Bailey)
24. Circleville (Williamson)
25. Comfort (Kendall)
26. Concan (Uvalde)
27. Concrete (DeWitt)
28. Content (Runnels)
29. Cool (Parker)
30. Cornersville (Hopkins)
31. Cost (Gonzales)
32. Country Campus (Walker)
33. Cross Cut (Brown)
34. Cut (Houston)

35. Cut And Shoot (Montgomery)
36. Cuthand (Red River)
37. Cyclone (Bell)
38. Deadwood (Panola)
39. Dimple (Red River)
40. Dinero (Live Oak)
41. Ding Dong (Bell)
42. Ditto (Atascosa)
43. Divot (Frio)
44. Dodge (Walker)
45. Domino (Cass)
46. Driftwood (Hays)
47. Drop (Denton)
48. Duster (Comanche)
49. East Direct (Lamar)
50. Eastgate (Liberty)

57. Flomot (Motley)
58. Floydada (Floyd)
59. Fort Spunky (Hood)
60. Globe (Lamar)
61. Happy (Swisher)
62. Harmony Hill (Rusk)
63. Hub (Parmer)
64. Lariat (Parmer)
65. Leona Schroder (Nueces)
66. Liberty City (Gregg)
67. Long Taw (Delta)
68. Loop (Gaines)
69. Loyal Valley (Mason)
70. Magic City (Wheeler)
71. Magnet (Wharton)
72. Markout (Kaufman)
73. Midline (Montgomery)
74. Mud City (Travis)
75. Mudville (Brazos)
76. Naclina (Nacogdoches)

Town (County)

77 Nada (Colorado)
78 Nameless (Travis)
79 Necessity (Stephens)
80 Nemo (Somervell)
81 New Deal (Lubbock)
82 New Home (Lynn)
83 Nobility (Fannin)
84 Nogalus Prairie (Trinity)
85 Odds (Limestone)
86 Oklaunion (Wilbarger)

127 Sundown (Hockley)
128 Sunny Side (Waller)
129 Sunset (Montague)
130 Swiftex (Bastrop)
131 Taft Southwest (San Patricio)
132 Tanglewood (Lee)

87 Old Center (Panola)
88 Old Glory (Stonewall)
89 Omen (Smith)
90 Ozona (Crockett)
91 Panhandle (Carson)
92 Pep (Hockley)
93 Pert (Anderson)
94 Pickton (Hopkins)
95 Pin Hook (Lamar)
96 Placid (McCulloch)
97 Plata (Presidio)
98 Pluck (Polk)
99 Poetry (Kaufman)
100 Point Blank (San Jacinto)
101 Queen City (Cass)
102 Quitaque (Briscoe)
103 Racetrack (Delta)
104 Radiance (Travis)
105 Ragtown (Lamar)
106 Randado (Jim Hogg)
107 Ranger (Eastland)
108 Rangerville (Cameron)
109 Realitos (Duval)
110 Regency (Mills)

111 Retreat (Navarro)
112 Rising Star (Eastland)
113 Rockhouse (Austin)
114 Rollover (Galveston)
115 Ropesville (Hockley)
116 Round Top (Fayette)
117 Roundup (Hockley)
118 Seclusion (Lavaca)
119 Segno (Polk)
120 Senior (Bexar)
121 Shovel Mountain (Burnet)
122 Slide (Lubbock)
123 Stagecoach (Montgomery)
124 Stampede (Bell)
125 State Line (Culberson)
126 Structure (Williamson)

133 Telegraph (Kimble)
134 Telephone (Fannin)
135 Tell (Childress)
136 Texla (Orange)
137 Texline (Dallam)
138 Thrifty (Brown)
139 Tintop (Matagorda)
140 Tin Top (Parker)
141 Tuxedo (Jones)
142 Uncertain (Harrison)
143 Universal City (Bexar)
144 Utopia (Uvalde)
145 Wayside (Armstrong)
146 Wealthy (Leon)
147 Welcome (Austin)
148 Welfare (Kendall)
149 Who'd Thought It (Hopkins)
150 Wink (Winkler)
151 Zephyr (Brown)

ALGOA (Galveston): on TX 6, eleven miles W of La Marque. First known as Hughes. Settlers were in the area in the 1880s. The daughter of one of the town developers named the town. She christened it for the British tanker *Algoaian*, which was docked at Galveston. A very interesting theory of the name's origin involves the same ship. Algoa is situated some eighteen miles from the Gulf. The devastating Galveston hurricane of 1900 supposedly hurled the ship this far inland, where it stayed for some sixteen months. There is evidence, however, that the name predates the hurricane.

AMBIA (Lamar): on FM 1506, five miles SW of Paris. The village was established in 1886 as a railroad stop and named by a justice of the peace from nearby Roxton. If the source is correct, the moniker came about in a rather disgusting manner: tobacco chewers liked to sit around and spit amber juice as they congregated at a local business.

ANGEL CITY (Goliad): on TX 239, ten miles W of Goliad. This was a viable community by 1931, laid out for tenant farmers. The name of the site derives from two possible sources. A tongue-in-cheek version attributes it to the violent fights that often accompanied early Saturday night dances. A more palatable rendition holds that two young women, dressed in white, watched a crew drill the town water well and inspired the name because their appearance reminded the workers of two angels.

ANNONA (Red River): on US 82, eight miles SE of Clarksville. I. D. and Mary Lawson moved to this area from Arkansas in the mid-1830s and settled on land granted to I. D. for his service in the Texas Revolution. The site was originally called Walker Station, after the owner of a mercantile store. When a post office was put in place, residents discovered that Walker duplicated another community name. Mythmakers claim that the village's present name came from that of a beautiful Native American maiden. The more realistic version is that Dr. George C. Wooten suggested the name, which, supposedly, comes from a Latin word meaning "depot" or "supply station."

AUSTONIO (Houston): on TX 21, fourteen miles SW of Crockett. Settlers were in the region in the 1840s, and the site was known as Pearville. Austonio acquired its label through a contest conducted in 1930. The name is a combination of Austin and San Antonio and was inspired by its location on El Camino Real (Old San Antonio Road). Mrs. Ruth Tucker submitted the winning entry.

BABY HEAD (Llano): on TX 16, ten miles N of Llano. The post office was established in 1879. The town was named for the mountain, which received this very unusual handle around 1850. A Comanche raiding party kidnapped a white baby and later, after killing the infant, decapitated it, mounted the head on a pole, and placed it on the mountain, where it was found by settlers.

BEAUKISS (Williamson): on Middle Yegua Creek, about one mile from the Lee County line in SE Williamson County. Samuel M. "Uncle Sammy" Slaughte, who was also the first postmaster, founded it in 1880; he suggested the name. One story for the origin of the name, although unsubstantiated, is that a married couple traveling by wagon through the area stopped on the road and kissed. There seems to be no other viable source for the origin of the community name.

BIG SQUARE (Castro): on FM 145, fifteen miles SW of Dimmitt. Named for the large, two-story houses built by members of the Stiles family, which settled the area in 1908.

BLOWOUT COMMUNITY (Blanco): fifteen miles NW of Johnson City. The settlement dates back to 1854. Its name came from Blowout Cave, located in a hillside east of Comanche Creek. The cave was at one time home to thousands of bats, and it was only natural that a large amount of guano would accumulate inside the cavern. It is assumed that ammonia and other gases from the decomposing guano built up in the cave and exploded when lightning struck near the entrance.

BONUS (Wharton): near jct FM 102 and 2614, fifteen miles N of Wharton. Established in the mid-1890s with the arrival of the railroad. Some claim William Dunavant named it for his Bonus Plantation. Others believe the first settlers were so pleased with the fertile soil that they called the place Bono, derived from the Latin for "good," and that the name Bonus subsequently evolved. Possibly the label emerged from the time railroad owners were promised a bonus for building a line into this area.

BOOTLEG (Deaf Smith): in SW Deaf Smith County. The village was developed in the early 1900s and was also known as Bootleg Corner. This rather intriguing moniker derived from one of two sources. One relates the naming to Moonshine Sheep Camp, where a still was patronized by cowboys and other travelers. Another theory concerns a "bootleg school" which was used by shady land agents to convince potential investors that a school was near their prospective purchase. The "school" was merely a small portable structure that could be moved from site to site as needed to make sales.

CAMP AIR (Mason): at jct US 377 and RM 1222, two miles SW of Katemey. Also known as Air. Although there were settlers in the area as early as 1862, the first real store and filling station was constructed in 1925. John Kyle, owner and builder of the facility, wanted to christen the site for himself, but soon learned that there was already another Kyle in Texas. He then supposedly named the place Air as a joke, claiming his store looked like a camp, and he had nothing but air. On the other hand, some believe Kyle chose the name because it was short and simple.

CAMP SWITCH (Gregg): between Kilgore and White Oak, off TX 42. The village was in place well before 1880 and was called Camp or Camps. The name was later changed to Camp Switch for a nearby railroad siding.

CAPS (Taylor): at int US 277 and FM 707, some ten miles from downtown Abilene. The town of Caps began in 1822 when newlyweds Ira and Anna Rollins Borders received a wedding present from J. Stoddard Johnston. The gift consisted of an acre of land that eventually became the town site. The place was called Borders Chapel until 1905, when citizens gathered to choose a new designation. Inspiration for the current name reportedly came about when someone threw his cap into the air and said, "Let's call it 'Caps'."

CASH (Hunt): on TX 34, five miles S of Greenville. Established in the mid-1890s. Originally named Sylvia in honor of the sister of E. H. R. Green, president of the Texas Midland Railroad. J. A. Money endeavored long and hard to have the line extended to this point. When his efforts bore fruit, Green, as well as local residents, wanted to name the station in honor of Money. Not wanting a train station by the name of Money, Green substituted the word Cash. As an added note: Mr. Money was the first postmaster of Cash.

CEE VEE (Cottle): on FM 1440, twenty-three miles NW of Paducah. A post office was granted to the community in 1928 and took its name from the C. V. Ranch, from which land for the town was provided.

CENTER CITY (Mills): on US 84, fourteen miles E of Goldthwaite. Settled about 1870. A survey conducted around the same time designated an aged oak tree standing in the town as the exact "center" of Texas. At the time, the town was called Hughes Store, but with this bit of news, the moniker was changed to its current designation.

CHOICE (Shelby): at jct FM 417 and 2140, seven miles SE of Center. The town was founded around 1904. Postal officials suggested three possible names for the settlement. The citizens, unable to decide, countered, "Pick your choice."

CIRCLE (Lamb): at int US 70 and FM 1842, five miles SE of Springlake. First known as Punkin Center. The curve in US 70 influenced the name change sometime after 1928.

CIRCLE BACK (Bailey): at jct FM 298 and 3397, sixteen miles S of Muleshoe. The community was established by 1918 and named for the Circle Back Ranch. The ranch took its tag from its stock brand, which was a circle on the animals' backs.

CIRCLEVILLE (Williamson): on TX 95, eighteen miles E of Georgetown. The town was settled in 1853 by three brothers, James, Joseph, and William Eubank, and christened for its semicircle of homes.

COMFORT (Kendall): at jct TX 27, US 87, and IH 10, sixteen miles NW of Boerne. Ernst Hermann Altgelt laid the town out in an old Native American village in 1854, believing it to be the place for everlasting comfort.

CONCAN (Uvalde): on TX 127, twenty-five miles N of Uvalde. The area was settled as early as 1840, and the name relates to a card game (coon can) that Mexicans used to play at an old gristmill.

CONCRETE (DeWitt): on US 183, eight miles N of Cuero. James Norman Smith laid out the town site, the oldest in DeWitt County, in 1846. Its name refers to the early adobe used in area construction.

CONTENT (Runnels): near RM 382, fourteen miles NE of Winters. Founded by storekeeper Daniel W. Hale in 1881 and named by him "for the contentment of this valley."

COOL (Parker): on US 180, eleven miles W of Weatherford. S. J. Davis and his wife bought land at this site in 1937 and the place was originally called Tile City, because most of the houses were constructed of tile made in Mineral Wells. It later became Fiddlers Ridge for the fiddle playing of Marvin McCracken. In mid-1942, residents gathered to determine a permanent, and acceptable, name for their home. Someone in the group yelled out, "Why not 'Cool' because it's cooler here than any other place in the county?" It became an incorporated community in 1960.

CORNERSVILLE (Hopkins): on TX 11, eighteen miles SE of Sulphur Springs. Dr. J. P. Anderson was an early settler, practicing medicine and operating a mercantile store in the region in 1869. The site was named for its situation near the "corners" of Hopkins and Franklin counties.

COST (Gonzales): on TX 97, six miles W of Gonzales. The town was developed by German settlers in the 1890s and was originally called Oso. Postal officials requested that the name be changed to one consisting of four letters. In 1897 residents dropped one "o" and added "c" and "t." No apparent reason for doing so is given.

COUNTRY CAMPUS (Walker): on TX 19, twelve miles NE of Huntsville. The community arose in 1942 as one of several World War II prisoner of war camps in the United States. After the war, the site became a housing unit for students attending nearby Sam Houston State Teachers College (now Sam Houston State University). This latter fact probably accounts for the community moniker.

CROSS CUT (Brown): at jct FM 279 and 2940, twenty-four miles NW of Brownwood. Founded in 1878 by John H. Bloodworth. The following year citizens applied for a post office. At the same time they suggested the name Cross Out, because the community was "across country" and "out" of the way of usually traveled roads. Either by chance or by design, Washington changed the second word to "Cut."

CUT (Houston): on TX 19, six miles S of Crockett. Originally called Paso or Paso Switch, the town was christened when the railroad cut through here about 1872, and the village was established as a watering stop for trains. The name was changed to Cut around 1900 for the aforementioned "cut" of the railroad.

CUT AND SHOOT (Montgomery): on TX 105, eight miles E of Conroe. Acquired its name in 1912. One thought is that the town moniker came from the time residents had a physical disagreement about, of all things, plans for a new church steeple! A small boy at the scene reportedly declared, "I'm going to cut around the corner and shoot through the bushes in a minute," referring to the hullaba-loo taking place. Just as ironic is another rendition, which states that churchgoing husbands went for knives and guns when a preacher was accused of being too friendly with their womenfolk. Ray "Cut N Shoot" Harris, who fought for the world boxing championship in 1958, was once county clerk here.

CUTHAND (Red River): at jct FM 1487 and 910, ten miles S of Clarksville. First called Enterprise when settlement began around 1850. Current name comes from the creek, which acquired its label when a member of the Kickapoo tribe cut his hand while working in the stream. Yet another version has it that the name remembers Old Cuthand, a Native American chief.

CYCLONE (Bell): on FM 964, eleven miles E of Temple. Several Czech families moved into the vicinity around 1803. It was chris-tened Cyclone because, when residents gathered to decide on its name, one of them quipped that "It would take a cyclone to get this bunch together."

DEADWOOD (Panola): on FM 2517, ten miles E of Carthage. The community was established under the name Linus in 1837. It took its present moniker in 1882, as the result of a joke on some residents who were trying to get the post office moved closer to the Sabine River. During a meeting regarding the situation of the facility, someone made the comment, "We've got the deadwood on them now."

DIMPLE (Red River): at int FM 2120 and TX 37, six miles N of Clarksville. The village had a post office in 1906, and Samuel R. Crockett, postmaster, suggested this name to honor a small girl in the community, apparently one with prominent dimples.

DINERO (Live Oak): on FM 534, ten miles SE of George West. Originally called Barlow's Ferry in 1846 for E. Barlow. The current title, which is Spanish for "money," dates back to the era of the Mexican general Santa Anna. As legend goes, Santa Anna and his forces were traveling through the area escorting a forty-mule team carrying gold. Meeting obstacles at this point, Santa Anna was forced to bury the gold and flee back to Mexico. The legend persists to this day, and the buried treasure is still hunted by seekers of wealth. Since the supposed secret cache is somewhere in the area, the hamlet took its name from the Spanish treasure. The name could also come from legends of silver mines in the vicinity, the excellent soil in the region, or the oil and gas in the area. Take your pick.

DING DONG (Bell): on TX 195, eight miles S of Killeen. The settlement date is unknown. Some residents believe the village received its name in jest, simply because it is located in Bell County. Others say it was christened for two cousins named Bell. As the story goes, when they let C. C. "Cohn" Hoover paint a sign for their store, the artist depicted two large bells on the sign with the lettering "Ding Dong" between the bells. Residents soon took the store name for the name of their village.

DITTO (Atascosa): five miles NW of Poteet. The history of this settlement dates back to the 1700s. Its early name was Agua Negra, which referred to the dark water of a natural spring containing iron oxide. The name was changed in 1881 when the postmaster applied for a new post office. He wrote the word "ditto" on the application form to indicate that the office should continue with the name Agua Negra. Postal officials misinterpreted his meaning, and the town became Ditto.

DIVOT (Frio): at int FM 1581 and 117, nine miles NW of Dilley. This was a viable community as early as 1906 and was known as Leona Settlement for its location near the Leona River. In 1908 the name was changed to Kingsville, honoring J. J. King. The present moniker came about, as many did, through a mistake. When first established, the hamlet was situated at a crossroads. Citizens opined that the logical name for the place was Pivot (to turn). Washington officials mistook the "P" for a "D."

DODGE (Walker): on FM 405, ten miles E of Huntsville. Although farmers had been tilling the soil since 1825, the community was not developed until 1872. It is on land granted to the railroad by William H. Parmer (Palmer?). When the railroad came through the area, citizens of Huntsville showed little interest. Because of their attitude, railroad officials decided to bypass them and set a station at another point. Since they were "dodging" Huntsville, officials christened their new site Dodge. Another submission is that the name came from Phelps-Dodge Company, the railroad construction enterprise.

DOMINO (Cass): on FM 3129, ten miles NE of Atlanta. The site was established in the late 1800s as a railroad stop. First called Alamo Mills, confusion soon arose with the town of Alamo. The new tag came about because, at the time, it was customary for passengers to play dominoes while waiting for the train. Conductors often referred to the place as Domino, rather than Alamo Mills, so the new name was an appropriate one.

DRIFTWOOD (Hays): on FM 150, twenty miles NW of San Marcos. Settlers were in the region as early as 1850 when the site was known as Liberty Hill. A community was in progress by 1886, but residents discovered that there was already a Liberty Hill in Texas, so they had to choose another name. Jim Howard, looking out the door at the driftwood lying about from a recent flood, felt this would be an appropriate moniker, since the post office building had to be constructed partly of driftwood.

DROP (Denton): on FM 1384, four miles NW of Justin. A post office opened on the site in 1886, and residents petitioned to have it named

Dewdrop. There was already a town by this name in the Lone Star State, so residents simply removed the first three letters of Dewdrop and came up with the current designation. Or, according to some, John Russell of Dallas claimed that his uncle Hardy Holmes, replying to a compliment paid the town, said, "Oh, this town is just a drop in the bucket." According to another source, "The Indians never stayed long in the camping places. Early settlers said these Native Americans just 'dropped' in and 'dropped' out, a practice that caused the town to earn its name." Take your pick.

DUSTER (Comanche): at jct FM 587 and 679, sixteen miles N of Comanche. Founded in the early 1880s. According to local tradition, when citizens met to discuss an official name for their post office, one fellow held up a sheet of paper and blew the dust off of it. He then suggested the name Duster.

EAST DIRECT (Lamar): at int FM 79 and 197, one-and-one-half miles E of Direct. Settlers were in the area at least by 1936. The settlement was named for its location "east" of the town of Direct.

EASTGATE (Liberty): near jct FM 1960 and 686, eight miles W of Dayton. The town plat was created in 1911 and made official in 1913. According to available sources, the town acquired its moniker because it was located at the "east gate" of a fence line where it crossed the railroad line.

ELWOOD (Van Zandt): near FM 47, thirteen miles NW of Canton. A Baptist church was on the site as early as 1898. The community's name came from combining the names of nearby *El*lis Chapel and *Wood*all School in 1917.

EMBLEM (Hopkins): on CR 71, twelve miles NW of Sulphur Springs. Founded by G. D. Kennemore in 1876. Originally called Soon Over by residents because they didn't hold much hope for their town's survival. As time passed, however, they changed their minds and desired a more suitable name. In front of the local store owned by W. T. Peck hung a large sign on which was an eagle, advertising a soft drink. The eagle inspired the name Emblem.

EMINENCE (Chambers): W of FM 563 and S of IH 10, in NC Chambers County. A post office was in place in 1898. The townspeople wanted their town to be widely known, so they christened it with this most "eminent" of names.

EULOGY (Bosque): near FM 56, nine miles NE of Walnut Springs. Charles Walker Smith, founder of the town, celebrated the opening of his store in July 1884 with a barbecue and square dance, a "eulogy" to the event. Another theory is that residents wanted to name the hamlet Smithville for Uncle Billye Smith. This name duplicated that of another town in Texas, so Julia Smith Mickey, Billye's sister, suggested Eulogy, stating that everyone "eulogized" Uncle Billye.

EXELL (Moore): off US 287 in SC Moore County. The community was developed prior to World War II and derived its name from inversion of the LX Ranch cattle brand of rancher Lee Bivins.

EXRAY (Erath): off TX 108, fourteen miles NW of Stephenville. While the area was pioneered prior to the Civil War, a community did not develop until around 1890. It was christened for its location at a crossroads.

FLOMOT (Motley): on FM 97 and 599, twenty miles NW of Matador. The settlement arose in the early 1890s and its name comes from *Flo*yd and *Mot*ley counties.

FLOYDADA (Floyd): at jct US 62 and 70, TX 207, FM 784 and 1958; county seat. First known as Floyd City and established in 1890 by M. C. Williams. The town site is situated on land donated by James and Caroline Price. In order to prevent confusion with the Hunt County town of Floyd, the town's original name was switched to Floydada after its post office opened. There are several versions as to the origin of the town's handle. Some believe it is a combination of Caroline Price's parents, Floyd and Ada, or James Price's mother, Ada. Some think the name was supposed to be Floydalia, but that, as often happened, an error was made somewhere between the town and Washington.

FORT SPUNKY (Hood): on FM 199 and 2174, twelve miles SE of Granbury. Originally known as Barnardville for George Barnard, who settled here in 1849. There was such rambunctious reaction among the citizens when they were awarded a post office that the community was tagged with this livelier name. Or, the moniker might have evolved from the fistfights that often broke out among the citizens.

GLOBE (Lamar): at int FM 79 and a LR, seven miles N of Paris. A post office opened on the site in 1899. T. H. Wheeler asked his family for name suggestions. One of his sons, eyeing a kerosene lamp, noticed the globe part of the lamp and recommended that as the name.

HAPPY (Swisher): on US 87, fifteen miles N of Tulia. A post office was in place there in 1891. Some believe the town was named for a creek, so called because travelers were very happy to find water. Another version, closely related to the first, is that a Native American, having journeyed a long distance, finally came upon water here and named the place "Happy Hunting Ground." Finally, there are those who contend the spot was named by J. B. Harper. A freighter, Harper and his brother were traveling through the region when they became lost in a snowstorm. For two days and nights they meandered, not knowing where they were. Then, just as they were about to give up hope, they spied a dim light in the distance. Making their way to the source, they found a cabin occupied by an elderly couple. The two weary, cold freighters were invited in, fed, and given hot coffee. In the course of conversation, Harper asked the name of the place. He was informed that it had no name and was invited to recommend one. Harper responded that he believed Happy would be a good name, because it would make anyone happy to see a light and fire on such a bad night. The community uses the slogan, "The town without a frown."

HARMONY HILL (Rusk): Fifteen miles NE of Henderson. The town was platted in the 1840s on land donated by John W. Kuykendall. The harmonious relations of early settlers probably inspired the name in 1856. As is sometimes the case, more interesting is its nickname, Nip 'N' Tuck, levied for an incident in which hounds chased a fox down the town's main street.

HUB (Parmer): at jct TX 86 and 214, ten miles E of Bovina. The site was occupied by 1925, and the name reflects the thought that it was the center for surrounding communities, ranches, and farms.

LARIAT (Parmer): on US 70/84, eight miles SE of Farwell. A post office was established here in 1925. The village began in 1913 as a railroad stop on former XIT Ranch land. W. A. Simpson, railroad agent, baptized the site for the cowboy's rope.

LEONA SCHRODER (Nueces): on FM 1833, thirty miles W of Corpus Christi. Two schools, Leona and Schroder, began operating in the vicinity around 1900. The community was named for the schools.

LIBERTY CITY (Gregg): at jct LR and FM 1252, sixteen miles S of Gladewater. The hamlet grew up sometime before the Civil War. It has been known variously as Mount Mariah for a church, Sabine for a school, McCary's Chapel for two churches, and Goforth for a local family. In 1902 or 1903 a community post office called Hog Eye was in operation. This unique, comical label came from either a hog thief or for a popular fiddler's tune at the time. In the 1930s the discovery of oil reserves in the area led to further development. W. W. Chapman and his brother Bert laid out a town site and residential area on land they had purchased. The spot was still without an official name when one day a stranger walked into the Chapman

Store and asked where he was. "Liberty City," one of the locals called out, off the top of his head.

LONG TAW (Delta): SW of Cooper in C Delta County. The settlement developed in the 1850s and was known as Good's Chapel. Early freighters, using animal-drawn wagons, referred to a haul as a "taw." There was an unnamed community here at the time, and freighters said that the drive from a bridge on the South Sulphur River to this spot was a long taw.

LOOP (Gaines): at jct TX 83 and FM 303, ten miles E of Seagraves. The first ranchers were in the region in the 1890s; Joe Sherman was the first settler on the site in 1905. The early community was once known as Blue Goose, although there is no source as to why this name was used. The current handle comes from the ranch brand, a loop, or an "O." Or, it might have emerged when a post office had been approved for the site, and Ted Beltcher, who was the first postmaster, was asked to suggest a name for the new facility. At the time he was performing a popular cowboy trick, that of whirling a rope into a loop, then jumping in and out of the loop as it spun. That gave him the idea for the name.

LOYAL VALLEY (Mason): on FM 2242, twenty miles SE of Mason. One of the oldest communities in the county, being settled by German immigrants who moved from the Fredericksburg area in 1858. The community moniker honors residents who remained loyal to the North during the Civil War. On the other hand, John O. Meusebach might have labeled the site for the "mutual cooperation and loyalty between the local settlers."

MAGIC CITY (Wheeler): in WC Wheeler County on the North Fork of the Red River. It was christened following the discovery of oil (magic gold) in Wheeler County in 1926. The name came from the fact that after the discovery, oil derricks multiplied like magic.

MAGNET (Wharton): E of TX 60, twelve miles S of Wharton. Around 1907 the Taylor-Fowler Land Company of Oklahoma carved out a town site and began promoting the area. One contention is that settlers tagged the place because they believed the good soil would draw other settlers. Another belief is that the land company promoted the town, and that by choosing this moniker, they hoped to attract more people to the little village. The closest town of any size, Bay City, was dry; Magnet was not. Maybe the saloons in the latter were the big attraction. Regardless, none of the dreams materialized, and today the hamlet consists of only a few farm dwellings.

MARKOUT (Kaufman): on FM 740, fourteen miles NW of Kaufman. A school was in session here in 1884. Some believe that the community name came about when the commissioners' court noted that the roads were "marked out" for use, which meant that they were carved out of the land, so to speak.

MIDLINE (Montgomery): on US 59, two miles NE of Splendora. The region was first settled in the late 1830s. The community takes its name for its location near the Montgomery-Liberty county line.

MUD CITY (Travis): on FM 969, four miles E of Austin. The settlement date is unknown. Little is left of this hamlet, whose claim to fame is that FBI agents once hid out here, waiting for the 1920s outlaws Bonnie Parker and Clyde Barrow (they didn't show). The hamlet acquired its designation because, when Cottonwood Creek flooded, the roads became so muddy that walking on them was virtually impossible.

MUDVILLE (Brazos): at int FM 50 and 1687, eleven miles W of Bryan. The area was settled in the 1860s and was once called Steele's Store for store owner Henry B. Steele. The current name comes from the mud that is common to this floodplain of the Brazos and Little Brazos rivers.

NACLINA (Nacogdoches): on TX 103, twenty miles SE of Nacogdoches. Developed around 1900s. Its name comes from *Nac*ogdoches and Ang*elina* counties.

NADA (Colorado): on TX 71, twenty-two miles SE of Columbus. The earliest settlers were believed to be J. William Schoellmann and his family, arriving in the vicinity in February 1881. First known as Vox Populi (Latin for "voice of the people"). The present name is an anglicized version of the Czech word *najda* ("hope"), an expression of the citizens' outlook for their new home. The Spanish *nada* ("nothing") could also apply in this sense.

NAMELESS (Travis): off FM 1431, five miles NE of Lago Vista. Settlers were on the grounds by 1869. When residents of the newly established community applied for a post office, officials rejected every name they proposed for the facility. After half a dozen names were turned back, someone took it on him- or herself to write the Post Office Department, "Let the post office be nameless and be damned!" Apparently, taking the writer at his words, Nameless became official in 1880.

NECESSITY (Stephens): on FM 207, twelve miles SE of Breckenridge. At one time, the site was known as Cotton Plant. The community was born during extremely difficult times in America's history: the Civil War and Reconstruction. To make matters worse, ranchers had to suffer through the severe drought of 1886. Apparently citizens named the settlement by reflecting on the hard times they had experienced, when everything was a necessity just for bare living.

NEMO (Somervell): at int FM 200 and 199, five miles E of Glen Rose. Settled in the late 1850s, the area was originally known as Johnson Station for Jimmie Johnson, early settler. The Post Office Department wanted a shorter name so, as legend has it, one man proffered Nemo, supposedly Latin for "no one," arguing that "If

Jimmie Johnson's name was not good enough, then no one's was."
Another belief is that W. H. Rinker, store owner, labeled the community just so it would rhyme with such surrounding settlement names as Bono and Rainbow.

NEW DEAL (Lubbock): on IH 27 and FM 1729, eleven miles N of Lubbock. The town began with the coming of the railroad in 1909. It was originally called Monroe for Monroe G. Abernathy, land promoter. It took its moniker in 1949 from the New Deal Consolidated School District, which was built during the New Deal days of President Franklin Roosevelt.

NEW HOME (Lynn): at int FM 211 and 1730, nine miles E of Lakeview. The community was viable by the 1930s and was first known as Deuce of Hearts for the ranch. The land on which the town site is situated was once part of the ranch, but when a church was built, another name seemed in order. Residents considered this their new home. Another source states that L. G. DePriest suggested the name because all the homes were new to the occupants. Actually, the abodes were no more than dugouts.

NOBILITY (Fannin): on TX 78, sixteen miles SW of Bonham. Settled around 1858. Original settlers wanted the rather pretentious name of Gentry. This was rejected because of duplication, so in 1881 they selected Nobility, which still maintained an air of supremacy. Another version is that the hamlet name relates to William Gentry, an early settler.

NOGALUS PRAIRIE (Trinity): on FM 357, thirteen miles NE of Groveton. Has been called Nogalus and Prairie View. Alabama and Georgia farmers were homesteading the region in the 1850s. A post office opened here under the name Nogallis Prairie. Local lore has it that two horse thieves were "hanged from a limb by the neck until dead." This incident brought about the community being dubbed "Nogallows." When a post office was granted, the spelling was changed from Nogallis to Nogalus.

ODDS (Limestone): on FM 147, seven miles W of Kosse. Settled about 1854 when David Barton arrived in the region. Originally called Buffalo Mott. In 1899 when another, more agreeable name was discussed, residents couldn't come to a mutual decision. They were then asked to write their suggestions on slips of paper and toss them into a hat. Still no agreement was reached. Because of the secret ballot, though, one attendee remarked that that was an odd way to name a town. The word "odd" caught the attention of the people and by adding an "s," they came up with the place name. While this is the generally accepted source of the hamlet name, there is a possibility that it took its tag from Odds, Kentucky.

OKLAUNION (Wilbarger): on US 183, 283, and 70, nine miles E of Vernon. Once called Mayflower. The current handle was suggested by Joe "Buckskin Joe" Wright, who founded the town in 1888, and commemorates the union by rail between the town and Oklahoma.

OLD CENTER (Panola): on FM 699, thirteen miles SE of Carthage. James Rowe and his brother developed the town site about 1830. When Texas secured its independence from Mexico in 1836, this area was part of San Augustine County. Still too big, legislators divided the region and created Shelby County. Center was to be the county seat, but Shelby County was also too large. The region was once more divided, and Panola County came into existence. Center was moved south to become the county seat of Shelby County, and the original Center became Old Center in Panola County.

OLD GLORY (Stonewall): on FM 1835, fourteen miles E of Aspermont. Developed in the 1880s and called Brandenberg by early German settlers. The name was changed during World War I in a show of patriotism.

OMEN (Smith): on TX 345, two miles W of Arp. First settled when Arnold O'Brien and family arrived in 1848. At various times the site was called Round Hill (1849), Canton (1851), Clopton (1852), Troup (1854?), and Old Canton (1879). W. W. Orr bestowed the present title in 1880, because he thought it might bring the people good luck.

OZONA (Crockett): on IH 10 and TX 163; county seat and the only town in Crockett County. Founded in 1891 and first called Powell Well for E. M. Powell, land surveyor. The city was named for the quality of its open air, or "ozone."

PANHANDLE (Carson): on US 60; county seat. Granted a post office in 1887, the town was platted the following year. Originally christened Carson City, honoring Samuel Price Carson, the first secretary of state of the Republic of Texas and namesake of the county. It was later called Panhandle City. In the early 1880s, it served as a buffalo hunters' camp. Billy Dixon was the first white settler in the county. Its present moniker was designated when it became a railroad terminus in 1888 and denotes its location.

PEP (Hockley): on FM 303, nine miles N of Petit. Originally a part of Yellow House Ranch of the vast XIT Ranch empire. The Yellow House Land Company sold this section in 1924, much of it to German immigrants interested in establishing a Catholic colony. J. G. Gerik opened a store here in 1925, when the colony was called Ledwig for Rev. Francis Ledwig, local minister. The name was changed to Pep in 1936 to reflect an admired characteristic of its residents. Or it could be a shortened form of the word "pepper."

PERT (Anderson): at int TX 155 and FM 2267, twelve miles NE of Palestine. A post office serviced the site in 1899. An early name for the settlement was Mount Vernon. Whoever changed the name to its present designation did so because he had faith that the community was going to be a "right pert" (spirited) town.

PICKTON (Hopkins): at jct TX 11 and FM 269, fifteen miles SE of Sulphur Springs. M. D. Jackson developed the site around 1856. A committee was appointed by local citizens to "pick" a name for the railroad station. They didn't have to consider choices very long, selecting Pick Town, which the railroad changed to Pickton, probably because of duplication somewhere down the line.

PIN HOOK (Lamar): on FM 195, eighteen miles NE of Paris. Developed around 1836 and quite likely named for a crook in the road passing through town.

PLACID (McCulloch): on FM 1028 and 2315, sixteen miles NE of Brady. J. A. Gault founded the community in 1903 after the arrival of the railroad. The name is descriptive of its quiet, serene location.

PLATA (Presidio): on FM 169, four miles S of Alamito. The community began life as ranching center in the 1880s. Once called La Plata, which comes from the Spanish for "silver." The town was named by the railroad when the line was built through here. The name was inspired either by the appearance of the ground—reflection—or evidence of silver ore in the region.

PLUCK (Polk): on FM 352, six miles NE of Corrigan. The community came into being around 1850 and was once called Stryker, after G. H. Stryker. George H. Deason suggested the current moniker because he felt it took "pluck" (stamina) to settle here. Or, maybe it was chosen by Washington officials through "general orneriness."

POETRY (Kaufman): at int FM 986 and 1565, six miles N of Terrell. A post office was established on the site in 1879. One theory about the current name revolves around a young man who worked on a local newspaper and loved poetry so much that he always filled his columns with verse. Another rendition is that the handle came from the fact that, at one time, many amateur poets met here to read and talk about poetry. Maybe a local merchant, Maston Ussery, suggested the name Poetry because the area in springtime reminded him of a poem. A fourth belief is the least logical, yet the most accepted. A drummer passing through noticed a small ragged boy followed by an equally scrawny dog. In those days, "tray" was a common term for a dog. The drummer commented, "There's a poor tray if I ever saw one." Residents were, at the time, trying to decide on a name for the town and hearing the drummer's words, changed "poor tray" to Poetry.

POINT BLANK (San Jacinto): at jct US 190 and TX 156, fourteen miles N of Coldspring. The community was settled by the 1850s. A French governess, Florence Dissiway, christened it because all directions to the site were point blank (unobstructed). She originally named it Blanc Point, which residents eventually changed to Pointblank.

QUEEN CITY (Cass): at jct US 59 and FM 74, three miles NE of Atlanta. The site was founded in 1877 as a railroad stop, possibly under the name of Lanark. Through some legal decision, the town site was declared void. John C. Hutchison and a group formed a stock company and established their own town. The name Queen City was inspirational for Hutchison and was adopted over protests of some citizens who had moved from Georgia as early as the 1840s. They wanted the town to be named for Marietta, Georgia. Their efforts were futile, however, and the town was incorporated on July 6, 1876, as Queen City.

QUITAQUE (Briscoe): on TX 86, sixteen miles SE of Silverton. The first settler in the region was the Comanchero trader José Piedad Tafoya in 1865. George Baker drove a herd of two thousand cattle to this region in 1865 and headquartered them on the Lazy F Ranch. In 1880 legendary cattleman Charles Goodnight purchased the Lazy F Ranch and renamed it Quitaque, thinking it was a Native American word for "end of the trail." Another tale goes that the name was derived from two buttes in the vicinity that resembled piles of manure. Still others claim the moniker was taken from the Quitaca tribe, whose name was translated by white settlers as "whatever one steals."

RACETRACK (Delta): at int FM 1530 and 1533, four miles SE of Pecan Gap. Developed in the early 1880s and christened for a race-track where horses ran on Sundays.

RADIANCE (Travis): on FM 1826, S of Oak Hill. Developed in the 1970s as a commune for practitioners of transcendental meditation. The name Radiance comes from Super Radiance Effect, the theory that communal meditation brings peace and understanding and will ultimately serve to cure many social ills.

RAGTOWN (Lamar): on FM 197, eighteen miles NW of Paris. Probably established earlier, but there are no maps indicating this site existed before 1900. According to tradition, the folk that lived here were so clean, they washed their clothes until they were nothing more than rags.

RANDADO (Jim Hogg): at jct TX 16 and FM 649, twenty-five miles SW of Hebbronville. The town site was part of an eighty-thousand-acre ranch owned by Hipolito García. In 1836 García built a headquarters, stone house, and other buildings on the site. Once established, the town was named for the highly ornate lassos, called *randas*, that were made on the ranch.

RANGER (Eastland): on IH 20, ten miles NE of Eastland. The town's name comes from the Texas Rangers, who camped about two miles northeast of the site in the 1870s. J. G. Searcy donated 160 acres to the railroad, thus marking the beginning of the small town.

RANGERVILLE (Cameron): on FM 1479, four miles SW of Harlin-gen. Established at least by 1922. It was named for the Texas Ranger camp maintained near the Old Military Road.

REALITOS (Duval): on TX 359, twelve miles SW of Benavides. Developed on the former Santos García Spanish land grant. In 1885 it was a "settlement, but also a ranch." The site supposedly acquired its moniker from the small camps of Mexican officers who were stationed in the area in the 1800s.

REGENCY (Mills): on a LR, twenty miles SW of Goldthwaite. Also known as Hannaville and Hanna Valley for the Hanna family, who settled in the vicinity in 1854. Supposedly, the Hanna men had intended this to be a temporary stop only and planned to move on to other territory in the future. As the story goes, the Hanna women persuaded their menfolk to put down roots here. It seems that the ladies were taken with the numerous songbirds flying about. When a post office was proposed for the site, postal officials, probably because of duplication, rejected the name Hanna Valley. The name Regency was levied on the community, possibly for Regency Falls.

RETREAT (Navarro): on FM 709, S of Corsicana. Settled in the 1840s and known as Beeman's School House. An old schoolhouse was moved several times from one location to another with the ebb and flow of the population. Consequently, citizens thought Retreat would be an appropriate name for the settlement.

RISING STAR (Eastland): at int US 183 and TX 36, twenty miles S of Cisco. Had its beginning in 1876 when six families moved here from Gregg County; was once called Copperas Creek. One version of the origin of the present designation is that T. W. Anderson applied for a post office in 1880. He submitted the name Rising Sun, but this was rejected because of duplication. He then sent in Star, which also existed elsewhere. Officials combined both suggestions and came up with Rising Star. The second version is that the town was designated by D. D. McConnell, when he described the area as a rising star be-cause of the bountiful crops reaped from the farmland.

ROCKHOUSE (Austin): on TX 159, four miles W of Industry. Settlement began in the region in the late 1850s. Victor Witte, from

Germany, built a stone house at La Bahia Prairie. As other German settlers moved in, the town took the name Rockhouse.

ROLLOVER (Galveston): on TX 87 on Bolivar Peninsula in E Galveston County. A post office was operating as early as 1897. The community was named for Rollover Pass, which was christened for the practice of ship captains during the days of Spanish rule. In order to avoid paying custom duties in Galveston, barrels of contraband were "rolled over" the Bolivar Peninsula.

ROPESVILLE (Hockley): on US 62/82, twenty-five miles SE of Levelland. The town site was platted in 1917 and was the first settlement in the county. Cowboys from the Spade Ranch wanted to name the town Ropes, the idea coming from their habit of building rope corrals to hold cattle for shipment. Postal officials rejected the name because it was too similar to Ropers, Texas. The cowboys then submitted Ropesville, which was accepted.

ROUND TOP (Fayette): at jct TX 237 and FM 1457, fifteen miles NE of La Grange. Stephen Townsend and his family, from Florida, settled here in 1826. The new settlement became known as Townsend. A post office was operating by 1835. The community moniker is a misnomer. It was named for a tower that stood atop a house owned by Alwin Soergel. The tower was octagonal in shape, not round.

ROUNDUP (Hockley): on US 84 and FM 2130, seventeen miles SE of Littlefield. Developed as a railroad-switching site in 1912, the name probably was inspired by its previously being a part of the Spade Ranch and was suggested by W. H. Simpson, a railroad official.

SECLUSION (Lavaca): SE of int FM 530 and 2437, twenty miles SE of Hallettsville. The village was settled in the 1840s and originally called Boxville. The name was changed to reflect its isolated location.

SEGNO (Polk): on FM 943 and 2798, twenty miles SE of Livingston. Settled in the late 1900s. A segno is a musical sign, marking the beginning and the ending of a repeated phrase. A musical background led Henry S. Knight, an early resident, to recommend this name. There is also the thought that there might have been a Native American named Sego and that residents later altered the spelling of his name.

SENIOR (Bexar): twenty-five miles SW of San Antonio in extreme S Bexar County. The site was settled in 1875 and received its name from children addressing the local storekeeper as "Señor."

SHOVEL MOUNTAIN (Burnet): Three miles W of US 281, six miles S of Marble Falls. Colonized in the mid-1850s and christened shortly after the Civil War when a settler found a shovel at the top of a nearby hill.

SLIDE (Lubbock): on FM 1730 and 41, thirteen miles SW of Lubbock. This is the second oldest community in the county. In the 1890s it was known as Block Twenty, but the name was changed in 1903, when a new survey discovered that nearly two hundred sections of land were farther west than first thought. Because of this, all settlers in the area and one school had to "slide" over.

STAGECOACH (Montgomery): on LR, twenty-eight miles SW of Conroe. The village began development in 1958 on a nineteenth-century stagecoach route and became known as Stagecoach Farms. When the community incorporated in 1980, it took the name Stagecoach.

STAMPEDE (Bell): on FM 2601, twelve miles NW of Temple. The site had a post office by 1883 and was named for a nearby creek, which was most likely christened for an early-day trail event.

STATE LINE (Culberson): on US 62/180, eighteen miles NE of Pine Springs. This community, christened for its location on the Texas-New Mexico border, consists of a few businesses and homes, nestled among extensive farm fields.

STRUCTURE (Williamson): on FM 619, ten miles SE of Taylor. Founded in the 1920s by Charles Ryan, who opened a store in a building that he had moved to the site. The place could well have taken its name from that relocated building. No other explanation is available.

SUNDOWN (Hockley): at jct FM 301 and 303, fifteen miles SW of Levelland. The town was laid out in 1928 and called Slaughter for Bob Slaughter, landowner. He didn't want the community to bear his family name and suggested Sundown. Another version is that a meeting was held to decide on a name. The session had gone on all day with no agreement reached. Finally, in desperation, one citizen suggested, "Aw, just name it Sundown, because that's what it is now."

SUNNY SIDE (Waller): two miles S of FM 529, twenty miles SE of Hempstead. Settled in 1866 and probably christened for its location on the sunny side of a knoll. Possibly, though, James Rainwater could have named it because he believed the sun would always shine on the site.

SUNSET (Montague): on TX 101 and FM 1749, fifteen miles S of Montague. Settlers homesteaded the region in the 1870s. The present name was suggested by the postmaster general. In days when travel was difficult, distance meant much more than it does today. The postal chief must have had that in mind when he commented to local residents, "You are so far towards the setting sun, why not the name Sunset?" An early surveying miscalculation placed Sunset in Wise County. A lawsuit filed in 1900 relocated the village to Montague County.

SWIFTEX (Bastrop): on TX 95, six miles N of Bastrop. Originally known as Swiftex Village when developed in the early 1940s to house military personnel stationed at Camp Swift. The current name is a contraction of Swift, Texas.

TAFT SOUTHWEST (San Patricio): SW of US 181 and the city of Taft. Taft Southwest was a segregated Mexican American community in the early decades of the twentieth century. The town's designation reflects its location.

TANGLEWOOD (Lee): on US 77, five miles NW of Lexington. Rev. Hugh Wilson settled the area in 1856 and founded the String Prairie Presbyterian Church. The town is said to have been named by two sisters who were reading a book entitled *Tanglewood Tales.*

TELEGRAPH (Kimble): on US 377, thirteen miles SW of Junction. A post office was established here in 1900. The town took its name from the fact that the first telegraph poles used in the county were cut in a nearby canyon.

TELEPHONE (Fannin): at int FM 273 and 2029, twenty-five miles NE of Bonham. The area hosted settlers as early as the 1870s, but the community was not established until about 1886. Pete Hindman, storekeeper, petitioned for a post office to be placed in his store. He submitted several names for consideration, but they were all rejected because of duplication. Trying to decide on a suitable title, the thought occurred that he was the only person in the community with a telephone.

TELL (Childress): at jct FM 94 and 2042, fifteen miles SW of Childress. Established in 1887 and first called Lee. Long ago this site was known as Tell Tale Flats because of the residents' habit of appearing before grand juries and "telling everything they knew." Tale and Flats were dropped in 1905.

TEXLA (Orange): at jct TX 62 and FM 2802, fifteen miles NW of Orange. The first post office opened here in 1905 and was named Bruce, after postmaster Charles G. Bruce. The site was renamed the following year by the owner of the R. W. Wier Lumber Company for the town's proximity to Louisiana.

TEXLINE (Dallam): on US 87, thirty-five miles NW of Dalhart. It developed with the arrival of the railroad in 1888 and was named for its location on the Texas-New Mexico line.

THRIFTY (Brown): on FM 2492, six miles N of Bangs. Settlement began with immigration of the Mullins family in 1858, and the town was at first called Jim Ned for an early settler. The current designation reflects the frugality of the early residents.

TINTOP (Matagorda): at int FM 1095 and 521, fourteen miles SW of Bay City. Founded about 1929. Originally spelled Tin Top, the moniker comes from the roofing material used on community buildings.

TIN TOP (Parker): on FM 2580, nine miles S of Weatherford. Settled in the mid-1880s as Smith for an early settler. It was later dubbed Irby, after rancher Benjamin F. Irby. The name Tin Top was derived from a cotton gin built here in 1909; it had a galvanized metal roof that was visible from a great distance.

TUXEDO (Jones): N of int TX 92 and FM 1661, ten miles W of Stamford. The town was established in 1905 with the coming of the railroad. It was originally known as Bonita, but when the post office was put in place, citizens discovered that there already was a Bonita, Texas. Warren Foster, an early settler, suggested the current name. Tuxedo comes either from the name of one of the railroad stockholders who lived in Waco or from someone who had a warehouse stocked with the formal attire.

UNCERTAIN (Harrison): on FM 2198, seventeen miles NE of Marshall on Caddo Lake. Established by the early 1900s. Also known as Uncertain Landing. Several possibilities for the origin of this community name abound. In the times of steamboat travel on Caddo Lake, one spot near here was extremely difficult for docking, thus earning the name Uncertain Landing. Maybe the name came from a comment made by fishermen: one day W. J. Sedberry and some friends were angling in the area and stated they weren't certain they would ever be able to find their way out. Another rendition is that the community was incorporated solely for the purpose of voting approval for the sale of alcoholic beverages. The state attorney general looked on the endeavor with a jaundiced eye and vowed that he would never let state incorporation laws be so flagrantly violated. Therefore, the community of Uncertain was uncertain of its legal status as a town. Along this same line, the town may have been so named from the fact that it was the only "wet" town in the area, and people coming here from nearby cities were often uncertain they would be able to get home.

UNIVERSAL CITY (Bexar): on Loop 1604, TX 218, in N Bexar County. Settled by 1932. A. Milner, developer, christened the community in view of the "universal appeal of the airfield" (Randolph Air Force Base).

UTOPIA (Uvalde): at jct RM 187 and1050, twenty-three miles N of Sabinal. The area was homesteaded by the 1850s. The Kincheloe family moved to the present site in 1873. In 1884 a plat for a town site called Montana was laid out, but the name had to be changed because of duplication. Postmaster George Barker chose the name Utopia, a choice possibly influenced by the imaginary land of perfection noted by sixteenth-century writer Sir Thomas More.

WAYSIDE (Armstrong): on RM 285, thirty-three miles SW of Claude. The community was founded in 1893 and originally named Beulah for one of the daughters of the McSpadden family, who donated land for the school district. Mrs. Hervey J. Bradford renamed the place Wayside in 1897 for its location on the "way-side" of the canyon.

WEALTHY (Leon): on FM 3, five miles W of Normangee. A post office was opened here in 1894. Originally known as Poor; understandably, citizens didn't like the name and changed it to its opposite sometime between 1894 and 1896.

WELCOME (Austin): on FM 109, fourteen miles NW of Bellville. Originally settled by Anglo immigrants in the late 1820s. Either theory of the name's origin reflects local hospitality. As one story goes, a traveler spent the night at a citizen's home, and the next morning attempted to pay for the accommodations. Surprised at his host's generosity in refusing money, the man gushed with words of appreciation, to which the host replied, "You're welcome." Another rendition is that J. F. Schmidt named the town for the friendly welcome given new settlers by the forest, flowers, and meadows and the hospitality of local residents.

WELFARE (Kendall): on a LR, eight miles N of Boerne. The post office opened here in 1880, and the site was called Bon Ton or Boyton. The name change was probably the spur-of-the-moment, whimsical choice of a few residents. There is thought, however, that the name comes from the German *wohlfahrt*.

WHO'D THOUGHT IT (Hopkins): off FM 1536, N of Sand Hill. The site was probably established sometime after 1900. Little of the hamlet remains, but it received its unusual handle from the remark an individual made when he first saw the place.

WINK (Winkler): on TX 115 and FM 1232, seven miles SW of Kermit. The community developed in 1926 when oil was discovered in the Hendrick oil field. Originally called Winkler for the county. Due to duplication the name was changed in 1927, still deriving the moniker from the county name.

ZEPHYR (Brown): on US 84, twelve miles E of Brownwood. The village was originally situated on Blanket Creek, a mile or so east of its present location. Surveyors are believed to have named the site in 1850, when they were caught in a "blue norther."

SOURCES

GENERAL REFERENCES

Handbook of Texas Online. Texas State Historical Association, tshaonline
.org/handbook/online.
Massengill, Fred I. *Texas Towns.* Terrell, Tex.: Fred Massengill, 1936.

CHAPTER I

Ibarra, Margie, director, Hondo Public Library, photocopied document, 23
January 2002.
Maguire, Jack. "Talk of Texas." *Austin American-Statesman,* 1 April 1984.
Pool, William C. *Bosque Territory: A History of an Agrarian Community.*
Clifton, Tex.: Chaparral Press, 1964.
Rampt, Barbara. McCulloch County (e-mail: 30 March 2002).
Sanders, Ora Lee, board member, Van Horn City-County Library, 6 March
1979.
Tarpley, Fred. *Place Names of Northeast Texas.* Commerce: East Texas State
University, 1969. (Furnished by Priscilla McAnally, assistant director, Paris
Public Library, Paris, Texas.)

CHAPTER 2

Campbell, L., Motley County clerk, correspondence, 12 February 1979.

Colwell, Frances, city secretary, White Settlement, Texas, copy of historical data, 22 December 1978.

Danheim, Verline, secretary, Cherokee County Heritage Association, letter, 1 February 1979.

Douthitt, Katherine Christian (ed.). *Romance and Dim Trails: A History of Clay County.* Dallas: William T. Tardy, Publisher, 1938.

Fuller, Hazel. Trinity County (e-mail: 21 June 2002).

Gerland, Jonathan K., director of archives, T. L. L. Temple Memorial Library and Archives, Diboll, Texas, 6 February 2002.

Linson, Roy. "WO Exes Return Home for 100th Anniversary." *The Longview Daily News,* 18 September 1985 (furnished by Longview Public Library).

Rains County Communities, available at rootsweb.com-texians/com.htm (from the *Rains County Leader,* 5 June 1986), accessed 27 March 2002.

Reed, Steve, "Blue Beckons." *Austin American-Statesman,* 1 April 1985.

Roehrig, Ned. Bell County community names (e-mail: 3 April 2002).

Tarpley, Fred. *Place Names of Northeast Texas.* Commerce: East Texas State University, 1969.

CHAPTER 3

Blakely, Mike. "Name Game Leaves Small Texas Towns with Distinct Identities." *Austin American-Statesman,* 18 February 1985.

Flemmons, Jerry. *Texas Siftings.* Fort Worth: Texas Christian University Press, 1995.

Geothe, Linda, assistant librarian, Cameron Public Library, photocopied document, 17 January 2002.

"Impact Lives, Dies with Liquor Sales." *Austin American-Statesman,* 29 May 1983.

Madison, Virginia, and Hallie Stillwell. *How Come It's Called That?* Albuquerque: University of New Mexico Press, 1958.

Simmons, Frank E. *Coryell County History Stories.* Oglesby, Tex.: unpublished, 1948.

Stewart, George R. *American Place-Names.* New York: Oxford University Press, 1970.

Tarpley, Fred. *Place Names of Northeast Texas.* Commerce: East Texas State University, 1969.

CHAPTER 4

Awbrey, Berry Dooley, Stuart Awbrey, and the Texas Historical Commission. *Why Stop? A Guide to Texas Historical Roadside Markers.* Houston: Taylor Trade Publishing, 2013.

Benthul, Dr. Herman F. *Wood County, 1850–1900.* Quitman, Tex.: The Wood County Historical Society, 1976.

Bonham County Public Library. *Fannin County Folks and Facts.* Dallas: Taylor Publishing Company, 1977.

Bradfield, Bill, and Clare Bradfield. *Muleshoe and More.* Houston: Gulf Publishing Company, 1999.

Brundidge, Glenn Fourman (ed.). *The Texas Sesquicentennial EditionBrazos County History: Rich Past-Bright Future.*

Cherokee County Historical Commission. *Cherokee County History.* Crockett, Tex.: Publisher unknown, 1986.

Douthitt, Katherine Christian (ed.). *Romance and Dim Trails: A History of Clay County.* Dallas: William T. Tardy, Publisher, 1938.

Elmore, Pat Shively. Rosalie question (e-mail: Jim Giddens, Paris, Texas, 29 March 2002).

"Folklore Says Town of Fred Was Named for Log Hauler." *Austin American-Statesman,* 26 December 2001.

Freier, Paul H. *A "Looking Back" Scrapbook for Calhoun County.* Port Lavaca, Tex: Publisher unknown, 1979 (collection of articles about the Matagorda and Lavaca areas).

Gibbs, Marian G., Falls County Historical Commission, letter, 20 October 1987.

Gough, Joy. *Collin County Place Names.* Published by Lois Jay Gough, 1996 (furnished by McKinney Memorial Library, undated).

Gray, Mrs. R. D. *Early Days in Knox County.* New York: Carlton Press, 1963.

Hall, Roy F., and Helen Gibbard Hall. *Collin County: Pioneering in North Texas.* Quanah, Tex.: Nortex Press, 1975 (furnished by McKinney Memorial Library, undated).

Haverhals, Leah. "The Name Game." *Austin American-Statesman,* August 2002.

A History of Hill County, Texas, 1853–1980. Published by the Hill County Historical Commission, 1980.

Horton, Deubrella, secretary to county judge, Jack County, photocopied document, 14 March 2002.

Lawrence, Kathryn R., director, Service League Library, Carthage, Texas, letter, 16 February 1979.

Myers, Cindi. "Speaking of Texas." *Texas Highways,* December 1994.

Parmer County Historical Society. *A History of Parmer County, Texas.* Vol. l. Quanah, Tex.: Nortex Press, 1974.

Phelps, Bailey. *They Loved the Land: Foard County History.* Foard County Historical Survey Committee, 1969.

Pool, William C. *A History of Bosque County.* San Marcos, Tex.: San Marcos Record Press, 1954.

Red River County Public Library, Clarksville, Texas, letter, undated.

Riggs, Carol, director, Texas Forestry Museum, Lufkin, Texas, photocopied document, 17 February 2002.

Robert J. Kleberg Public Library, Kingsville, Texas, letter, undated.

Robinson, David. *A Little Corner of Texas.* Tulsa, Okla.: John Haden Publishers (furnished by Yvonne Ross, history clerk, Live Oak County Library, George West, undated).

Roehrig, Ned. Bell County community names (e-mail: 3 April 2002).

Roscoe, City of, leaflet, undated.

Sanders, Betty, and R. S. Sanders. *Cowpokes and Sod Busters—A History of Rural Communities in Haskell County, Texas, 1885–1940* (furnished by Haskell County Library, Haskell, Texas, undated).

Sherman Public Library, Sherman, Texas, genealogy reply, 18 January 2002.

Simmons, Frank E. *Coryell County History Stories.* Oglesby, Tex.: unpublished, 1948.

Sparkman, Ervin L. *The People's History of Live Oak County, Texas.* Mesquite, Tex.: Ide House, 1981 (furnished by Yvonne Ross, history clerk, Live Oak County Library, George West, Texas, undated).

Spikes, Nellie Witt, and Temple Ann Ellis. *Through the Years: A History of Crosby County, Texas.* San Antonio: The Naylor Company, 1952.

Stambaugh, J. Lee, and Lillian J. Stambaugh. *A History of Collin County, Texas.* Vol. 2. Austin: The Texas State Historical Association, 1958.

Tarpley, Fred. *Place Names of Northeast Texas.* Commerce: East Texas State University, 1969.

Throckmorton Chamber of Commerce, correspondence, undated.

Wood, Sylvia, assistant librarian, Delta County Public Library, Cooper, Texas, letter, 18 January 2002.

CHAPTER 5

Baylor County Historical Society. *Salt Pork to Sirloin: The History of Baylor County, Texas from 1879 to 1930.* Seymour, Tex.: Nortex Offset Publications, Inc., 1972.

Bonham County Public Library. *Fannin County Folks and Facts.* Dallas: Taylor Publishing Company, 1977.

Bowles, Flora Gatlin. *A No Man's Land Becomes a County* (furnished by Jan Laughlin, Goldthwaite, Texas, undated).

Bradfield, Bill, and Clare Bradfield. *Muleshoe and More.* Houston: Gulf Publishing Company, 1999.

Castillo, Delia, archivist, Wharton County Historical Museum, Wharton, Texas, letter, 29 April 2002.

Dedication of Two Historical Markers (Old Montalba and Tennessee Colony), 12 September 1971 (furnished by Palestine Public Library, Palestine, Texas, undated).

Edwards, Brenda J. Grandview (e-mail: 12 December 2001).

Flemmons, Jerry. *Texas Siftings.* Fort Worth: Texas Christian University Press, 1995.

The History of Franklin County (furnished by Charlene Donoghue, Franklin County Genealogical Society, Mount Vernon, undated).

Kunkel, Grace, Bastrop, Texas, letter, 14 December 1978.

Moorhouse, R., librarian, Baylor County Free Library, Seymour, Texas, correspondence, undated.

Neal, Bill. *The Last Frontier: The Story of Hardeman County.* Quanah, Tex.: Quanah Tribune-Chief, 1966.

Penitas, City of, Clerk's Office, historical document, undated.

Prather, Beth, librarian, Coke County Library, Robert Lee, Texas, 5 February 2002.

Simmons, Frank E. *Coryell County History Stories.* Oglesby, Tex.: unpublished, 1948.

Swift, Roy L., chairman, Wilson County Historical Commission, Floresville, Texas, letter, 15 February 1979.

Szilagy, Pete. "Lake Town Gun Barrel City Seeking Identity." *Austin American-Statesman,* 29 January 1984.

Tanner, Laine. *What's in a Name?* Hereford, Tex.: Pioneer Book Publishing, Inc., 1971.

Test, Janis C., head of information services, Abilene Public Library, Abilene, Texas, letter, 25 February 2002.

Thompson, June. "Chalk Hill Got Name from White Chalky Clay." *Henderson Daily News,* 26 November 1995 (furnished by Rusk County Library, Henderson, undated).

CHAPTER 6

Awbrey, Berry Dooley, Claude Dooley, and the Texas Historical Commission. *Why Stop? A Guide to Texas Historical Roadside Markers.* Houston: Gulf Publishing Company, 1999.

Blakely, Mike. "Lone Star Legacy." *Austin American-Statesman,* 18 February 1985.

Brundidge, Glenna Fourman (ed.). *The Texas Sesquicentennial Edition Brazos County History: Rich Past-Bright Future.*

Cherokee County Historical Commission. *Cherokee County History.* Crockett: Public Development Company of Texas, 1986.

Fowler, Gene. "Border Folk-Hero: Catarino Garza." *Texas Highways,* September 2002.

A History of Hill County, Texas, 1853–1980. Published by the Hill County Historical Commission, 1980.

Killen, Mrs. James C. (ed.). *History of Lee County, Texas.* Quanah, Tex.: Nortex Press, 1974.

Maguire, Jack. "Talk of Texas." *Austin American-Statesman,* 2 November 1980.

Notes on the Places of Williamsom County, publication information unavailable (furnished by Claire Maxwell, Taylor Conservation and Heritage Society, Taylor, Texas, 6 April 2002).

Rains County Communities, available at rootsweb.coun/txrains/com.htm, accessed 27 March 2002.

Tarpley, Fred. *Place Names of Northeast Texas.* Commerce: East Texas State University, 1969.

Vinson, Billy C., director, Limestone County Historical Museum, Groesbeck, Texas, letter, 7 March 1979.

CHAPTER 7

Deland, David, webmaster, *www.calfcreek.net,* 3 April 2002.

Garrison, Quillian, Angleton, correspondence, undated.

Havins, T. R. *Something about Brown (A History of Brown County).* Brownwood, Tex.: Banner Printing Company, 1958.

Kendall County—Yesterday and Today (furnished by Shirley R. Stehling, district and county clerk, Kendall County, Boerne, Texas, undated).

A Pictorial History of Polk County, Texas (1846–1910). Published by the Heritage Committee, Polk County Bicentennial Commission, and the Polk County Historical Survey Committee (furnished by Murphy Memorial Library, Livingston, Texas, undated).

"Putting Paint Creek on the Map," Haskell County Library, Haskell, Texas, letter, undated.

Quimby, Myron J. *Scratch Ankle, U.S.A.—American Place Names and Their Derivation.* New York: A. S. Barnes and Company, 1969.

Smith, Susan. "The Awakening of a Sleepy Village." *Austin American-Statesman,* 26 May 2002.

Stovall, Frances, et al. *Clear Springs and Limestone Ledges.* Austin: Nortex Press, 1986.

CHAPTER 8

Harris, George, chairman. Henderson County Historical Commission (e-mail: 28 March 2002).

The History of Mabank, Texas. Mabank, Tex.: The Mabank Sesquicentennial History Book Committee, 1987 (furnished by Paul Dotson, librarian, the Library at Cedar Creek Lake, Cedar Creek Lake, Texas, 26 March 2002).

Raabe, Steven J., Path, letter, 7 April 2002.

Ramsey, Allen E., Santo, letter, 1 January 1979.

Roberts, Mrs. J. B., Plainview, Texas, letter, 25 February 1979.

Stephenson, Doris, district and county clerk, Martin County, Stanton, Texas, correspondence, undated.

Tarpley, Fred. *Place Names of Northeast Texas.* Commerce: East Texas State University, 1969.

Wilkinson, Bill, mayor, Double Oak, Texas, letter (furnished by C. Erik Wilkinson, reference librarian, Denton, Texas, undated.)

CHAPTER 9

Barber, Calvin H., county clerk, Rusk County, Henderson, Texas, correspondence, 11 January 1979.

Benthul, Dr. Herman F. *Wood County, 1850–1900.* Quitman, Tex.: The Wood County Historical Society, 1976.

Crofford, Lena H. *Pioneers on the Nueces.* San Antonio: The Naylor Company, 1963.

Gibbs, Mrs. Clane R., compiler. *Candle Lights of Oatmeal Community.* Oatmeal Homecoming, 14–15 July 1951 (furnished by Herman Brown Free Library of Burnet County, Burnet, Texas, undated).

Henderson, Nat. "Center Scene." *Austin American-Statesman,* 27 August 1984.

Nueces County Historical Society. *The History of Nueces County.* Austin: Jenkins Publishing Company, 1972.

Stephenson, Aline, county clerk, Polk County, Livingston, Texas, photocopied document, undated.

Tarpley, Fred. *Place Names of Northeast Texas.* Commerce: East Texas State University, 1969.

Vallentine, G., chairman, Gonzales County Historical Commission, correspondence, undated.

Weisiger, Sidney R. "Vignettes of Old Victoria," publication information unavailable (furnished by Karen Locher, Local History Department, Victoria, Texas, undated).

Wyatt, Frederica, city secretary, Junction, Texas, correspondence, undated.

CHAPTER 10

Adams, L. I. *Time and Shadows* (furnished by Mabel Leyda, librarian, Tyrrell Historical Library, Beaumont, Texas, 7 December 1978).

Bennett, Carmen Taylor. *Our Roots Grow Deep: A History of Cottle County.* Floydada, Tex.: Blanco Offset Printing Company, 1970.

Bonham County Public Library. *Fannin County Folks and Facts.* Dallas: Taylor Publishing Company, 1977.

Bradfield, Bill, and Clare Bradfield. *Muleshoe and More.* Houston: Gulf Publishing Company, 1999.

Castillo, Delia, archivist, Wharton County Historical Museum, Wharton, Texas, letter, 29 April 2002.

Cave, Teresa, library assistant, Kaufman County Library, Kaufman, Texas, photocopied documents, undated.

Clark, Gary, and Kathy Adams Clark. *Backroads of Texas.* Minneapolis: Voyageur Press, 2016.

Deswysen, Ed. "How Ben Bolt Got Its Name." *Corpus Christi Caller-Times,* 1 May 1960 (furnished by Alice Public Library, Alice, Texas, undated).

Dotson, Pam, librarian, the Library at Cedar Creek Lake, Cedar Creek Lake, Texas, photocopied document, 26 March 2002.

Farmer, Garland R. *The Realm of Rusk County.* Henderson, Tex.: The Henderson Times, 1951.

Gray, Mrs. Elmer, letter, 12 January 1979.

History of Howard County, 1882–1982 (furnished by Vera Gene Hyer, reference librarian, Howard County Public Library, Big Spring, Texas, 24 January 2002.

A History of the First Seventy-Five Years of Castro County, Texas, 1891–1966. Diamond Jubilee Celebration, 11–20 August 1966, Zonell Maples, county clerk, undated.

A History of Waller County. Published by the Waller County Historical Commission, 1996 (furnished by Judy Robinson, Waller County Historical Museum Administrator, Brookshire, Texas, 1 May 2002).

Kiley, Mike. "A Horse Named Marfa Puts West Texas Town on the Map." *Austin American-Statesman,* 5 May 1983.

Kirr, Susan. "Marfa: Giant of a Town." *Texas Highways,* October 2001.

Lee, Evelyn, city secretary, Early, Texas, 28 November 1978.

Love, Anne Carpenter. *History of Navarro County.* Dallas: Southwest Press, 1933.

Ludeman, Annette Martin. *La Salle County: South Texas Brush Country.* Quanah, Tex.: Nortex Press, 1975.

Mabry, Kay, librarian, Centennial Memorial Library, Eastland, Texas, letter, 21 January 2002.

Madison, Virginia, and Hallie Stillwell. *How Come It's Called That?* Albuquerque: University of New Mexico Press, 1958.

Maguire, Jack. "Tales of Texas." *Austin American-Statesman,* 21 March 1982; 10 April 1983.

McQueen, Clyde. *Black Churches in Texas: A Guide to Historic Congregations.* Publication information unavailable (furnished by Judy Robinson, Waller County Historical Museum administrator, Brookshire, Texas, 1 May 2002).

My Hometown: Cisco, Texas (furnished by Louise Pryor, librarian, Cisco Public Library, undated), available at our-town.com/ britlcisco.htm.

"North Gulch." *Texas Monthly Magazine,* April 1982.

"Rains County Communities." *Rains County Leader,* 5 June 1986, available at rootsweb.com/txrains/ com.htm, accessed 27 March 2002.

Roehrig, Ned. Bell County community names (e-mail: 3 April 2002).

Scarbrough, Clara Stearns. *Land of Good Water, A Williamson County, Texas, History.* Georgetown, Tex.: Williamson County Sun Publishing Company, 1973 (furnished by Myreta Matthews, chairperson, Williamson County Historical Commission, Liberty Hill, Texas, 28 December 1978).

Segal, Bennett. "The Jungleman Never Swung into Tarzan, Texas." *Austin American-Statesman,* 2 September 1983.

Smith, Karon Mac. "On the Watershed of the Ecleto and the Clear Fork of Sandies." *The South Texas Drummer,* 18 January 1979.

Spikes, Nellie Witt, and Temple Ann Ellis. *Through the Years: A History of Crosby County, Texas.* San Antonio: The Naylor Company, 1952.

Swift, Roy L., chairman, Wilson County Historical Commission, Floresville, Texas, letter, 11 December 1978.

Tanner, Laine. *What's in a Name?* Hereford, Tex.: Pioneer Book Publishers, Inc., 1971.

Tarpley, Fred. *1001 Texas Place Names.* Austin: University of Texas Press, 1980.

———. *Place Names of Northeast Texas.* Commerce: East Texas State University, 1969.

"Valentine, Texas, Sends Love." *Southern Living,* February 1984.

Williams, Annie Lee. *A History of Wharton County: 1846–1961.* Austin: Von Boeckmann-Janes Company, 1964.

Winfrey, Dorman H. *A History of Rusk County.* Waco, Tex.: Texian Press, 1961.

Wolfram, Joydelle Garrett, secretary-treasurer, Falls County Historical Survey Committee, Marlin, Texas, letter, 8 May 1979.

CHAPTER 11

"Africa Community," available at http//boards.ancestry.com/mbexec/msglrw/TmB.2aCl/968.1, accessed 28 March 2002.

Angell, Jim, compiler. "Did You Know . . .?" *American Profiles,* 11–17 August 2002.

Awbrey, Barry Dooley, Claude Dooley, and the Texas Historical Commission. *Why Stop? A Guide to Texas Historical Roadside Markers.* Houston: Gulf Publishing Company, 1999.

Bandy, Janelle, Lubbock, letter, 11 March 2002.

Blakely, Mike. "Lone Star Legacy." *Austin American-Statesman,* 18 February 1985.

Bonham County Public Library. *Fannin County Folks and Facts.* Dallas: Taylor Publishing Company, 1977.

Bradfield, Bill, and Clare Bradfield. *Muleshoe and More.* Houston: Gulf Publishing Company, 1999.

Casey, Clifford B. *Mirages, Mysteries and Reality—Brewster County, Texas: The Big Bend to the Rio Grande.* Seagraves, Tex.: Pioneer Book Publishers, Inc., 1972.

Cave, Teresa, library assistant, Kaufman County Library, Kaufman, Texas, photocopied documents, undated.

Clark, Gary, and Kathy Adams Clark. *Backroads of Texas.* Minneapolis: Voyageur Press, 2016.

Crosby County History, 1876–1977 (furnished by Crosby County Library, Crosbyton, Texas, undated).

Fayette County, Texas, Heritage. Vol. l. La Grange, Tex.: Fayette County History Book Committee, 1996 (furnished by Sherice Knape, Fayette Heritage Museum, La Grange, Texas, 16 January 2002).

Felker, Rex A. *Haskell County and Its Pioneers.* The Haskell County Bicentennial Committee. Quanah, Tex.: Nortex Press, 1975.

Flemmons, Jerry. *Texas Siftings.* Fort Worth: Texas Christian University Press, 1995.

Gonzales County Library System, Gonzales, Texas, photocopied documents, undated.

Gray, Mrs. R. D. *Early Days in Knox County.* New York: Carlton Press, 1963.

Gregg, Rosalie (ed.). *Wise County History: A Link With the Past.* Vol. l. Decatur, Tex.: Nortex Press, 1975.

Hall, Roy F., and Helen Gibbard Hall. *Collin County: Pioneering in North Texas.* Quanah, Tex.: Nortex Press, 1975 (furnished by McKinney Memorial Library, undated).

Harmon, Dave. "Memories, Strong Family Ties Keep This Sleepy Community from Melting into the Brush." *The (McAllen) Monitor* (furnished by Donald Egle, reference librarian, McAllen Memorial Library, 14 February 2002).

The History of Liverpool, Texas, and Its People. Houston: D. Armstrong Book Printing Company, 1996 (furnished by Paul M. Strohm, Librarian, Angleton Branch Library, 17 January 2002).

Kelley, Dayton (ed.). *Handbook of Waco, McLennan County, Texas.* Publisher unknown, 1972 (furnished by Sue Kethley, librarian, Waco-McLennan County Library, 29 November 1978).

Killen, Mrs. James C. (ed.). *History of Lee County, Texas.* Quanah, Tex.: Nortex Press, 1974.

Ludeman, Annette Martin. *La Salle County: South Texas Brush Country.* Quanah, Tex.: Nortex Press, 1975.

Madison, Virginia, and Hallie Stillwell. *How Come It's Called That?* Albuquerque: University of New Mexico Press, 1958.

Schultz, R. M. Fargo (e-mail: 27 March 2002).

Simmons, Frank E. *Coryell County History Stories.* Oglesby, Tex.: Unpublished, 1948.

Sparkman, Ervin L. *The People's History of Live Oak County, Texas.* Mesquite, Tex.: Ide House, 1981 (furnished by Yvonne Ross, history clerk, Live Oak County Library, George West, Texas, undated).

Sparks, Rick, Dayton Chamber of Commerce, Dayton, Texas, article, 10 January 2002.

Stambaugh, J. Lee, and Lillian J. Stambaugh. *A History of Collin County, Texas.* Vol. 2. Austin: The Texas State Historical Association, 1958.

Tanner, Laine. *What's in a Name?* Hereford, Tex.: Pioneer Book Publishers, Inc., 1971.

Tarpley, Fred. *Place Names of Northeast Texas.* Commerce, Tex.: East Texas State University, 1969.

Taylor, Carol, librarian for genealogy/local history, W. Walworth Harrison Public Library, Greenville, Texas, 4 March 2002.

Welch, Vickie, city secretary, Troy, Texas, letter, undated.

Winfrey, Dorman H. *A History of Rusk County.* Waco, Tex.: Texian Press, 1961.

CHAPTER 12

Banta, Bob. "Mud City: FBI Once Hunted Outlaws in Hamlet." *Austin American-Statesman,* 5 August 1982.

Bennett, Carmen Taylor. *Our Roots Grow Deep: A History of Cottle County.* Floydada, Tex.: Blanco Offset Printing Company, 1970.

Bishop, Eliza H., chairman, Houston County Historical Commission, letter, 19 December 1978.

Blakely, Mike. "Lone Star Legacy." *Austin American-Statesman,* 18 February 1985.

Bowmer, Martha (ed.). *Bell County Revisited.* Temple, Tex.: Temple Jaycees, 1976 (furnished by Lena Armstrong, librarian, Belton County Library, Belton, 10 January 1996).

Bradfield, Bill, and Clare Bradfield. *Muleshoe and More.* Houston: Gulf Publishing Company, 1999.

Brundidge, Glenna Fourman (ed.). *The Texas Sesquicentennial Edition Brazos County History: Rich Past-Bright Future.*

Evans, Grace (Moran). *Swisher County History.* Wichita Falls, Tex.: Nortex Press, 1977.

Gray, Elaine, president, Llano County Historical Association, Plano, Texas, correspondence, 2 January 1979.

Harwell, Linda. (e-mail: 28 March 2002).

Havins, T. R. *Something about Brown (A History of Brown County).* Brownwood, Tex.: Banner Printing Company, 1958.

The History of Gregg County (furnished by Longview Public Library, undated).

Kendall County . . . Yesterday and Today (furnished by Shirley R. Stehling,
district and county clerk, Boerne, Texas, undated).

Leftwich, Dan. "A Neighbor Working toward a Better World." *Onward,* 3
June 1986.

Love, Annie Carpenter. *History of Navarro County.* Dallas: Southwest Press,
1933.

McConal, Jon. "These Folks Stay Cool All Summer." *Star Telegram* (Fort
Worth), 27 June 1994 (furnished by Weatherford Public Library, undated).

McGuire, Jack. "Talk of Texas." *Austin American-Statesman,* 20 June 1982;
5 October 1980.

Morris, Eleanor. "Round Top Shows Pioneer Culture." *Austin American-
Statesman,* 11 December 1983.

Ord, Paul (ed.). *They Followed the Rails: A History of Childress County.*
Childress, Tex.: The Childress Reporter, 1970.

Parmer County Historical Society. *A History of Parmer County, Texas.* Vol.
1. Quanah, Tex.: Nortex Press, 1974.

Pool, William C. *Bosque Territory: A History of An Agrarian Community.*
Clifton, Tex.: Chaparral Press, 1964.

"Queen City, Texas: Come Grow with Us" (brochure) (furnished by Vickie L.
Ray, city secretary, Queen City, 11 December 2001).

Quick, May, Presidio County Museum, letter, 5 April 2002.

Reed, Carrie, county clerk, Parker County, Weatherford, Texas, correspondence, 6 March 1979.

Runnels County Historical Markers, available at rootsweb.com/~txrunnel/
markers.htm, accessed 30 March 2002.

Salter, Bill. "Welfare Postcards Have Unique Lines," publication information unavailable (furnished by Shirley R. Stehling, district and countyclerk,
Boerne, Texas, undated).

Scarbrough, Clara Stearns. *Land of Good Water: A Williamson County,
Texas, History.* Georgetown, Tex.: Williamson County Sun Publishing
Company, 1973 (furnished by Myreta Matthews, chairperson, Williamson
County Historical Commission, Liberty Hill, Texas, 28 December 1978).

Shelton, Harver, and Homer Hutto, compilers. *First 100 Years of Jones
County, Texas.* Stamford, Tex.: Shelton Press, 1978.

Smith, Doris, assistant director, Carson County Square House Museum,
Panhandle, Texas, letter, 4 December 1978.

Smith, J. Dora, Leon County Court deputy clerk, Centerville, Texas, correspondence, undated.

Stanley, F. "The Glenrio, New Mexico, Story." Nazareth, Texas, 1973 (furnished by Rebecca Walls, library director, Deaf Smith County Library, Hereford, Texas, 23 January 2002).

Stewart, George R. *American Place-Names.* New York: Oxford University Press, 1970.

Stillwell, Edd. Old Center, Texas (e-mail: 28 March 2002).

Stovall, Frances, et al. *Clear Springs and Limestone Ledges.* Austin: Nortex Press, 1986.

Syers, Ed. *Backroads of Texas.* 3rd ed. Houston: Gulf Publishing Company, 1993.

Tanner, Laine. *What's in a Name?* Hereford, Tex.: Pioneer Book Publishers, Inc., 1971.

Tarpley, Fred. *Place Names of Northeast Texas.* Commerce, Tex.: East Texas State University, 1969.

"Uncertain Origins: Baffling Name of East Texas Hamlet Still Brings Arguments." *Austin American-Statesman,* 23 June 1985.

Vallentine, G., chairman, Gonzales County Historical Commission, correspondence, undated.

Vinson, Billy C., director, Limestone County Historical Museum, Groesbeck, Texas, letter, 7 March 1979.

Wasowski, Andy. "The Texas Name Game." *Texas Highways,* April 1988.

Wells, Eulalia Nabers. *Blazing the Way.* 2d ed. Comanche County Historical Museum. Comanche, Tex.: Comanche Litho-Print, 1996.

Weyand, Leonie Rummel, and Wade Houston. *An Early History of Fayette County.* La Grange, Tex.: La Grange Journal Plant, 1936.

Williams, Annie Lee. *A History of Wharton County: 1846–1961.* Austin: Von Boeckmann-Janes Company, 1964.

Womack, A., Cass County clerk, Linden, Texas, correspondence, undated.

INDEX

ABOUT THE AUTHORS

Don Blevins was a member of the Texas State Historical Association, the Writers' League of Texas, and the Coalition of Texas Writers. He published six books and wrote articles for more than fifty magazines including *American History Illustrated* and *True West*. A native of Johnson City, Tennessee, Don was a longtime resident of San Marcos, Texas. He passed away in 2014.

Paris Permenter and **John Bigley** are the authors of thirty-five books for travelers and pet lovers. The husband-wife team penned *Day Trips from Austin, Day Trips from San Antonio,* and *Day Trips from Houston,* as well as *Insiders' Guide to San Antonio* and more. The Hill Country residents are members of the Society of American Travel Writers.